THE LEARNING CYCLE
ELEMENTARY SCHOOL
TEACHING

THE
Learning Cycle AND

ELEMENTARY SCHOOL
SCIENCE TEACHING

JOHN W. RENNER
Professor of Science Education
Adjunct Professor of Physics
University of Oklahoma

EDMUND A. MAREK
Associate Professor of Science Education
University of Oklahoma

SPECIAL CONSULTANT
DON G. STAFFORD
Professor of Chemistry
East Central University
Ada, Oklahoma

HEINEMANN
PORTSMOUTH, NH

Heinemann Educational Books, Inc.
70 Court Street   Portsmouth, NH   03801

London Edinburgh Melbourne Auckland
Singapore New Delhi Ibadan Nairobi
Johannesburg Kingston Port of Spain

© 1988 by John W. Renner and Edmund A. Marek

10 9 8 7 6 5 4 3 2 1

Library of Congress Cataloging in Publication Data

Renner, John Wilson, 1924–
    The learning cycle and elementary school science
teaching.

    Includes bibliographies and index.
    1. Science—Study and teaching (Elementary)—United
States. 2. Learning. 3. Child development—United
States. I. Marek, Edmund A. II. Title.
LB1585.3.R395 1986   372.3′5044   86-31867
ISBN 0-435-08300-7

Front-cover photo by Christine Kuehn
Designed by Maria Szmauz
Printed in the United States of America

CONTENTS

PREFACE vii

I EXPLORATION
ONE ■ WHAT CHILDREN CAN THINK ABOUT 3
TWO ■ HOW CHILDREN LEARN 29
THREE ■ WHAT CHILDREN LEARN 45

II CONCEPTUAL INVENTION
PROLOGUE TO THE LEARNING CYCLES FOR THE BIOLOGICAL, EARTH, AND PHYSICAL SCIENCES 59
FOUR ■ LEARNING CYCLES FOR THE BIOLOGICAL SCIENCES 67
FIVE ■ LEARNING CYCLES FOR THE EARTH SCIENCES 93
SIX ■ LEARNING CYCLES FOR THE PHYSICAL SCIENCES 117
SEVEN ■ LEARNING CYCLES FOR THE KINDERGARTEN CHILD 143

III EXPANSION OF THE IDEA
EIGHT ■ PREPARING LEARNING CYCLES 155
NINE ■ THE EDUCATIONAL SIGNIFICANCE OF THE LEARNING CYCLE 165
TEN ■ RESEARCH WITH THE LEARNING CYCLE 185

APPENDIX ■ PROTOCOLS FOR FORMAL OPERATIONAL TASKS 203

ACKNOWLEDGMENTS 215

INDEX 219

PREFACE

When educational reformers recommend changes in elementary school science, they generally focus on changes in content. They seem to believe that changing the content of the elementary school science program will produce students better educated in science than they now are. But the foundation-sponsored curriculum developments of the 1960s are public testimony that focusing on content in science education is *not* the way to reform.

One curriculum development project of the 1960s focused on content changes necessary in the curriculum, but it did not stop there. That project also gave its attention to *how* science should be taught and *what* elementary school students can learn. The Science Curriculum Improvement Study (SCIS), directed by Robert Karplus, Professor of Physics, University of California, Berkeley, hypothesized that teaching science requires more than content. Teaching, said the SCIS, also requires a teaching plan derived from both the discipline of science and the manner in which students learn. Karplus called the teaching process invented to satisfy those requirements the *learning cycle*. This book is about the learning cycle.

But the book includes much more than the material necessary to lead readers to develop a teaching procedure. It also explores content to be taught and how that content is developed into learning cycles. Also included in this book is a procedure for teachers to use in judging those concepts of which students at the several grade levels can construct meaning. In other words, this book is devoted to leading readers to understand what *knowledge construction* means and how students are led to accomplish it.

Our belief is that as *essential* for teachers as the knowledge of science content is, knowledge is not enough. To teach science, teachers also need to understand students and how they learn.

This book is devoted to assisting teachers in developing that understanding as well as increasing their knowledge of what science content can and should be taught.

Many of our colleagues in the schools—teachers, consultants, and administrators—have contributed to this book. We sincerely thank them. There is one person who deserves a special thank you. Dr. Don G. Stafford was a coauthor through two editions of an earlier book on elementary school science and has graciously consented to permit material from that early book to be used here. Thank you, Don.

I

EXPLORATION

CHAPTER ONE

WHAT CHILDREN CAN THINK ABOUT

A six-year-old child is standing near a school-room window on a November day watching big fluffy flakes of snow drifting lazily to the already white ground.[1] The child's teacher comes and stands beside her and says, "Isn't the snow pretty?" The little girl replies, "Yes, and tomorrow it will be Christmas!" "Why do you think that?" the teacher asks. "Because," says the child, "it snows at Christmas time!" The child in this incident was certainly reasoning. She had decided that snowing can bring Christmas as easily and properly as the Christmas season can bring snow. The little girl did not reason as an adult would, but she was certainly putting all the data she had together and reaching a conclusion.

Consider this incident with a two-year-old child (Piaget, 1951, pp. 230–31).

J. wanted for her doll a dress that was upstairs; she said "Dress" and when her mother refused to get it, "Daddy get dress." As I also refused, she wanted to go herself "to mummy's room." After several repetitions of this she was told it was too cold there. There was a long silence, and then: "Not too cold." "Where?" "In the room." "Why isn't it too cold?" "Get Dress."

As far as Jacqueline (J.) was concerned there was no difference in the logic between a warm room making securing the dress possible and getting the dress making the room warm. Jac-

---

[1] We are grateful to Ms. Marguerite Packnett, a kindergarten and first-grade teacher at Wilson School, Norman, Oklahoma, for the substance of this incident.

Figure 1-1 Young children usually do not believe the number of checkers stays the same when moved from a row to a stack.

queline used the same type of reasoning that the child in the snowing-Christmas incident used.

An adult and a five-year-old child are seated next to each other at a table (Figure 1-1). The adult carefully lays out a row of six red checkers and a second row of six black checkers. Opposite each red checker is a black one. The adult asks the child to count the number of red and black checkers. The child states that there are six red checkers and six black checkers. The adult asks, "Are there as many red checkers as there are black checkers?" The child says there are. The adult next says, "I am going to put the red checkers in a stack like this." The red checkers are now neatly stacked one on top of the other. "Now," says the adult, "do I have more red checkers, more black checkers, or is the number of the red checkers I have the same as the black

checkers?" The child looks at the checkers and says, "There are more red checkers." "Why do you think so?" "Because the red checkers are taller." This child believes that just because the checkers are physically stacked there are now more.

Many times when those not familiar with children's reasoning observe a scene like this, they believe that the child did not understand the language. They think that if the adult had asked the "amount" of checkers rather than the "number" of checkers, the child would have reported correctly. If you feel this way, we urge you to get six black and six red checkers—or nickels and pennies or other similar objects—and a child between four and six years old and try the task just described. We have tried changing materials, language, putting the checkers in a pile as opposed to a stack, and anything else we could think of; the results were the same. Sometimes a child will say that there are more checkers in the row than in the stack. We do not know why. We did the checkers task with twelve children between five years and five years four months old; nine of the twelve responded incorrectly.

When adults observe children using reasoning like that shown by the children in incidents like those just described, they often conclude that young children do not reason. Quite evidently young children do reason; they reason differently from adults, but they do reason. Very frequently their reasoning leads them to conclusions that are at variance with the world, and then they—and possibly the world—become confused.

Why do children demonstrate the type of reasoning reflected in the three examples above? What other characteristics do young children— and older children—display that can reveal why they reason as they do and what leads them to *construct* the understanding of the world they hold? The purpose of this chapter is to lead you to construct a model of how children learn and what they can learn.

Before providing you with data that will permit you to answer this question, we need to explain a term used in wording the question. We referred to leading children to *construct* their own understandings. What does that mean? We all "know" a lot of things, but much of what we "know" is not useful to us because it has no meaning. Asking children to memorize poems with abstract meanings for recitation to adult groups is an example of asking them to "know" something that usually has no meaning for them. No doubt, we have all memorized something that had no meaning for us to get over some hurdle—a test, for example. *Such material is not knowledge; knowledge must have meaning.*

When we interact with a new object, event, or situation, we participate in all aspects that are available to us. We select what *we* believe are the relevant, important, and salient facts, ideas, and relationships from that interaction and put them all together into a whole that is meaningful to us. The complexity of that meaningful whole obviously changes with our experiences; this is the point of the reasoning model discussed here. We develop knowledge from the kind of interaction just described. Such knowledge is usable with new objects, events, or situations because we, ourselves, built or *constructed* our understanding from our interactions. Our understanding is ours and not someone else's, which we were told about. We can have assistance in constructing our knowledge about something, but if we are permitted, we will construct our own knowledge of the object, event, or situation. Even if we are *instructed* in exactly what we should know and how we should know it, we probably still construct our own understanding, because most of what we memorize, we forget—what is left is what we have constructed for ourselves. We believe that every student in school should have the opportunity to engage in *knowledge construction*; this is what everyone does outside the classroom and in later years when school is finished.

When you became proficient in understanding the model that leads children at different ages to construct knowledge, you will have a tool that you can use to select and construct curricula, and a tool from which you can derive the principal teaching procedures you will use. In other words, you will have a *theory base* from which you can practice your profession.

When considering children's learning, there is more than one theory-base that can be used. This book, in general, is based upon a cognitive theory-base for learning. That theory-base is concerned with the mental processes involved in knowing: perception, imagery, reasoning, and so on. Specifically, this book is based upon the developmental theory of the Swiss psychologist-epistemologist, Jean Piaget. He and his associates have been studying the development of cognitive processes in children (and publishing their findings) since the 1920s, and have accumulated the greatest amount of data extant today. Keep in mind that Piaget's theory is basically cognitive and is essentially a model of intelligence. In fact, Piaget has stated (1969, p. vii) that the basic aim of his work has been "to explain the development of intelligence and to comprehend how from elementary forms of cognition superior levels of intelligence and scientific thinking came about." Frequently, it has been said that the theory of Piaget is a model of intellectual development, which it is. But do not confuse the intelligence that is Piaget's concern with that which is measured by an IQ test. What Piaget has in mind is intelligence that directs our interaction with our surroundings and the persons and things in it. He is concerned with the development of the entire intellect.

ACTIONS AND OPERATIONS

Knowledge is not a copy of reality. To know an object, to know an event, is not simply to look at it and make a mental copy or image of it. To know an object is to act upon it. To know is to modify, to transform the object, and to understand the way the object is constructed. An operation is thus the essence of knowledge; it is an interiorized action. (Piaget, 1964a, p. 176)

In the quotation, Piaget states that to know an object or event, the learner must act upon it; there are, however, different ways of acting. Very young children simply hit, grab, squeeze, and do all manner of physical things in interacting with an object. Their actions are entirely overt. Next comes a time when "the young child simply runs off reality sequences in his head just as he might do in overt action" (Flavell, 1963, p. 158). The child has made, according to Flavell, a step-by-step mental replica of concrete actions and events. In other words, the child who is capable of actions with objects and events is interacting with them or running off mental

"reality sequences" with them; that child is really trying to reproduce reality.

Eventually the child has had enough experiences, and a dramatic event occurs. Piaget explains it in this way:

When he [the child in the example] was . . . a small child—he was seated on the ground in his garden and he was counting pebbles. Now to count these pebbles he put them in a row and he counted them one, two, three, up to ten. Then he finished counting them and started to count them in the other direction. He began by the end and once again he found ten. He found this marvelous that there were ten in one direction and ten in the other direction. So he put them in a circle and counted them that way and found ten once again. Then he counted them in the other direction and found ten once more. So he put them in some other arrangement and kept counting them and kept finding ten. There was the discovery that he made.

Now what indeed did he discover? He did not discover a property of pebbles; he discovered a property of the action—which he introduced among the pebbles. The subsequent deduction will consist of interiorizing these actions and then combining them without needing any pebbles. (Piaget, 1964a)

The child in the example had made the dramatic move, from making a step-by-step mental replica of reality to mentally transforming and modifying what reality is. This child had begun to do what Piaget calls *mental operations*; he had begun to construct his own knowledge. The primary difference between actions and mental operations is that actions mentally reproduce reality, while operations do something further with that reproduction.

Consider the example cited earlier of the child and the two lines of checkers. The child who believes that there are more checkers in the stack is simply making a mental replica of the height of the stack compared to the length of the line of checkers. That child cannot *reverse* the thinking process to include the fact that the line is also much shorter than the stack. All the child can do is make a mental replica of the reality of both objects. But the child who can do mental operations can mentally reverse the stack-of-checkers image to the line-of-checkers image. This learner can indeed transform the data received from the environment; this learner has interiorized the action of producing a stack from the line. Piaget describes a mental operation as *"an interiorized action.* But in addition, it is a *reversible* action; that is, it can take place in both directions, for instance, adding or subtracting, joining or separating" (Piaget, 1964a, p. 177). Think of a mental operation this way: it is *mentally* doing something with the data received from the environment.

A child plants a seed in a cup and tapes another seed to the outside. When the plant appears in the cup the child who planted it does not see the connection between the seed on the cup and the plant. Defend whether this is evidence of an action or a mental operation.

LEVELS OF INTELLECTUAL DEVELOPMENT

In 1920 Piaget accepted a position in the Binet Laboratory in Paris. His assignment was to develop standardized French versions of certain English reasoning tests. While carrying out this responsibility he made two major findings that led him into the detailed study of intelligence. He found that children of about the same age frequently gave the *same wrong answers* to a particular question. In addition, "there were different kinds of common wrong answers at different ages" (Ginsburg and Opper, 1969, p. 3). These findings led him to believe that the thinking of younger children was *qualitatively* different from that of older children. In other words, younger children actually believe that the world

works in a way different from what older children believe.

These findings led Piaget to reject a quantitative definition of intelligence, which is derived from measuring the number of correct responses on an IQ test. According to Piaget's theory, a young child may be just as bright as an older one, but the qualities of the types of thought of which the two groups are capable are distinctly different. Adults often believe that older children are brighter than younger children because the thought type of older children more closely approximates adult thought. This notion is built around the assumption that children are miniature adults. The Piaget model rejected this idea and stated that a certain age range has a distinct quality of thought. According to the Piaget model of intellectual development, humans pass through stages or phases of thought in moving through life. Thought in each stage has certain properties that differ from those in other stages.

Many years of exacting study of children at all ages have gone into Piaget's stages-of-intellectual-development model. Phillips explains Piaget's method for gathering his data like this:

He observes the child's surroundings and his behavior, formulates an hypothesis concerning the structure that underlies and includes them both, and then tests that hypothesis by altering the surroundings slightly—by rearranging the materials, by posing the problem in a different way, or by even overtly suggesting to the subject a response different from the one predicted by the theory. (1975, p. 3)

Piaget's data about the reasoning patterns of humans begins at birth and extends into the third decade of life. Obviously, the data gathered from birth and for several years thereafter are based only on his observations.

Perhaps, for our purposes, Piaget's procedure for gathering data could be described as giving the child a task to perform that involves materials and reasoning, letting the child perform the task, and then asking the child what he/she did and why he/she did it that way. What is important for you as a teacher is that *Piaget's model of intellectual development is derived from direct association with learners of all ages.* Any model used by teachers to guide them in selecting and employing content and materials must be relevant to children.

The data which Piaget and his co-workers have gathered have led to the formulation of a model of intellectual development that includes four unique levels. The quality of thought in each of these levels (stages, phases, periods) is distinctly different from the quality of thought in each of the other levels. In other words, the content children at each level can learn is unique. Do not interpret this statement to mean that all children in a particular level think *exactly* alike, but rather, that the thinking of children in the same level has common properties.

The first level
The first stage of intellectual development in Piaget's model begins at birth and continues until the child is approximately two-and-a-half years old. Piaget has called this period the *sensorimotor stage.* During this stage the child learns that objects are permanent—just because an object disappears from sight does not mean that it no longer exists. Acquiring the characteristics of object permanence explains, for example, why a child approximately a year old will cry when his mother leaves. This separation anxiety, however, does not occur earlier because until that point, "out of sight, out of mind" adequately describes the child's perception. During the sensorimotor period, language begins to develop (Phillips, 1975, pp. 25–60), a development that is far too complex to explore fully in this book. Basically, however, the child learns how to attach sounds to the objects, symbols, and experiences he/she has had. But inventing appropriate sounds for something depends, as does later learning, on the child's experiencing that something.

During the sensorimotor period, the first signs begin to emerge showing that intellect is *developed* and not spontaneous. Now, certainly, the way a child in the sensorimotor stage goes about learning is quite different from the way an adult learns. But throughout all the stages of Piaget's model, the fact becomes obvious that later learning cannot occur unless early learning has been accomplished. This means that, for culturally deprived children who have not had the benefit of a rich environment to assist them in developing the beginnings of a language system, the school may need to provide many experiences that go far beyond conventional reading-readiness programs before traditional "school" activities can begin. There is little likelihood that you will be working with children in the sensorimotor stage. You need to be aware, however, that this is the stage in which intellectual development begins to emerge, and until the child accomplishes certain goals in this stage, later learning must wait. Perhaps we, as teachers, need to spend more time determining what the learner is ready to learn and less time being concerned with the specific content being covered.

Much confusion has developed about the ages at which children move from stage to stage within the intellectual development model. Piaget has repeatedly said that the ages he has suggested are only approximations and has gone so far as to say that to "divide developmental continuity into stages recognizable by some set of external criteria is not the most profitable of occupations" (Piaget, 1963, p. 139). The external criterion most often used is chronological age, but using it can be misleading.

There is only one stage in Piaget's model whose starting point can be precisely stated—the sensorimotor stage. As noted earlier, it begins at birth and ends around two-and-a-half years of age. A two-and-a-half-year-old child will begin to enter the *preoperational stage;* his exit from this type of thinking begins around seven years of age. In other words, the model does not state precise ages at which a learner will progress from stage to stage. Piaget explains that, although the order of succession is constant, the chronological ages of these stages varies a great deal (Piaget, 1964a). As you read the remainder of this discussion about Piaget's model of intellectual development, keep in mind that a child does not move completely from one stage to another at one time. The evidence available suggests that a learner can easily be in the sensorimotor phase on some traits and in the preoperational phase on others. Rather than thinking that a child moves from one stage to another, think of the child as moving into a particular stage on certain traits. As development progresses, the child moves more deeply into one stage on some traits and begins to move into the next higher stage on other traits. In other words, there is not a chronological line children cross indicating that they have moved completely from one stage to another like that when an individual is permitted to vote at age eighteen.

I n this paragraph the notion of "trait" is referred to. What is a trait? Based only on what you know so far, describe what you think are the "traits" referred to.

The second level

Think back to the discussion regarding the difference between "action" and "operation." The name of the second stage in the Piagetian model, *preoperational*, is wonderfully descriptive of what the mental activities of children occupying that stage are like. Children of this age are confined to making step-by-step mental replicas of the environment and running off reality sequences in their heads. However, doing something with those reality sequences—that is, performing mental operations—cannot be accomplished by the preoperational child. Perhaps the best description of preoperational

thought is that it is perception-bound.[2] Preoperational children see, decide, and report. They think, but thinking *about* what they think is beyond their intellectual ability. The preoperational stage of thought is one that exists before (pre-) mental operations are possible.

A complete description of all the intellectual characteristics of the preoperational child is far beyond the scope of this book. If you wish to investigate the characteristics of preoperational children further, we suggest that you consult *The Origin of Intellect: Piaget's Theory* by John L. Phillips, Jr., referred to throughout this chapter, or Piaget's *The Psychology of Intelligence*, in which he explains his intelligence model and the characteristics of the stages within the model.

As children begin to move from sensorimotor thought, certain changes occur in their cognitive abilities. Piaget explains these changes like this:

At the end of the sensori-motor period . . . there appears a function that is fundamental to the development of later behavior patterns. It consists in the ability to represent something by means of a "signifier" . . . which serves only a representative purpose . . . we generally refer to this function that gives rise to representation as "symbolic." However, since linguists distinguish between "symbols and signs," we would do better to adopt their term "semiotic function" to designate those activities having to do with . . . signifiers as a whole. (Piaget and Inhelder, 1969, p. 51)

This quotation describes an important difference between the sensorimotor child and the preoperational child. Carefully consider the phrase "which serves only a representational purpose." This is what is meant by a "signifier"; it represents what is going to happen. Thus,

[2] The authors wish they could take credit for inventing this phrase, but they cannot. They first heard it used by Dr. Celia Stendler Lavatelli in the film *Piaget's Theory: Conservation*, produced by John Davidson Films, San Francisco.

when the preoperational child hears the bell of the ice cream truck, it signifies to the child that ice cream is available. To the sensorimotor child, however, the sound of the bell and his taste of ice cream are not mentally separated. Hearing the sound of the bell also means the taste of the ice cream. A sensorimotor child sees a sibling put on his coat and thinks the sibling is going to school. In other words, the overt sign—the signifier—is not differentiated from what the sign means.

A preoperational child can think about signifiers and distinguish them from the objects, events, or situations they signify. This ability allows the teacher to use some definite characteristics in working with preoperational children. There are at least five of these characteristics—called semiotic (or symbolic) functions—whose appearance is almost simultaneous. Each of the five is described, from the simplest to the most complex, in the following discussion.

1. Deferred imitation: This is the ability of a child to observe an event, object, or situation and later imitate what he/she has observed. Children who have observed how a rabbit wrinkles its nose and later try to do it when asked are using this preoperational characteristic. The establishment of habits uses a good bit of deferred imitation.

2. Symbolic play: This trait is most adequately described by the preoperational child's game of pretending, a game that is not found at the sensorimotor level. Using this trait allows a teacher to have a play-store in the classroom, for example.

3. Drawing: Here the child is able to represent his experiences graphically. Many times the symbols used are not clear to an adult, but the child can explain them. Piaget believes that this trait is an intermediate stage between play and mental image. If you doubt the importance of mental images to thinking, try to imagine thinking without them. (That, too, is a mental image!)

4. Mental image: This is, of course, what must be available to children before they can describe anything they have experienced. Whenever a teacher says, "Tell me what happened" or, "Tell me what you saw," the ability to use the mental-image trait is assumed.

5. Verbal evocation: The increasing ability of children to use language makes it possible for them to describe events that have already happened.

When children describe or comment on something that has recently happened, they are using at least the mental images and verbal evocation traits. Obviously the five semiotic functions are interconnected.

Why is the semiotic function of young children important enough for their teachers to know about? Answering this question requires the evolution of a principle for using the Piagetian model in the classroom. If children are to develop increasingly complex mental abilities and content understanding (undergo intellectual development) they must have maximum opportunities to interact with their environment. Preoperational children *can* use symbolic play, drawing, and all the other semiotic functions. Instruction, therefore, must also use these traits.

The teaching principle that can be deduced from Piaget's model says that teaching at any level of intellectual development must use the mental abilities unique to that particular level. If teachers insist that children "know" something when they do not have the mental abilities to understand what is being pushed at them, children have only one choice—they memorize. When the trivia contest is over, most of what they have memorized they promptly forget. We will examine this point further as we look at the last two levels in Piaget's model.

Describe a classroom activity that would use each of the five semiotic function traits.

For the purposes of applying the Piagetian model in selecting and using content and instructional methodology, six basic characteristics of the preoperational child—in addition to the semiotic function—warrant examination. The characteristics are:

1. Egocentrism
2. Irreversibility
3. Centering
4. States in a transformation
5. Transductive reasoning
6. Conservation reasoning

Egocentrism is one of the preoperational child's most prominent traits. The child sees the world from only one point of view—his own. The world revolves around the child, who is completely unaware of being a prisoner to only one way of viewing it. The preoperational child cannot see another's point of view and coordinate it with his own and that of others. Children's perceived opinion—a reality sequence—is what they believe, and they feel no responsibility to justify a belief or to look for contradictions in it. Preoperational learners have developed a certain language pattern, which they use to communicate with others, but they do not have the ability or see the need to adapt that language pattern to the needs of their listener.

The second trait of the preoperational child, which has great importance from the curriculum, teaching-methodology frame of reference, is that of *irreversibility*. In order for a human to begin to perform intellectual operations he/she must be able to reverse his/her thinking. Irreversibility of thought is beautifully illustrated by this dialogue with an eight-year-old boy (Piaget, 1964b, p. 86):

Have you got a brother?
Yes.
And your brother, has he got a brother?
No.
Are you sure?
Yes.
And has your sister got a brother?
No.

You have a sister?
Yes.
And she has a brother?
Yes.
How many?
No, she hasn't got any.
Is your brother also your sister's brother?
No.
And has your brother got a sister?
No.

The dialogue continues until finally the child recognizes that he is his brother's brother. This dialogue with a four-year-old girl also nicely illustrates the irreversibility concept (Piaget, 1964b, p. 85):

Have you got a sister?
Yes.
And has she got a sister?
No, she hasn't got a sister. I am my sister.

Reversibility means that a thought is capable of being returned to its starting point. For example: $8 + 6 = 14$ and $14 - 6 = 8$. The thought started with 8 and returned to 8. Preoperational children cannot reverse their thinking. Consider what this says to those planning a mathematics program for the early primary grades. Much of our society has a real hang-up about mathematics. Perhaps understanding many of the mathematics concepts presently taught in an early elementary mathematics education requires mental reversibility. Since children cannot use reversibility, they cannot develop the understanding demanded. They have no choice, therefore, but to use rote memory if they wish to survive the trivia contests (tests). Could it be that such an experience creates "hang-ups" about mathematics that individuals never conquer?

Isolating the irreversible trait in a young child's thinking is not difficult, and it is informative. A procedure using clay will enable you to do it. The materials you will need are simple—two equal quantities of modeling clay or plasticene (we found that using different-colored pieces facilitates communication with the child).

F orm the pieces of clay into two balls and explain to the child that you want to start the experiment with one ball just the same size as the other. In other words one ball should contain *just as much* clay as the other. Allow your subject to work with the two balls until *the child believes* they contain the same amounts of clay. Now, deform one of the balls; a good way to do this is to roll one of the balls into a long, cylindrical shape or a pancake.

Next, ask several children (five-year-old children are probably best) if there is more clay in the ball, more in the roll, or if there is the same amount in each (be sure to give each child all three choices). Ask each child why the answer given is the one he/she believes is correct. Record the responses you receive.

A child who has not developed the thinking trait of reversibility will tell you that there are different amounts of clay in the two shapes. Our experience has been that most preoperational children will select the cylinder (or pancake) shape as the one containing more clay.

The preoperational subject is not able to make the thinking reversal from the cylinder-shaped object that now exists back to the clay sphere that did exist. The child cannot do the analyzing and synthesizing that would permit him or her to reconstruct the sphere mentally, although the child knows that the sphere existed. This can be proved by asking the child to restore the roll of clay to its original shape; a sphere will be produced and the child will now tell you that there is the same amount of clay in each. Children of this age think, but their thinking is so irreversible, they cannot think *about* their thinking.

Why does the preoperational learner usually focus attention on the cylinder-shaped object rather than on the ball? This can be explained by using another trait in the preoperational model—centering. When one clay ball was deformed, the child's attention was probably fixed on the detail of length, and rigid, preception-bound mental abilities prevented him/her from seeing anything else about the transformed object. Educational experiences provided for young children must avoid using materials, activities, or both that encourage the centering trait. If colors are used, for example, they should all be attractive and appealing. Teachers must not be surprised when children focus their attention on one aspect of an object, event, or situation; they are only acting as preoperational learners can be expected to act.

Centering is a characteristic of preoperational children, and those working with them should expect to find it. Does a child's inability to reverse thinking cause him/her to center, or does the child's centering trait cause irreversibility? Who knows? Besides, is it important? Both traits exist—and which comes first is really not relevant because obviously they are not mutually exclusive.

The extreme perception-boundness of a preoperational child is well illustrated by the trait known as *states in a transformation*. Figure 1-2 represents a wooden rod that is held vertically (position 1) and then released (positions 2, 3, 4, and 5). The rod eventually comes to rest at position 6. Obviously, the rod was in a state of rest when it was held in position 1 and is again at rest in position 6. If a series of pictures is

Figure 1-2 The ability of children to see states in a transformation can be assessed with the falling rod experiment.

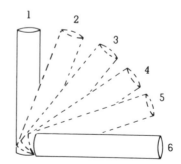

taken of the falling object, it would be seen to pass through many other states, represented by positions 2, 3, 4, and 5. In other words, the series of states in the event results in a transformation, from the stick standing erect to the stick lying in a horizontal position.

If preoperational children are shown the experiment, after having been informed that they will be asked to draw a diagram of it, they will not draw what is shown in Figure 1-2, nor will they indicate in any way what successive states the stick went through in being transformed from position 1 to position 5. Our experience in asking children to do this task has been that they draw only positions 1 and 5. They see only the beginning and final states and do not see the transformation. This particular preoperational trait (which also shows irreversibility and centering) is particularly important when young children are studying science and doing experiments, as, for example, a plant-growing experiment. There is little need to try to get them to see the importance of the several states in the transformation; *they cannot do it.* They will perceive the first and final states and nothing else. The process that allowed the final state to be a function of the intermediate states cannot be understood by preoperational children. That state seems to call into doubt the insistence that young children do detailed experiments; they will see the beginning and the end, but as long as they are preoperational, they will not learn anything about the process of experimentation.

At the beginning of this chapter you read three incidents that each involved young children making decisions using reasoning that seemed strange. One child thought that, because it was snowing, tomorrow it would be Christmas; another, that a cold room was not cold because she wanted something from it; and the third child that stacking up a row of checkers increased their number. Such reasoning seems strange, even silly, to an adult, but it is very real to a child. These three children are not reasoning from a general to a particular case (deduction)

nor has a series of particular cases led them to a generalization (induction). Rather, the three children are reasoning from one particular case— e.g., it's snowing—to another particular case— e.g., tomorrow will be Christmas. Reasoning from particular case to particular case is called *transductive* reasoning. This type of reasoning begins to appear in the child with the beginning of language and generally lasts until after four years of age. It is sometimes found late in the preoperational period, however, as in the case of the child in the snowing example.

In our study of children, we have often used Piaget's classification tasks. One of these involves showing a child a great number of wooden beads, all of one color (we usually use red), and a few of another color (say, blue). Ask the child if there are more wooden beads or red beads. A truly preoperational child will tell you there are more red beads, and when asked why, will often answer: "Because they are prettier"—a perfect transductive response. As a teacher, do not be surprised if you encounter such transduction in kindergarten and first-grade children. If you do, be patient; usually it disappears with the increased experiences a school environment can provide over what the preschool environment could.

R eread the checkers example and write a complete explanation of why that child is using transductive reasoning.

Identifying whether or not the preoperational thinker can see the relationship between states in a transformation is a simple task; you do the falling stick experiment with the children and then ask them to tell you what happened. You have just explained why the checkers activity allows a child to demonstrate transductive reasoning, and other tasks will also do it. Identifying egocentrism, irreversibility, and centering, however, is not as easy as using the falling stick experiment.

There is a procedure, however, that can be used to identify the traits of preoperational children. You have already met two of the techniques used—the activities involving checkers and clay balls. Those activities illustrate the inability of a preoperational child to mentally hold the image of an object and to see that distorting the object does not change the amount of material it contains. "Mentally holding" the original image of an object is called *conservation reasoning*. Preoperational children do not conserve; they make decisions about the distortion of the object on the basis of what they perceive. This rigid, perception-boundness, however, is due to their irreversible thinking, tendency to center, extreme egocentrism, inability to see a transformation between states, and transduction reasoning. Isolating a child who does not use conservation reasoning will allow you to describe his stage of intellectual development in terms of the preoperational traits we have already described *and* the trait of conservation reasoning. According to Piaget: "The clearest indication of the existence of a preoperational period . . . is the absence of notions of conservation until about the age of seven or eight" (Piaget and Inhelder, 1969, p. 97).

Conservation, then, is an overt manifestation of whether or not a child is a preoperational thinker. As we said earlier, this stage of development begins at about two-and-a-half years of age. In describing the beginning of a child's ability to conserve, Piaget has also provided information about the end of the preoperational period:

There always comes a time (between 6 and one-half years and 7 years 8 months) when a child's attitude changes: he no longer needs to reflect, he decides, he even looks surprised when the question is asked, he is certain of the conservation. (Piaget, 1963, p. 140).

The beginning of the ability to conserve and the beginning of the child's entry into the third stage in the Piagetian model—*concrete operations*—occur, then, in the late first or early second grade. For purposes of designing a first-grade curriculum for most of the year, a teacher can consider that the children are preoperational.

The clay balls experiment measures the ability to conserve solid amount, and the checkers experiment assesses whether or not the child can conserve number. There are four additional tasks we have found useful. These tasks are: the conservation of liquid amount, length, weight, and area. Descriptions of all six tasks and how they are administered follow. As you read these descriptions, keep in mind the definition of "conservation," which may be stated thus: Children who conserve can hold a concept about an object in their minds while a second object, like the first, is distorted, and they can see that the distorted object is still like the nondistorted object in many specific ways.

Conservation of number task. You have already met this task.[3] Have the children line up six black checkers in one row and six red checkers in another row, as shown in Figure 1-3. Ask the child if he/she agrees that there are as many red checkers as there are black checkers. After the child agrees, stack the red checkers, one on top of the other, and leave the black checkers as they were; the checkers will now appear as in Figure 1-4. After you have rearranged the check-

---

[3] The utilization of these tasks is illustrated in the film, *Piaget's Theory: Conservation*, produced and distributed by John Davidson Films, San Francisco. The directions for these tasks have been tried by several hundred elementary school teachers, and we appreciate their suggestions and contributions.

Figure 1-3   **Figure 1-4**

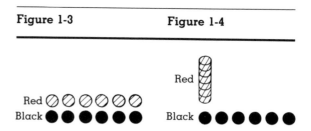

ers, ask if there are more red checkers, more black checkers, or if the numbers of black and red checkers are the same. If the child reports that the numbers are the same, number is conserved. *Be sure to ask why the child believes as he/she does, not only on this task but also on all the others.* Getting the child to explain his/her answer will tell you a great deal about the state of the child's intellectual development.

Conservation of liquid task.   Pour the same amount of water into two containers of equal size (see Figure 1-5). For convenience, you may wish to color the water in one container red. Ask if the child agrees that the containers are the same size and that they contain the same amount of liquid; if the child wishes to adjust the water levels, let this be done. After agreement has been reached that the amounts are equal, have the child pour one of the liquids into a taller, thinner container (see Figure 1-6) and ask if there is more colored water, more clear water, or if the amounts are equal. A report that the amounts are equal shows that the child conserves liquid amount; a report that there is more water in one of the containers demonstrates a lack of liquid-conservation ability.

Conservation of solid amount task.   This task has already been referred to. Prepare two pieces of clay, each containing the same amount, and roll them into balls of equal size (see Figure 1-7). For convenience during the discussion with the child, you may wish to use two colors of clay, blue and red, for example. Ask the child if there is the same amount of blue clay as red

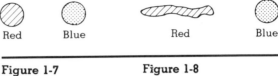

Red   Blue   Red   Blue

Figure 1-7   **Figure 1-8**

clay; let the child make any adjustments in the balls he/she feels are necessary to convince the child the balls are of equal size. Next, deform the piece of red clay by rolling it into what you may want to call a "snake" (see Figure 1-8). Ask the learner if there is more clay in the ball, in the snake, or if there is the same amount in each. Recognizing that the amount of the solid remains constant indicates solid-amount conservation ability.

Conservation of area task.   Begin this task by showing the child two pieces of green construction paper of *exactly* the same size. Explain that the pieces of paper represent two fields of grass and that they must be exactly the same size. Give the child the opportunity to examine the two pieces of paper and to make adjustments on them if necessary. The child must be convinced that the two fields are exactly the same size. Be sure to ask the child to explain to you why one field contains as much grass as the other. That act of explaining convinces the child that he/she must think about the papers as grass (a preoperational child can do this; think about the semiotic functions) and will indicate that the child understands the "sameness" concept in this task.

Next show the child some wooden cubes (about 2.5 centimeters on a side). Explain that you are going to pretend that each of these cubes is a barn. Give the child the opportunity to examine the "barns" until the child is convinced they are all the same size. Place a barn on each field (see Figure 1-9) and ask the child whether, in each field, there is still the same amount of grass that has not been covered, or whether one field or the other has more grass. After adding

Figure 1-5   **Figure 1-6**

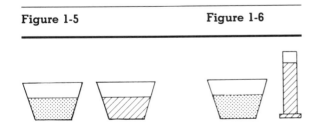

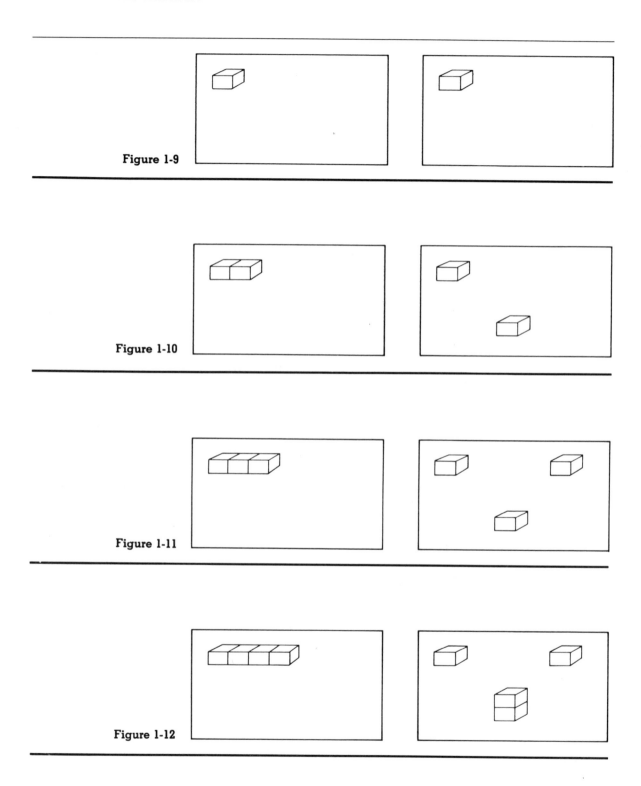

Figure 1-9

Figure 1-10

Figure 1-11

Figure 1-12

---

a barn to each field and having the child tell you which has more uncovered grass, *always* ask why the child believes the answer given is true. Record the child's answer. Now place one more barn on each of the fields, but on one field of paper place the barns very close together and on the other separate them (see Figure 1-10). Again ask the child if there is still the same amount of uncovered grass in each field and why. Use a third barn as shown in Figure 1-11 and again ask questions about the amount of uncovered grass.

Not infrequently, the only justification a child gives to explain why the grass area is the same in both fields is that the numbers of barns on the two fields are equal. These data suggest that the child is conserving number and not area. To determine whether or not this is what the child is doing, follow the procedure shown in Figure 1-12; here one of the barns has been placed on top of another. Ask the child the question as before. The child who responds to the arrangements in Figures 1-9, 1-10, and 1-11 by stating that the amounts of uncovered grass are equal but those in Figure 1-12 are unequal has demonstrated the ability to conserve area.

Conservation of length task. This task requires a wooden dowel forty centimeters long and four dowels of the same diameter each ten centimeters long. The exact lengths and numbers of the shorter dowels are not important, but the combined lengths of the smaller dowels must equal the length of the long dowel. Two identical toy cars are also helpful. Place the long dowel and the shorter pieces parallel, so that the combined length of the pieces just equals the length of the long piece (see Figure 1-13). Be sure the child agrees that the line of pieces is exactly the length of the long piece; let adjustments be made if necessary. Inform the child that the dowels represent roads and there is going to be a race. Place identical toy cars (say, a red car and a blue car) at the same ends of the roads and then pose this question: "If the cars

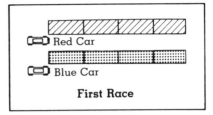

First Race

Figure 1-13

travel the same speed, which car, the red one or the blue one, will reach the end of the road first? Or will they reach the ends of the roads at the same time?" If the child does not ultimately agree that the cars will reach the ends of the roads at the same time, abandon the task.

Next, move two pieces of the four-piece road as shown in Figure 1-14 and ask the question about the race. If the child states that the cars will reach the ends of the roads at the same time, he/she conserves length.

Conservation of weight task. Give the child two balls containing equal weights of clay; two colors of clay, such as red and green, facilitate communication in this task (see Figure 1-15). Add and subtract clay from each of the balls until the child agrees that the balls weigh exactly the same. Next, take the two balls of clay from the child and flatten one of them into a pancake or distort it in some other way. *Don't let the child lift the two clay objects after this distor-*

Figure 1-14

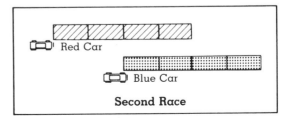

Second Race

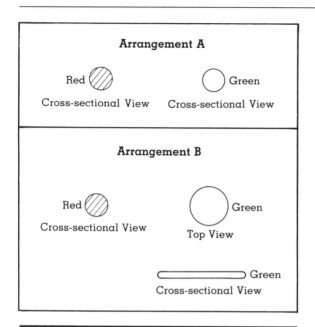

Figure 1-15

tion. Next, ask the learner if the green clay weighs more, the red clay weighs more, or if the weights are still the same. Failing to recognize that the weights of the red and green clay objects are still equal shows that the child does not conserve weight.

The conservation tasks you have just read are neither meaningful nor functional until you employ them with children. You are probably thinking that the tasks are so simple anyone can do them. All this proves is that you are not preoperational!

A dminister the six conservation tasks to three children and record your results. A five-year-old, a seven-year-old, and a nine-year-old will probably give you an age range that will allow you to see preoperational thought and thought moving into the concrete operational stage. After the children you examine respond to the question you ask, be sure to give them the opportunity to explain their reasoning to you.

Your results will increase in meaning if you combine them with those of your colleagues. The combination of data will also show you that age alone does not determine when a preoperational learner leaves this stage. Additionally, the data combination will show you that just because a child conserves on one task does not necessarily mean that he/she will conserve on others. Our experience with the tasks suggests that the first conservation usually made is of number, the second of liquid amount, and the third of solid amount.

The data shown in Table 1-1 are informative when studied within a frame of reference. The 252 children represented in this table are a random sample of children from the Norman, Oklahoma, school system. Those doing the evaluations used identical task directions and objects, and standardized their questioning techniques.

If you adopt a policy of interpretation that all twelve children of any particular age must complete a specific task satisfactorily before the group can be regarded as exercising conservation reasoning in that task, conservation reasoning appears rather late for some tasks. In evaluating data from the responses of children to a type of task just slightly different from conservation reasoning, Piaget used the following procedure: "We have followed the accepted custom of considering a test successfully passed when 75 percent of the children of the same age have answered correctly" (Piaget, 1964b, p. 100). This means that in Table 1-1 conservation reasoning is achieved when nine children (in the twelve-child sample) in any cell respond satisfactorily. (The number in each cell of Table 1-1 reflects those responding correctly.) In each column, however, the number should not fall substantially below nine once it has been achieved. We have taken the position that eight is not seriously below nine but that seven is; our interpretation is, of course, arbitrary. If you disagree, please make your own interpretation and operate with it on what follows.

If Piaget's "75 percent rule-of-thumb" is adopted, the data in Table 1-1 take on a meaning

TABLE 1-1

Age in Months	Sample Size	Conservation of					
		Number	Solid Amount	Liquid Amount	Length	Area	Weight
60–64	12	3	2	2	—	1	1
65–68	12	7	2	—	2	2	3
69–72	12	6	3	4	1	2	1
73–76	12	8	7	7	3	6	3
77–80	12	8	5	5	3	2	6
81–84	12	9	5	5	—	3	5
85–88	12	11	11	9	6	9	10
89–92	12	11	9	11	9	8	11
93–96	12	9	9	8	7	6	8
97–100	12	12	12	11	9	8	11
101–104	12	12	11	8	5	7	8
105–108	12	11	9	9	7	8	10
109–112	12	11	10	10	7	7	6
113–116	12	11	11	10	7	7	7
117–120	12	12	12	10	7	6	9
121–124	12	9	12	11	7	8	9
125–128	12	11	11	10	9	7	11
129–132	12	12	11	11	12	10	10
133–136	12	12	12	12	8	7	12
137–140	12	12	10	10	10	10	12
141–144	12	12	12	12	12	12	12

Source: John W. Renner, Judith Brock, Sue Heath, Mildred Laughlin, and Jo Stevens, "Piaget Is Practical," *Science and Children*, October 1971, p. 23. These data were gathered by a group of experienced test administrators, all of whom cannot be acknowledged. The authors are especially grateful, however, to elementary school teaching colleagues.

that tells those concerned with curriculum a great deal. Conservation of number, for example, is not achieved until 84 months of age (seven years). What does that tell you about using numerical experiences with children in science experiments? Conservation of length is not achieved until 136 months (11 years 4 months). Teaching a system of measurement usually begins by teaching length, and its conservation is assumed. Where do you usually find the teaching of systems of measurement? Is the conservation of length assumption valid?

Whatever the outcome throughout the conservation tasks, the children are being evaluated on their ability to reverse their thinking, decenter their attention, cease using transductive reasoning, and overcome all of the other character-istics of a preoperational thinker. A child who does not reverse his thinking does poorly in science experiments; he can only observe and report what he saw. All the conservation tasks indicate a child's ability to carry out reversals of thinking; those reversals get more difficult as the complexity of the tasks increases.

Explain the mental reversals in each conservation task, and how difficult an experiment each successful conservation allows a child to perform.

The conservation concept is a potent tool in the hands of a teacher who knows how to use it. That teacher can identify preoperational and concrete operational learners and immediately know something about their thinking processes. The type of curricula that can be used with this type of thinker can then be identified. There is no use, for example, in asking a preoperational thinker to become involved in an educational activity that requires thinking reversals; preoperational thinkers *cannot* do them. They can observe, perceive, and report their perceptions. They need educational experiences that use the semiotic functions.

Piaget and Inhelder (1969, pp. 92–93) describe the preoperational child as able to use "a successful adaptive action," but this ability "is not automatically accompanied by an accurate mental representation of the situation or of the action performed." The following example makes this theoretical statement very clear.

Children of four and five often go by themselves from home to school and back every day even though the walk may be ten minutes or so in length. Yet if you ask them to represent their path by means of little three-dimensional cardboard objects (houses, church, streets, river, squares, etc.) or to indicate the plan of the school as it is seen from the main entrance or from the side facing the river, they are unable to reconstruct the topographical relationship, even though they constantly utilize them in action. Young children's memories are in some sense motor-memories and cannot necessarily be represented in a simultaneous unified reconstruction. The first obstacle to operations, then, is the problem of mentally representing what has already been absorbed on the level of action. (Piaget and Inhelder, 1969, pp. 93–94)

The last sentence in this quotation represents the principal point that teachers must understand when working with preoperational children. Young children *cannot* mentally represent what they can do at the level of action. That means, for example, that young children can look at the roots of a plant growing into dirt, but they cannot mentally represent that those roots came from the seed. Furthermore, if asked to draw the plant and roots as they are growing, they will not be very successful. Young children

can count three blocks and two blocks and when the blocks are pushed together they will probably count five blocks. But when that action is listed on the chalkboard as $3 + 2 = 5$, they cannot mentally represent that *operation* as the same as the *action* of pushing the blocks together and counting five. Perhaps the best summary statement that can be made about preoperational children is that they cannot represent cognitively what they can do in action.

You have probably been given more information about preoperational children than you wanted! There is a reason, however, for treating the preoperational period of intellectual development this thoroughly: understanding preoperational thought greatly facilitates developing an understanding of the third level in the Piagetian model.

The third level

Somewhere between the ages of six and seven, when they are asked the questions in the conservation tasks, most children are absolutely certain that the quantities are conserved. In fact, they look surprised that such questions would be asked. Children between the ages of eighty-one and eighty-four months (see Table 1-1) can use conservation reasoning because they can use the mental operations of thought reversal, decentering, and seeing states in transformation, and they *begin* to use deductive and inductive reasoning as opposed to transductive reasoning. In addition to these mental operations, there are other operations in which these children can engage, such as seriation, classification, and correspondence. Consider teaching a child a measuring system. The conservation of length is a necessity and so is correspondence; placing a measuring stick down once corresponds to measuring that much length. To *understand* number, children must be able to seriate; they must realize that placing six after five and before seven means that six is truly *more* than five and *less* than seven. Classification ability must be present before children can understand that song birds, ducks, and geese are different although they are all birds. There is little doubt—although we know of no research that tests it—that the ability to use conservation reasoning requires using such operations as serial ordering, classification, and correspondence.

The foregoing paragraph can be interpreted to say that there is an entire set of mental operations that *begin* to become available to children at around seven years of age. When children reasoning at this intellectual level apply the mental operations just discussed to a problem or situation, they do so linearly. That is, they use the operations in a step-by-step fashion. They do not apply the operation to the entire situation about which they are reasoning or any part of the problem in relation to the entire problem. They reason only one step at a time. Piaget describes the operations and the manner in which they are used as " 'concrete' because they relate directly to objects and not yet to verbally stated hypotheses" (1969, p. 100). The name of this stage of intellectual development is *concrete operational.*

Piaget's pointed remark that these operations are concrete because they relate directly to objects is a directive to schools about what they ask children to do. Students cannot learn unless they deal with reality. Actual objects, actual events, actual situations are mandatory. In many elementary science programs, children are asked to "learn" about the atom. Now, to understand the atom and what it means, you must understand data that support the existence of the atom. No one has ever seen an atom; it is abstract, not concrete. Concrete operational learners cannot understand abstractions. What they do understand is data from reality. Concepts that are built from concrete experiences are *concrete concepts.* Research has shown (Renner et al., 1976, ch. 9) that concrete operational learners can develop understanding of concrete concepts, but they do not develop understanding of concepts based upon abstractions. Understanding what this research finding means is vital to teachers.

All school subject matter must be evaluated within the frame of reference of concrete and abstract. If the material the children are to learn can be derived from reality—actual objects, events, or situations, or all three—children in the concrete operational stage can understand it. If the material is not from reality, the children interacting with it will not experience learning. *Do not believe* that children will learn concepts if they are given only the data from some concrete event, object or situation, or all three. They must become involved in gathering the data, evaluating the data they have been given, discussing the sources that produced the data, or in some way have an actual concrete experience with the particular data that are to lead them to the concept to be learned. The most beneficial experience is, of course, gathering the data themselves; vicarious experiences do not have the efficacy that actual experiences have. We believe there is much nonconcrete content in many elementary school science programs that needs to be eliminated.

Piaget originally stated that children begin to move into the concrete operational stage between six and seven years of age. The data in Table 1-1 tend to corroborate this generalization. The original investigation carried out by Piaget and his colleagues led them to state that children began to move out of the concrete stages of thought "at about 11 or 12 years . . ." (Piaget, 1963, p. 148). In 1972, however, Piaget wrote an article (Piaget, 1972) in which he stated that the students used in the original investigation were taken from "the better schools in Geneva." He further stated that he felt the ages of eleven to twelve years, which he had concluded were the ages when children began to leave the concrete thought period, were derived from data taken from "a somewhat privileged population." He proposed, rather, that the point at which the exit from concrete thought begins is "between 15 and 20 years and *not* 11 and 15 years."

Our own research data tend to corroborate Piaget's statement that concrete thought is still present in many students even older than 15 years. Recently (Renner et al., 1977, pp. 24–27), 811 students in grades ten through twelve and between the ages of 13.75 years and 18.58 years completed tasks whose results revealed the type of thought in this group. Concrete thought was demonstrated 57 percent of the time. Data (Renner et al., 1976, ch. 7) also show that approximately 50 percent of entering college freshmen also use concrete thought most of the time. Such data vividly demonstrate that teachers must thoroughly understand concrete thought. It usually begins in the late first or early second grade and persists in the majority of students through high school.

The presence of concrete reasoning means that actual experience with those concepts that are to be learned is the *only way understanding develops*. To be sure, students capable of concrete reasoning can memorize the definition of an atom, or of how to divide fractions, and perform—and perform or act is what they do—with such memorized content in the classroom. But when they need to use that content in another context, whether in the classroom or outside it, they cannot repeat the performance. The general public gives many reasons for this lack of success. Generally, these reasons come down to: "The schools are not bearing down enough!" All sorts of remedies are suggested by parents, school personnel, and, lately, politicians to try to "make the kids learn." The "back-to-the-basics" folks want the children to do more and more of the same kind of activity even though it did not result in learning the first time they attempted it. By some magic, the second time is supposed to produce results. Frequently, test scores do go up the second time around, but these increased test scores leave no lasting effect. The second time through the same content, children are able to memorize a little more. But that, too, they will soon forget. These learners did not learn any more because they have not achieved the early learning necessary to build the understanding required to make new or additional learning possible. "Back-to-the-basics" advocates do not realize that the real basic in school is providing children with learning ex-

periences at their own intellectual level from which they *can* learn. The "back-to-the-basics" group does not understand what "cannot learn" means.

E arlier in this chapter we made the statement that you would understand why so much time was being spent on the preoperational stage of thinking. Stop reading at this point, pick up your pencil, and organize your thoughts about why understanding the preoperational stage is so important. Record those thoughts.

The fourth level

Preoperational thinkers often indulge in the wildest kind of fantasy, which often has no basis in fact. If the world does not suit them, they just imagine the type of fanciful world they want. Concrete operational thinkers, however, are concerned with the actual data they extract from objects, organizing these data, and doing mental operations with them. These learners do not formulate abstract hypotheses from their experiences; they confine their thinking to events in the real world. They can classify, compare, seriate, and perform all the various thinking acts that will lead to the extraction of information from objects if they are given experience with concrete objects. In short, children in the concrete operational stage of thinking rarely depart from reality, as do preoperational thinkers, even though these departures have no lawful or logical basis.

At some time between fifteen and twenty years of age, many people find they can do a type of thinking that is not completely dependent upon reality, but which depends instead upon "simple assumptions which have no necessary relation to reality or . . . beliefs" (Piaget, 1963, p. 148). According to Piaget, such an individual "thinks beyond the present and forms theories about everything, delighting especially in considerations of that which is not" (1963, p.

148). These quotations describe a kind of thinking that can best be named abstract. Those using this kind of thinking do not need to have direct experience with reality; they can assume that it exists and use that assumption as though it were reality. Piaget states that a person performing abstract thinking has become capable of *hypothetico-deductive* thought, which consists of implications and contradictions established between propositions. Such a person can think about the consequences (implications) of his/her thinking.

Another descriptive term that could be used for this stage of thought—hypothetico-deductive thinking and thinking with assumptions—is "propositional reasoning." A proposition says: If the assumption or deduction (about such and such) is true, then it follows that (such and such is also true); therefore (this or that action is dictated or suggested). In other words, thought on this level in the Piaget model has a particular *form*. Here again the title given this stage is descriptive. Piaget has called it *formal operational*.

Quite evidentally, formal thought is much more sophisticated than concrete thought. Inhelder and Piaget (1958, p. 16) describe this difference in sophistication like this:

Although concrete operations consist of organized systems (classifications, serial ordering, correspondence, etc.), they proceed from one partial level to the next in step-by-step fashion, without relating each partial link to all others. Formal operations differ in that all of the possible combinations are considered in each case. Consequently, each partial link is grouped in relation to the whole; in other words, reasoning moves continually as a function of the "structured whole."

In this quotation, the "whole" must be interpreted to mean the entire problem, event, or situation the learner is attempting to understand. A good example is the structure of the atom. The structure means nothing if one cannot see the role of each part of the atom—electrons, protons, neutrons, and so on—in relation to the entire atom. The atom is the structured whole. Concrete thinkers can see that negative charges attract positive charges, and they can also vaguely understand the role of electrical-charge repulsion. They then ask why the negative charges around the positively charged nucleus are not pulled into the nucleus. They cannot see each part in relation to the whole; they only reason one step at a time. Since the atom is a concept that requires formal thought, it is a *formal concept*. You met the notion of a concrete concept earlier. Formal thought takes into account the total number of *possible* combinations in any problem, event, or situation; a *combinatorial system* is present. This formal ability is called "reasoning with the structured whole."

Perhaps the best example of reasoning with the structured whole is found in the English grammar system taught in schools. To see the correct grammatical form of a word to use, the user must be able to generate mentally all possible combinations of the individual word within an entire sentence. The sentence is the structured whole, and each element in it must be compared to that whole. Such reasoning is not available to concrete operational thinkers. Formal thought is also needed to see the relationship between the force, weights, and distances in a first-class lever and to visualize the distance between the earth and the other planets in the solar system. Understanding the description of the DNA molecule—often presented in books for the upper elementary grades and junior high school—also requires using the structured whole found in formal thought. A recently published list of the kinds of understanding elementary school students should acquire referred to the suitability of using the periodic table of elements in the fifth grade. The published document suggested that students be "introduced" to the periodic table (the whole) and to such ideas as elements, symbols, compounds, and number of atoms in a molecule (the parts). To understand any of the latter ideas in terms of the periodic table, a student must be able to judge them in relation to the periodic table. In other words, each part—elements and atoms—must be mentally extracted from the whole—the periodic chart—and judged according to that whole. This intellectual activity requires a high degree of formal thought. In fact, many college freshmen have trouble developing an understanding of the periodic chart and its relationship to such ideas as elements, atoms, compounds, and symbols. Most certainly, therefore, even an introduction to the periodic chart is not an appropriate topic for fifth graders.

To understand an idea that has no necessary relationship to reality, a student must be able to use formal operational thought. The key word in distinguishing concrete operational thought from formal operational thought is *reality*. The concrete operational thinker can think *only* about reality—experiences the thinker is having or has recently had. The formal operational thinker "is concerned with reality, but reality is only a subset within a much larger set of possibilities" (Phillips, 1975, p. 131). That larger set of possibilities exists because those capable of formal operational reasoning can think on the basis of assumptions, "delighting especially in the considerations of that which is not" (Piaget, 1963, p. 148). This description shows that formal thought is capable of departing from reality, but those departures are lawful and based on assumptions. Reasoning from assumptions—whether or not they are true is unimportant—is as legitimate to formal thought as reasoning from reality is to concrete thought.

Science content and intellectual levels

By now the type of science content appropriate for the elementary school should be apparent. Children begin to display concrete thought in late first or second grade. Before that time, the science experiences provided for them must lead children to observe and report what they have seen. Since preoperational children do not see

states in a transformation, doing experiments in the kindergarten or first grade is nonproductive. But some simple experiments can be done in late first grade. A group of first graders thought that water disappeared from a small aquarium because the fish drank it. They built a second aquarium just like the first without fish and observed it for a period of two weeks. This was a simple experiment. Concrete operational students can do experiments that become increasingly more complex as grade level increases, but they *must* have direct experience with the materials, and the concept being taught must be drawn directly from the data that the experience produces.

As we have pointed out, Piaget claimed that most learners enter the formal reasoning period between fifteen and twenty years of age. When children have just begun to enter the formal thought period—or have just begun to leave the concrete thought period—they will succeed with the conservation of volume task (see the Appendix). We administered the conservation of volume task to seventeen randomly selected sixth graders from one school and sixteen randomly selected sixth graders from a second school in the Norman, Oklahoma, system. Of that group, twenty-nine were twelve years old, and four were thirteen years old. Only six—18 percent—of these thirty-three students were successful with the conservation of volume task. These data show that students can *begin* to enter formal thought before fifteen years of age but that very few do.

Earlier we quoted data demonstrating that among 811 students in grades ten through twelve, concrete thought was found 57 percent of the time. In that sample, each student had the opportunity to demonstrate complete formal thought three times. In other words, a total of 2,433 (811×3) formal thought demonstrations was possible. A total of 1,038 formal thought demonstrations was found (43 percent). The distribution of formal and concrete reasoning among

TABLE 1-2

THE PRESENCE OF CONCRETE AND FORMAL
THOUGHT AMONG STUDENTS IN GRADES 10
THROUGH 12

	Sample: 412 Males	399 Females		
Score	10	11	12	Total
4	0	3	2	5
5	11	19	5	35
6	18	26	14	58
7	32	34	19	85
8	34	53	27	114
9	34	40	29	103
10	26	54	40	120
11	20	57	33	110
12	8	43	28	79
13	7	26	20	53
14	5	11	16	32
15	1	8	8	17
	196	374	241	811

Scores 4–8: Concrete Operational Reasoning
    Grade 10: 95 (48.5%)
    Grade 11: 135 (36.1%)
    Grade 12: 67 (27.8%)
         Total: 297 (36.6%)

Scores 9–11: Transitional Reasoning
    Grade 10: 80 (40.8%)
    Grade 11: 151 (40.4%)
    Grade 12: 102 (42.3%)
         Total: 333 (41.1%)

Scores 12–15: Formal Reasoning
    Grade 10: 21 (10.7%)
    Grade 11: 88 (23.5%)
    Grade 12: 72 (29.9%)
         Total: 181 (22.3%)

ages of *students using concrete and formal reasoning moving from stage to stage in the Piagetian model.*

What happens or can be made to happen that will encourage a child to begin to move out of one stage and into another? Piaget lists three factors (1964a, p. 178) that contribute to movement from stage to stage—maturation, experience (physical and logical-mathematical), and social transmission. He contends that any one of the three factors is not enough by itself to account for sufficient change to encourage a child to move from one period to the next.

The simplest definition of maturation is the process of maturing or growing. In relating growth to the increase of intelligence, what has to grow and mature is the nervous system. The maturation of the nervous system gives each of us the opportunity to see, hear, feel—in short, to experience—more and more objects, events, and situations within our environment.

There are two types of experience that influence intellectual development. The first is physical experience, which includes simply poking, breaking, lifting, and squeezing objects, putting objects into water, throwing objects into the air, and engaging in all manner of activities that allow learners to gather data about their physical environment. Walking in the mud is as important as hearing pleasant sounds. There is, however, a second kind of experience, which Piaget calls logical-mathematical. He believes that through this experience, "knowledge is not drawn from the objects but it is drawn by the actions effected upon the objects" (Piaget, 1964a, p. 179). Earlier, we gave the example of the young child who discovered that, regardless of how stones were arranged, there were always ten. These experiences require mental operations and have to do with the logic and order of the environment. Discouraging children from touching, feeling, and interacting with the environment in the classroom deprives them of the needed physical experience that leads to mental development.

the 811 students is shown in Table 1-2. In this table, the *complete* thought pattern of *each student* (a total of 811), rather than the three thought demonstrations each student gave (2,433), was used. The data in Table 1-2 show the percent-

Asking children not to use objects and to think only about numbers provides them an impoverished logical-mathematical experience.

Transmission means to pass along. Social transmission means to pass along what your own society is like, and the most common kind of social transmission is oral language: talking. But social transmission also occurs through the institutions of society—schools, churches, museums. Indeed, everywhere a child can interact with society, social transmission and concomitant intellectual development is taking place. The interaction concept is so important to us that we use social interaction as a synonym for social transmission.

There is also a fourth factor that influences movement from stage to stage in the Piagetian model. This factor will be discussed in chapter 2.

Write a paragraph on what prohibiting children from talking and having inadequate materials does to a child's opportunities for moving upward through the stages in Piaget's model of intellectual development.

Research has shown that school experiences can accelerate the movement of children from the preoperational to the concrete operational stage and the movement of junior high school students and college students from the concrete to the formal operational stage (Renner et al., 1976). Whether or not such acceleration is desirable is questionable. (Piaget has called this "the American question.") We believe that whether or not acceleration is desirable depends on what is meant by acceleration. Most assuredly, young children can be trained to give satisfactory answers to the conservation tasks. We once trained a group of kindergarten children on the conservation of liquid task.[4] They became so proficient that regardless of the liquid or containers used,

---

[4] Our thanks to Maxine S. Edwards, an elementary school teacher, for her excellent work on this project.

they always gave the correct response. Next, we used salt instead of a liquid. Salt takes the shape of the container and pours just as a liquid does, yet when salt was used the children failed the task. This experiment demonstrates that merely providing correct answers on the conservation task does not lead to intellectual development.

Schools teach content in science, mathematics, social science, and the other disciplines. Our position is that if acceleration occurs through the study of the disciplines taught, it is a positive experience for children. But to accelerate a child for the sake of acceleration is not, in our judgment, advisable. How then can the discipline of science be used to lead students simultaneously to learn that discipline and to increase their levels of intellectual development? The data needed to answer that question will be presented in chapter 2.

References

Flavell, John H. *The Developmental Psychology of Jean Piaget.* Princeton, N.J.: Van Nostrand, 1963.

Ginsburg, Herbert, and Sylvia Opper. *Piaget's Theory of Intellectual Development.* Englewood Cliffs, N.J.: Prentice-Hall, 1969.

Inhelder, Barbel, and Jean Piaget. *The Growth of Logical Thinking.* New York: Basic Books, 1958.

Phillips, John L., Jr. *The Origin of Intellect: Piaget's Theory.* 2d ed. San Francisco: Freeman, 1975.

Piaget, Jean. *Play, Dreams and Initiation in Childhood.* New York: Norton, 1951. Original French edition published in 1945.

———. *Psychology of Intelligence,* Paterson, N.J.: Littlefield, Adams, 1963.

———. "Development and Learning." *Journal of Research in Science Teaching* 2(3):176–86, 1964a.

———. *Judgment and Reasoning in the Child.* Paterson, N.J.: Littlefield, Adams, 1964b.

———. Foreword to Hans G. Furth. *Piaget and Knowledge: Theoretical Foundations.* Englewood Cliffs, N.J.: Prentice-Hall, 1969.

———. "Intellectual Evolution from Adolescence to

Adulthood." *Human Development* 15(1):1–12, 1972.

Piaget, Jean, and Barbel Inhelder. *The Psychology of the Child*. New York: Basic Books, 1969. For those wishing to pursue the topic of the symbolic function in depth, this reference is highly recommended.

Renner, John W., Don G. Stafford, Anton E. Lawson, Joe W. McKinnon, F. Elizabeth Friot, and Donald H. Kellegg. *Research, Teaching, and Learning with the Piaget Model.* Norman, Okla.: University of Oklahoma Press, 1976.

Renner, John W., Dianna K. Prickett, and Michael J. Renner. *Evaluating Intellectual Development Using Written Responses to Selected Science Problems*, pp. 24–27. Norman, Okla.: University of Oklahoma, 1977.

CHAPTER TWO

HOW CHILDREN LEARN

The title of this chapter implies that it will lead you to achieve a rather ambitious, nearly pretentious, goal: understanding how learning takes place. Before presenting data that will, we believe, lead to that understanding, some "ground rules" need to be established.

The first of these ground rules relates to what we call learning. Not infrequently adults—including some teachers—believe that, just because learners can repeat something, they understand it. Thus, such demonstrations as counting, saying the alphabet, writing a name, reciting a poem, repeating the multiplication tables, or naming the parts of a plant are often mistaken for learning; and they may be. Such intellectual tasks as these, however, can simply be the result of repeating something often enough until it is memorized, which represents training rather than a basic understanding of the material. This assertion can easily be checked by asking a child who demonstrates the ability to recite, for example, the multiplication tables, *why* $6 \times 9 = 54$. If the child explains that 6×9 means six added nine times, or nine added six times, and that the total is 54, learning and understanding are present. If such an explanation is not forthcoming, the child has been trained to recite, not educated to understand.

In our judgment learning implies understanding. Therefore, unless understanding of the type found in the above example is present, learning has not taken place. There are many tasks in our society that require only training to perform. There are also tasks in school for which training is necessary. Suppose you wish to show your fourth grade class how to use simple microscopes. Taking the time needed to explain the lens system in the microscope is not advisable for two reasons. First, the operation of the lens system is a formal concept and cannot be understood by concrete operational fourth graders. Second, knowing how the microscope works is not the object of introducing the instrument; the object is to lead children to understand how to place an object under a microscope to view it. The conclusion is obvious: train students in how to use the microscope. Understanding lenses *at this point* is not necessary. But remember, training *does not* necessarily lead to an understanding of what the students are being trained in, *nor is it intended to.* Likewise, we believe that teachers should be *educated* and that to discuss "teacher training" is incorrect.

The second ground rule deals with the reality of the title of this chapter. The title implies that you really can know how children learn. This is not true. We make judgments about how children learn by observing how they act when exposed to a given object, event, or situation. From our observations we abstract patterns, which lead us to postulate how learning takes place. In short, we build a *model*—or theory—of how learning comes about. This chapter deals with the explanation of such a model.

The third—and last—ground rule is related to the first one. *We have constructed all of our understanding for ourselves.* From birth to death we are *knowledge constructors.* No one can give us *our* understandings; others can give us *their* understanding but not until we learn how to function with a particular object or in a particular event or situation have we developed our *own.* Two names are often used to identify this idea: the *development learning* model or the *knowledge construction* model. Learning how to function with a particular object or with a particular event or situation is really learning how

to construct your own knowledge about it. How does the process of knowledge construction occur?

A LEARNING MODEL

Suppose you asked a five-year-old to compare two automobiles. The child would probably compare their size, color, and the other properties obvious to a preoperational child. A concrete operational thirteen-year-old may talk to you about tire size, speed, engine size, and other properties the five-year-old had not mentioned. If you next asked an engineer to compare the same two automobiles, you would probably get a completely new set of comparisons.

Each of the three observed the same two automobiles: why would they compare different properties? Because each of the three is at a different level intellectually and was, therefore, concerned about, or attended to, different properties. Each saw different properties because each—due to differing intellectual levels—had different mental abilities, procedures, or systems to use in processing the data received from the environment. The notion of how data from the environment[1] are processed is central to the theory of Piaget.

From birth each of us develops mental processes to use in dealing with incoming data from the environment. Piaget calls these mental data-processing procedures *mental structures;* the differences in mental structures distinguish one intellectual level from another. That intellectual level obviously gets more and more complex as we grow older. As children move through the intellectual stages in the Piagetian model, they can process more and more complex data from

---

[1] "Environment" is used as an umbrella term in this chapter to mean whatever the learner is involved with at a particular moment. Thus, an infant's input data might come from a rattle, while a third grader's data might come from a frog. Both are represented here by the term "environment."

the environment. This explains why the child, the adolescent, and the adult would probably give different and increasingly complex comparisons when observing two automobiles.

Mental-structure building probably begins at birth, but early structures are simple. When a baby looks at a toy and picks it up, the baby becomes able to repeat that action with any object that he or she can grasp and lift. A system for looking-grasping-and-picking-up has been established. This system is, of course, a small mental structure, which Piaget calls a *scheme*. The quality of the schemes that develop early is undoubtedly dependent upon the quality of the nervous system we inherited from our parents. Notice, however, that the baby's scheme included the stimulus (looking) and all the other processes that led to the complete act. A scheme, according to Piaget, is "whatever is repeatable and/or generalizable in an action." (1970a, p. 42). As a child grows older, he/she constructs more and more schemes; these eventually become integrated with each other and form cognitive structures. That is, the basic, or generic, unit of the cognitive structure is the scheme (Phillips, 1975, p. 12). This relationship is shown in Figure 2-1.

As more and more cognitive structures are built, more and more data from the environment can be incorporated into them, and the individual moves *through*—according to the Piaget model—the intellectual stage *and/or* into the next one. The process of incorporating data into existing structures is known as *assimilation*. A teacher must keep in mind that only learners themselves can assimilate incoming data from the environment; *no one can do it for them.* The learner must experience the hardness of a brick, watch mealworms go through a life cycle, or observe a lens form an image. Then and only then does assimilation take place. *Giving a child information does not lead to assimilation.*

Suppose a preoperational child is asked to assimilate a concrete operational idea or concept. The schemes of the child will not permit that assimilation to occur. But some assimilation probably does occur, and preoperational learners construct preoperational understandings of those parts of the idea that they can observe and for which they do have processing schemes. The child's schemes change—transform and modify—the input from the environment. Most certainly, this is not the type of understanding that the teacher—or other adults—intended should be achieved, and such an occurrence is generally responsible for adult exasperation with young children when they do or say things that are in direct contrast to what the adult believed they understood. The child heard the language, but he/she did not assimilate the idea. This does not upset the child; he/she is probably concerned, rather, that something is wrong with the adult but does not—cannot—know what is wrong. That is, the content of the event does not concern the child, but the social outcome in relation to the adult may.

The concrete operational child, however, is concerned about the content of an event because now he/she is probably aware that what has been assimilated is not being understood. No such awareness exists with preoperational learners. They believe that what they assimilated from the object, event, or situation was what they should have assimilated. But concrete operational learners are aware that there is a mismatch between their mental structures and what they

Figure 2-1 As learning progresses, schemes and structures change. That relationship, therefore, is *variant*.

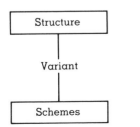

have assimilated, and their awareness causes them concern. These learners are in what Piaget called a state of *disequilibrium*, which is revealed by such statements as "What's that?" "How did that happen?" "Why did that object turn brown?" or any others indicating that the learner is concerned about what is under consideration—an object, event or situation—and does not fully understand it. Do not equate disequilibrium with frustration; they are not synonymous. But if disequilibrium is allowed to persist, frustration can develop, and the learner's interest will probably disappear.

Just as mental structures or schemes can change input from the environment, input can also cause mental structures to change. The disequilibrium caused by the mismatch of input and mental structures can cause new schemes to be built, or structures to be modified, combined, or both, in order to enable an altered structure to emerge. The entire process, the adjustment or change of mental structures, is called *accommodation* and is brought about by the disequilibrium that resulted from assimilation. But when structures have been adjusted to accommodate the new inputs (or intrusions) from the environment, the learner has once again reached a stage of equilibrium.

Describe a situation in which you made an assimilation and found yourself in disequilibrium. What did you do to put yourself back in equilibrium?

The procedure by which mental structures are revised is the process of equilibration. Revised mental structures make possible assimilations that were not possible before, and represent the movement of the learner more deeply into a particular intellectual stage or into an advanced stage. The child can now undertake learning that he/she could not have accomplished before the new, revised structures were present. The new learning, however, depends upon accommodation, which is the result of

disequilibrium; but disequilibrium is caused by assimilation. In the truest sense, therefore, without assimilation there is no accommodation and no new learning. Remember, however, that the impetus promoting accommodation is disequilibrium.

Teachers need to be aware that the key to the entire process of bringing about disequilibrium is assimilation, and that this must be done by the learner—no one else can do it for him. To emphasize that disequilibrium is focused on the learner, Piaget has frequently used *self-regulation* (1969, p. vi) as a descriptor of equilibrium. By using the theory-base of Piaget to develop a view of teacher responsibility in promoting learning, it is clear that the teacher's first responsibility is to involve the learner in an assimilation that will cause disequilibrium.

Assimilation and accommodation cause a change in the learner's mental structures, which represents an *adaptation* of the learner to the inputs received from the environment. But adaptation is accomplished only "when there is equilibrium between accommodation and assimilation" (Piaget, 1963, p. 7). According to Piaget, the learner has found an "accord of thought with things" (1963, p. 8). That a learner makes an adaptation and puts thought in accord with things—inputs from the environment—is certainly at least a part of learning.

But no thought exists in our cognitive structures by itself. Every adaptation that results from assimilation and accommodation is always related to all other earlier adaptations that resulted in structures. In other words, the new structure is placed among all the other structures in some type of mental-structure *organization*. An obvious definition for organization is the relationships that exist between a new mental structure and previous mental structures. Piaget defines organization as the "accord of thought with itself" (1963, p. 8).

Explain why organization and adaptation are complementary processes.

Earlier, we made the point that the impetus promoting mental-structure construction and reconstruction is disequilibrium. Disequilibrium is *caused* by assimilation and *causes* accommodation. In Piaget's theory, equilibrium is dynamic, not static. It is consistently being caused or causing. In addition, as disequilibrium diminishes, the newly constructed or reconstructed structures become more and more stable, and we begin to see inconsistencies and gaps in them that we did not see before. These gaps and inconsistencies are perhaps what lead us to say "yes, but . . ." after we believe we have mastered a new concept. The "yes, but . . ." response can cause a new assimilation, which in turn can produce a new disequilibrium. Phillips explains the entire process in this way:

Each equilibrium state . . . carries with it the seeds of its own destruction, for the child's activities are thenceforth directed toward reducing those inconsistencies and closing the gaps. (Phillips, 1975, p. 16)

Piaget refers to assimilation, accommodation, adaptation, and organization as the functional *invariants* of intelligence (1963, pp. 3–8). By that he means that, regardless of the age of the learner, the process is the same. It begins with assimilation and stops with organization and adaptation. The material with which the human organism functions and the sophistication with which functioning occurs change as a learner gets older; these, of course, are dependent upon the learner's intellectual stage. The invariant relationships that exist among assimilation, accommodation, and adaptation are shown in Figure 2-2. Those relationships are called the intellectual *function*. Although we cannot establish that Piaget ever referred to functioning as the learning process, we look upon it as such.

While the process of functioning itself is an invariant, mental structures are not; they are consistently changing (see Figure 2-1). Those changes probably begin the instant we are born, continue throughout our entire lives, and are

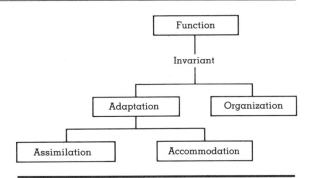

Figure 2-2 Functioning in Piaget's model is an invariant.

responsible for our movement through the intellectual stages. To us, mental structures—although to our knowledge Piaget has not said this—represent learning. Piaget has said that "a structure is a system of transformations" (1970b, p. 5). Now, when we ask children to "learn something" we have asked them to transform the inputs from the environment into their own mental structures. This will happen only if each child has a system that can make the required transformations. Suppose children are to be taught how to weigh a liquid. They need to understand that the beaker must be weighed empty, then with the liquid in it, and the two values subtracted. Unless children can use the necessary mental operations to make all of the transformations required in this process, they cannot understand that at the end, they will know the weight of the liquid. Using mental structures to make such transformations on the data received from the environment represents to us the process of learning; knowing how to describe the mathematics involved in a first-class lever does not. A teacher must understand the type of mental structures available to learners at different ages.

Think back to chapter 1. The mental schemes the preoperational child is able to use are the semiotic functions. These schemes allow learners to observe and report, but what they report they observe is not necessarily what a concrete or formal operational observer would report. The mental structures available to the concrete operational learner are represented by serial ordering, conservation, correspondence and classification, used in a linear, step-by-step fashion. The formal operational thinker functions with the structured whole. Mental structures, therefore, are mental operations used in transforming into meaning the data received from our environment. According to Piaget, ". . . operational structures are what seem to me to constitute the basis of knowledge . . . the central problem of intellectual development is to understand the formation, elaboration, organization and functioning of these structures" (1964, p. 177). It is this "central problem" that we classroom teachers must learn to solve, but we must also learn to implement a solution. In other words, how do we base classroom teaching upon the Piagetian functioning model?

W rite working definitions of assimilation, accommodation, adaptation, disequilibrium, organization, and functioning. Keep your definitions in a convenient reference place while you study the next section.

A TEACHING MODEL

You have just explored a learning model called the *developmental* or *knowledge construction* model. We believe that a teacher cannot teach students unless that teacher understands a model of how students learn. Without that understanding, all a teacher can do is to expose students to content and, using tricks and "motivational techniques," hope they will glean enough from the exposure to pass the tests. This can happen when a teacher does not have a theory-base about learning upon which to base teaching procedures that will promote learning. The learning

model you have just explored is such a theory-base. Where does a teacher start planning to use the theory-base?

The knowledge-construction theory-base begins with the process of assimilation. During assimilation, learners acquire all the information they can about what is to be learned. We believe that in science, or any discipline, students learn concepts. Think about concepts as the major ideas in a discipline: "Energy makes things happen in our environment," "Chemical change cannot be reversed," "Food producers, food consumers, and decomposers constitute a community." During assimilation, students absorb the essence of concepts such as these. Before students can begin assimilating the essence of concepts, however, the teacher has to decide what concepts to teach. We will discuss how to do that in detail in chapter 3. For the present, therefore, assume that you have a list of concepts that are to be taught in a particular grade or to a particular group of children. How do you promote assimilation?

If preoperational and concrete operational learners are to absorb the essence of a concept, they *must* experience that concept. Students must use materials that they can touch, feel, hear, and observe; they must use every sense possible in finding out everything they can about them. Piaget has often said (Dyrli, 1973, p. 23) it is the materials that children learn from. The materials relating to the concept must be made to interact with each other; frequently the teacher needs to supply directions about how this should be done. These directions do *not* tell the students what they should learn from the materials, however, nor does the teacher "*explain*" the concept to be learned at the beginning of the assimilation. Students are simply exploring the materials on their own or by following teacher-provided directions. This phase of the learning has been called *exploration* (Karplus and Thier, 1967, p. 40). We believe that exploration of the materials promotes assimilation. What follows are directions that students should use to explore the concepts of electrical circuit and electrical current (Renner, Stafford, and Coulter, 1977).

Exploration
You will need a wire, a dry cell, and a light bulb. The objects are shown in the picture. Make a system of the three objects (see Figure 2-3). What evidence do you find that the objects will interact? After you find evidence of interaction, draw a picture of how you connected the wire, the dry cell, and the light bulb.

First, use one wire to produce interaction. Then use two wires.

Draw a picture of how the two wires, the dry cell, and the light bulb were connected when you saw evidence of interaction.

Compare the two pictures you have drawn. How are they alike? How are they different?

At how many *different* points did you have to touch the dry cell before you observed evidence of interaction? At how many places did you touch the light bulb before you saw evidence of interaction?

Each of the six pictures in Figure 2-4 shows a system made up of a wire, a dry cell, and a light bulb. The objects in the system are connected differently in each picture. Why does the system remain the same system?

Study the various ways in which the objects in the system are arranged. Predict which of the arrangements will produce evidence of interaction. Record your prediction in a table like the one shown in Figure 2-5. Each end of a dry cell is called a *pole*. Notice that one pole is marked "+" and the other is marked "−." The "+" stands for *positive*, and the "−" stands for *negative*.

You are predicting whether each of the ar-

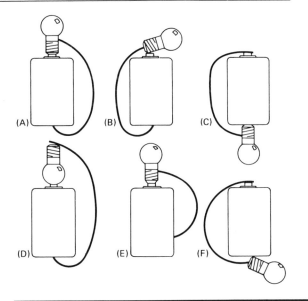

Figure 2-4

rangements of the objects in the system will give evidence of interaction. Write "yes" or "no" in your table to show whether or not you expect to see evidence of interaction.

Earlier, you answered questions about the number of places a dry cell and a light bulb have to be touched before you observed evidence of interaction. Refer back to the answers to those

Figure 2-3

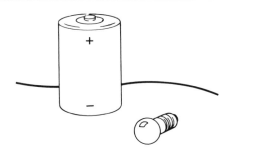

Figure 2-5

Picture	Prediction (yes or no)	Experiment (yes or no)
(A)		
(B)		
(C)		
(D)		
(E)		
(F)		

questions. If you wish to change any of your predictions, do it now.

From now on, do not change any of your predictions. You are going to do experiments with a wire, a dry cell, and a light bulb to test your predictions. Arrange the objects in the system just as they are shown in pictures (A), (B), (C), (D), (E), and (F). Record in your table whether or not you found evidence of interaction by writing "yes" or "no."

Do not be concerned if you predicted incorrectly for some arrangements of the objects. Figure out why you predicted incorrectly. Record what you decided about incorrect predictions.

The foregoing directions for the exploration—this phase of the learning is sometimes called "Gathering Data"—are quite specific in directing children how to interact with the materials. Take careful note that nowhere in those directions are the words *electrical current* and *electrical circuit* used, nor are the students told what concepts they are to find. The directions lead the students to find data that lets them absorb the essence of the concepts. The directions—and particularly the data in the table shown in Figure 2-5—also do one additional thing: they lead students into a state of disequilibrium. Our experience in using these exploration directions in classrooms has been that students find several contradictions between the "Prediction" and "Experiment" columns. Those contradictions lead them to ask, "Why did that happen?" "Will it happen again?" and so on. Such questions are evidence that disequilibrium has occurred; the students are now ready to be led to accommodate themselves to the concept to be learned.

The teacher next asks the students to sit down and to contribute the data they have gathered to a class discussion. The teacher and the students put all these data together and *invent* an explanation that represents the concept to be learned. The teacher then supplies the language. This phase of the learning has been called *conceptual invention* (Karplus and Thier, 1967, p. 40). An example of what might happen in the conceptual invention—or just invention—phase follows.

Invention

A wire, a dry cell, and a light bulb can be arranged in a system which does something. There is evidence of interaction.

With the lighting of the light bulb, energy is being used. The dry cell supplies the electrical energy. But in order to see evidence of interaction you had to arrange the wire, the dry cell, and the light bulb in a certain way.

The wire, the dry cell, and the light blub were arranged in a special way. With this arrangement you observed evidence of interaction. Such an arrangement is called an

electrical circuit.

The light bulb will not light without the dry cell. The dry cell is the energy source in the circuit. The *interaction* of the wire, the dry cell, and the light bulb causes something to happen in the circuit. That interaction causes

electrical current.

Any evidence of electrical interaction requires current. When the starter on a car begins to hum, current is there. When a refrigerator, an electric razor, or a television set operates, current is also present. Current is present when the electric light is turned on.

People sometimes refer to electric current as "juice." The word "juice" suggests a mental picture. Those who use the word are trying to make a model of electric current.

Assimilation and accommodation have now taken place. The students have acquired two new concepts. Usually only one concept is acquired at a time, but in this case, two concepts are inherent in the same materials. Usually there is no surprise when the concept is introduced, no "ah-ha." The students expect some unifying idea and have probably been referring to the circuit as "thing" or some other suitable word. The students absorbed the concept before they identified it. When the identification was made known, they were not surprised and automatically owned the concept. Their accommodation of that particular concept was complete. The name "Getting the Idea" or "The Idea" is sometimes used for the conceptual invention phase.

The students are now ready to integrate these new concepts with other ideas. They expand the new ideas they have just acquired to include other ideas. We have called this phase of the learning *expansion of the idea*. We have found that using student directions for this phase is helpful and gets the expansion underway. Once the expansion has begun, students often suggest other ideas that contribute greatly to their retention of the newly acquired concept. It is extremely important that, during the expansion, the language—the labels—of the new concept be used. The students need to continue to accommodate the labels for the concept they have absorbed. In the following expansion, notice the use of the language.

Expansion of the Idea
You will need a dry cell, a light bulb, two brass clips, three pieces of wire, a holder for the dry cell, and a socket for the light bulb.

Put the objects together as shown at the left of Figure 2-6. As you will observe, the light bulb gives no evidence of interaction. Next, touch wire (A) and wire (B) together. What happens?

Put different kinds of objects between wire (A) and wire (B) (Figure 2-6, right). Touch the two wires to the objects. Which objects permit electrical current to light the bulb?

When the current lights the bulb, the circuit is a *complete circuit*. Make a record of the kinds of materials you used in your circuit. Indicate which materials made a complete circuit.

Refer once again to the pictures (Figure 2-6). When a system of electrical objects is arranged like the system in the first illustration, the arrangement is called an *open circuit*. The circuit is a *closed circuit* when something is put between wire (A) and wire (B) and the light bulb lights.

The foregoing investigation demonstrates how the functioning model of Piaget is implemented in the classroom. The exploration phase fosters assimilation and disequilibrium, the conceptual invention phase provides for accommodation, and the expansion-of-the-idea activities accomplish organization. These three phases of learning—exploration, conceptual invention, and expansion of the idea—represent the *learning cycle*. The phases of the learning cycle are diagrammed in Figure 2-7, which shows that the activities in the exploration start broadly and narrow their focus at conceptual invention. The expansion-of-the-idea activities then broaden the invented concept.

The learning cycle is certainly a curriculum development procedure; when constructing curricula developers must organize student activi-

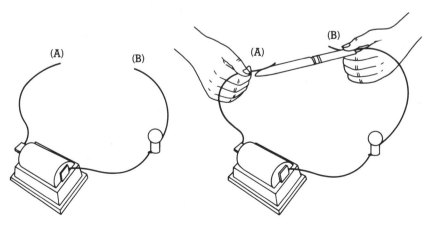

Figure 2-6

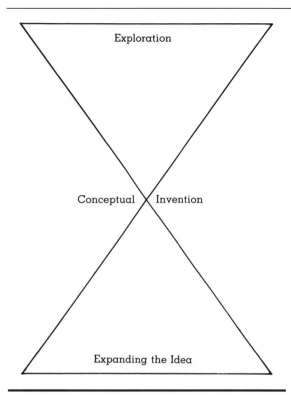

Figure 2-7 The Learning Cycle

The learning cycle has a solid theoretical basis that can guide teachers in their responsibilities because it focuses upon the principal goal of education: learning. The learning cycle was derived from a model of how learning takes place that we believe every educator should understand. This understanding—how knowledge is constructed—could and should form the theory-base for all education. Educational theory is frequently ridiculed as impractical; but you have just experienced how practical it is. The theory introduced here can be used to construct curricula to teach students; we contend that this is educationally very practical.

S elect a science concept suitable for a grade you want to teach. Prepare a learning cycle to teach that concept. Write out all directions as in the example given here.

AN ALTERNATIVE

In the example of the learning cycle presented here, student directions were supplied. However, there is another procedure that can be used during the exploration and expansion phases of the learning cycle. In the exploration, the students can be given the materials and told to put them together—make them interact—and observe and record what happens. Our experience has been that most students will be able to light a bulb if given a dry cell, a wire, and a bulb. The teacher can next provide a second piece of wire, another bulb, or one or more additional dry cells and encourage children to look at each other's work and share ideas. After a suitable time invention can proceed. The expansion phase opens a plethora of possibilities. Different kinds of materials from which they can attempt to make circuits can be furnished to the children. Will string make a circuit? How about nylon fish line? The expansion really proceeds with great enthusiasm and diversity once it gets underway. The alternate form of the learning cycle could

ties around the three phases. It is also a teaching procedure. In the exploration phase, the students are permitted to gather their own data and fully explore the materials; this phase is student-centered. The teacher provides directions and materials, answers and asks questions, gives hints and clues, helps with repairing materials and equipment and generally keeps the exploration going. The conceptual invention phase is teacher-centered. The teacher establishes the environment, asks for and accepts the data gathered, suggests an organization plan for the data if necessary, and ultimately introduces the language for the concept. The role of the teacher in the expansion-of-the-idea phase is like that in the exploration phase; in addition, the teacher must use the language of the concept and *insist* that the students use it also.

be implemented by providing only materials without explicit oral or written instruction. The final results are about the same.

If the results of doing the experiment are about the same with or without directions, why provide directions for the students to follow? Because the time required to teach a concept without directions is longer than with directions; directions increase the efficiency of classroom-time use. Teachers, administrators, and parents often feel uneasy if students "do not have something to read" that guides their activities. Children sometimes have a difficult time beginning an investigation and continuing it if they are not provided with some direction. Uncertainty about what to do *can* cause anxiety in some children and can turn to frustration.

There is no doubt in our minds, however, that free exploration of materials, without adult interference, produces assimilation resulting in greater personal learning than when directions are used. Whenever you give children directions, you are restricting their assimilation because they will usually attend only to those items the directions request them to. Free exploration of materials does not have that restriction because children are dependent upon themselves for their directions. Whether you employ the direction-oriented or free-exploration method depends on your teaching situation and what you are comfortable with. The learning-cycle teaching procedure leads to assimilation, disequilibrium, accommodation, and organization; our research (Renner, Abraham and Birnie, 1986) confirms that.

ANOTHER MODEL

Up to this point, we have examined two factors concerned with learning. The first is mental functioning, which is invariant (see Figure 2-2), and which led us to curriculum construction and a teaching procedure called the learning cycle. Intellectual functioning led to the second factor concerned with learning: the formation and reconstruction of schemes and mental structures. But there is also a third factor related to mental structures and functioning that we have not considered.

The third factor can best be understood by considering data that resulted from administering the conservation-of-volume task (see the appendix) to 1,108 students in grades ten through twelve. Just as the conservation of volume task directs, two identical glass cylinders were filled to the same height with water. Each of the students was given two solid metal cylinders having exactly the same shape and size but different weights. The students were told that the two metal cylinders were going to be put into the partially filled glass cylinders, that the metal cylinders would sink, and that this would result in the water levels rising. They were then asked, *before* the cylinders were submerged, whether one of the metal cylinders would push the water level up more and which cylinder would do this, or if the metal cylinders would push the water levels up equally. A total of 484 of the 1,108 students (44 percent) stated that one metal cylinder would push the water level up more than the other.

This example demonstrates what Piaget referred to as *content*. Phillips (1975, p. 8) defines content as "observable stimuli and responses," and Flavell as "the external behavior that tells us functioning has occurred" (1963, p. 18). In the conservation of solid amount task using clay balls, for example, young children often state that there is more clay in the pancake. The results of these two conservation tasks tell the interviewer that the children have assimilated the situation and how the interviewer's content directed them to behave. Do not be misled into believing that the proper questions were not asked or that the two subjects did not understand what they were expected to do. Neither redirecting the question nor making the questions "smaller" will change the responses, which were dictated by content. To change the response, the entire functioning, structure-build-

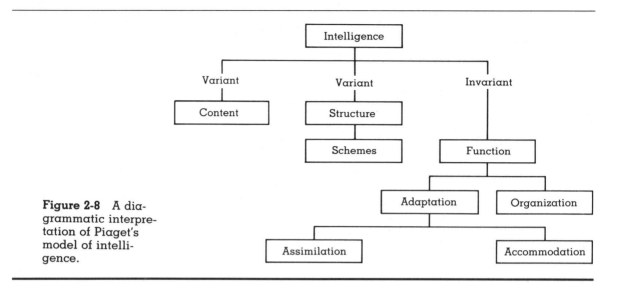

Figure 2-8 A diagrammatic interpretation of Piaget's model of intelligence.

ing process must be activated and disequilibrium brought about. In other words, the content factor is a variant inextricable from the structure and function portions. We have found it extremely useful to think about content as the way the child believes the world works. A young child really believes that flattening a ball of clay produces more clay, just as an adolescent believes that a heavy object pushes down harder on water than a lighter object, and moves the water level up more. Those responses represent content, the way the individual believes the world looks.

Mental structures, content, and function, Piaget postulates, represent *intelligence*. According to Piaget, intelligence is not a *static* attribute that each of us possesses. Rather it is a dynamic factor, which changes through the construction and reconstruction of mental structures and content that begins with assimilation, disequilibrium and accommodation. We have diagrammed the Piagetian intelligence model in Figure 2-8. The diagram was not prepared by Piaget or his associates. It is our interpretation of the relationships among the factors that constitute intelligence; that is, mental structures,

content, and functioning. Reading the diagram from top to bottom explains the overall intelligence theory, but when implemented through the learning cycle in a classroom, it begins with assimilation.

Prepare explanations of content, structure, and functioning that are satisfactory to you. Now compare your explanations with those of your peers. Agree upon suitable explanations of those concepts.

COMBINING MODELS

In chapter 1 we considered Piaget's model of intellectual development, often called the *developmental model*. In this chapter we have explored the intelligence model. Certainly these two factors—level of intellectual development and intelligence—are related. We have found that performance on the Piagetian tasks to measure formal operational thought (see the appendix) is positively correlated with a measurement of static IQ; the correlation coefficient is 0.44.

But that correlation does not relate to the relationship between the intellectual development and intelligence models discussed in this book.

To uncover this relationship, you must think about what the stages of intellectual development really mean. While you are doing that, however, remember that mental functioning is an invariant—we always assimilate, disequilibrate, accommodate, and organize. How does assimilation by a preoperational child differ from that by concrete and formal operational thinkers, who assimilate different aspects of the same object, event, or situation? Why are their assimilations different? Because they have different schemes and mental structures to use in assimilation; that is, they have different systems to use in transforming data received from the environment.

Furthermore, each person thinks the world works in a different way. The preoperational child believes that pouring water from one size of container to another increases or decreases the amount of water. The concrete operational child thinks that such a suggestion is silly. Of course, the amounts are the same: "All you did was pour it from one container to another, you did not add any or take any away." That same concrete operational child, however, will also tell you that heavier objects "push down" on water more than less heavy objects do and push the level of the water up more than less heavy objects, even when all other variables—size, shape, height of water—are the same. The formal operational thinker considers this latter task rather silly because, "It's the volume not the weight that controls how much water an object displaces." In other words, the content is different for each of the three.

Content and mental structures determine intellectual level. These mental structures, however, also control what can be assimilated in order to change content and mental structures. Perhaps considering this will make seeing why content and mental structures are called variants easier. Our interpretation of the relationship between the intellectual development and intelligence models is shown in Figure 2-9.

FACTORS AFFECTING PROGRESS FROM ONE INTELLECTUAL STAGE TO ANOTHER

Throughout this chapter and chapter 1 we have said that learners move from stage to stage. How does this happen? Obviously, learners must assimilate, but what factors promote assimilation? According to Piaget (1964, p. 178), there are four factors that can be used to promote assimilation and advance learners through the stages. Those factors are maturation, experience, social transmission, and equilibration.

The first factor—maturation—is really physiological maturation of the nervous system and plays an indispensable role in promoting intellectual development. Maturation greatly influences how we receive and react to stimuli. We know that, while succession through the stages is constant, the average ages at which they occur vary greatly from one society to another. For example, children in rural areas of Iran enter the stage of concrete operations later than children in Geneva, Switzerland (Piaget, 1964, p. 178) or Norman, Oklahoma. There is no reason to believe that the nervous systems of rural Iranian children have a slower maturation rate than those of other children. What causes this developmental lag among cultures?

One explanation, advanced from the second factor, is needed to assist children through the intellectual levels; that factor is experience. There are two kinds of experience that are needed—physical and logical-mathematical. "Physical experience consists of acting upon objects and drawing some knowledge about the objects by abstraction from the objects" (Piaget, 1964, p. 179). In logical-mathematical experience, knowledge is "drawn by the action effected upon the objects." In other words, knowing that

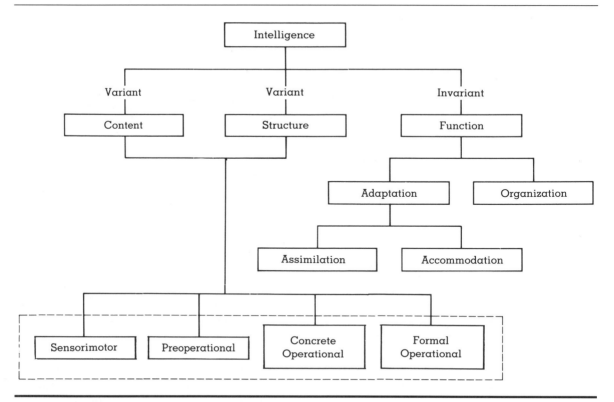

Figure 2-9 An interpretation of the relationship between Piaget's intelligence and developmental models.

changing the shape of a clay ball does not change the amount of the clay in the ball is logical-mathematical experience. Knowing the properties of the clay and the ball is physical experience. Preoperational children cannot assimilate from logical-mathematical experience but profit greatly from physical experience, while concrete operational children will profit from many logical-mathematical experiences.

The third factor—social transmission—simply means that children must interact with each other and with adults. They must communicate within society. School discussions, group work, and other such techniques promote social transmission; isolation and independent work do not.

Social transmission obviously promotes assimilation. Piaget has also referred to this factor as linguistic or educational transmission. In using language to provide children with information, linguistic transmission alone is not sufficient. Piaget explains this danger like this:

. . . the child can receive valuable information via language or via education directed by an adult only if he is in a state where he can understand this information. That is, to receive the information he must have a structure which enables him to assimilate this information. This is why you cannot teach higher mathematics to a five-year-old. He does not yet have structures which enable him to understand. (Piaget, 1964, p. 180)

The value of social transmission in promoting intellectual development, therefore, is dependent upon the child's mental structures.

We have discussed the fourth factor that promotes intellectual growth—equilibration—several times in this chapter. Equilibration is needed to promote mental structure and content changes. These changes really represent movement more deeply into a stage or from one stage to another. Equilibration is dependent upon experience and social transmission because without them, there is no assimilation. Without assimilation there is no disequilibrium, no structure change, no equilibration and no intellectual growth. The importance of assimilation is once again paramount.

Describe a science activity at a proper grade level that would promote experience, social transmission, and disequilibrium.

TROUBLE WITH A COMMON LEARNING MODEL

For many years the most common learning model used in schools has been stimulus-response (S-R). This model is the basis for programmed learning, whose most vocal spokesman had been B. F. Skinner. Behavior modification and most forms of training use S-R as their theory base. The S-R theory assumes that a learner will respond if the stimulus is adequate. The S-R theory confines its attention to inputs (stimuli) and outputs (responses) and "the direct relationship between them, ignoring the internal connection" (Piaget, 1971, p. 76). Piaget believes that ignoring the internal connections between the stimulus and the response is improper, and he has stated so.

I think the stimulus-response schema, while I don't say it is false, is in any case entirely incapable of explaining cognitive learning. Why? Because when you think of a stimulus-response schema, you think usually that first of all there is a stimulus and then a response is set off by this stimulus. For my part, I am convinced that the response was there first. . . . A stimulus is a stimulus only to the extent that it is significant, and it becomes significant only to the extent that there is a structure which permits its assimilation, a structure which can integrate this stimulus but which at the same time sets off the response. (Piaget, 1964, p. 182)

The foregoing quotation explains why those preparing programmed-learning materials must be careful that no question involves too much material. The stimulus (the question) must be able to be assimilated into existing structures. If the learner has not had the opportunity to build new structures through assimilation (which programmed learning does not provide), he/she must answer the question from existing structures built by accommodations not necessarily related to the new stimulus. To lead a learner to respond to a stimulus (answer a question) from mental structures only remotely related to the stimulus requires the questioner to use a great deal of care. The S-R model forms only a small part of Piaget's mental structure model.

So far we have concentrated on how learning takes place and how learning and intellectual development are related. Earlier in this chapter we defined concepts as major ideas. What are the educational ramifications of this definition? Chapter 3, "What Children Learn," will be devoted to exploring this question.

References

Dyril, Ochard Egil. "Piaget Takes a Teacher's Look." *Learning* (October, 1973): 22–27.

Flavell, John H. *The Developmental Psychology of Jean Piaget.* Princeton, N.J.: Van Nostrand, 1963.

Karplus, Robert, and Herbert D. Thier. *A New Look at Elementary School Science.* Chicago: Rand McNally, 1967.

Phillips, John L., Jr. *The Origin of Intellect: Pi-*

aget's Theory. 2d ed. San Francisco: Freeman, 1975.

Piaget, Jean. *The Origins of Intelligence in Children.* New York: Norton, 1963.

————. "Development and Learning." *Journal of Research in Science Teaching* 2(3): 176–86, 1964.

————. Foreword to Hans G. Furth. *Piaget and Knowledge: Theoretical Foundations.* Englewood Cliffs, N.J.: Prentice-Hall, 1969.

————. *Genetic Epistemology.* New York: Norton, 1970a.

————. *Structuralism.* New York: Harper & Row, 1970b.

————. *Science of Education and the Psychology of the Child.* New York: Viking, 1971.

Renner, John W., Michael R. Abraham, and Howard H. Birnie. "The Occurrence of Assimilation and Accommodation in Learning High School Physics." *Journal of Research in Science Teaching* 23(7):619–34, 1986.

Renner, John W., Don G. Stafford, and Vivian Jensen Coulter. *Models,* pp. 44–48. The *Learning Science Program,* Book 6. Encino, Calif.: Benziger Bruce & Glencoe; New York: Macmillan, 1977. Parenthetical references to figures have been added.

CHAPTER THREE

WHAT CHILDREN LEARN

The first chapter in this book discussed the levels of thought through which all people pass as they experience mental development and construct their own knowledge about the world. We found in chapter 1 that the quality of thought of each level of development is different from that of the other levels. If this is so, individuals at the different levels can think about the specific phenomena that require the quality of thought of the level(s) below them. In chapter 1 we stated that the science content children in each level of development *can* learn is unique.

Piaget explained the foregoing idea clearly (1964):

So I think that development explains learning, and this opinion is contrary to the widely held opinion that development is a sum of discrete learning experiences. For some psychologists development is reduced to a series of specific learned items, and development is thus the sum, the cumulation of this series of specific items. . . . In reality, development is the essential process and each element of learning occurs as a function of total development, rather than being an element which explains development.

DEVELOPMENT AND LEARNING

Development explains learning; what a potent educational idea! Preoperational children can learn only content and "school stuff" that uses preoperational thought, not concrete or formal operational thought. Concrete operational students *cannot* comprehend content that demands formal operational thought. Why is this true? The answer lies in two elements of the Piagetian intelligence model presented in chapter 2, *assimilation* and *mental structures*.

Think about the meaning of assimilation developed in chapter 2. Assimilation is the process by which learners—school or nonschool—ingest what they are experiencing. If the term ingest has no meaning for you, try *perceive*. The learner becomes aware of what is expected during the process of assimilation. Assimilation was accomplished by the mental structures described in chapter 2 as systems of transformation. Now, transformation to us means changing, adjusting, or in some way mentally manipulating what has been assimilated so that it has meaning. During the entire process, the learner is in a state of disequilibrium that causes mental structures to change: accommodation takes place and equilibrium is restored. However, if the learner's mental structures—or schemes—do not have the quality that permits transformation, no disequilibrium and accommodation occur, or disequilibrium occurs and the student can do nothing about it. In this instance, teachers frequently provide the content in a form that can be memorized for recitation or repeated in an examination; but no understanding is present in student mental structures because no accommodation has taken place. What has been memorized is quickly forgotten.

Preoperational children have a beautiful trait that prevents them from becoming disequilibrated. That trait is *transductive reasoning*. If you are unsure what transductive reasoning is, return to chapter 1 and read about it. When preoperational children assimilate something that cannot be transformed, they seek a specific reason to explain what they cannot mentally transform. Thus, in the conservation-of-number task, the stack of checkers made from the row cannot be related to the row; that action cannot be transformed. The preoperational child centers his/her attention on the height of the stack, and by using transductive reasoning, explains that there are more in the stack (or the row) because "the stack is taller." Other transductive responses preoperational children give are: "There are more checkers in the row because it is longer," and "There are more checkers in the row because it is red." The incoming data cannot be transformed; no disequilibrium occurs because of transductive reasoning.

The presence of transductive reasoning in preoperational children *probably* permits them to remain sane. Just imagine being in a world constantly bombarding you with objects, events, and situations that you cannot explain, although those around you keep asking you to. Such an environment would probably lead you to begin doubting yourself and your relationships with the world. But preoperational children do not seem to have this problem. They transform and modify the data they receive with transduction and explain away all discrepancies the world forces on them. Transductive reasoning keeps them from becoming disequilibrated. But in chapter 2 we made the point that accommodation is brought about by disequilibrium, and that the visible or measurable products of accommodation are usually called learning. Furthermore, to move deeply into one intellectual stage and to construct the mental structures necessary to eventually enter the next stage, we have said that disequilibrium and accommodation are necessary. How, then, do preoperational children become concrete operational if they do not become disequilibrated and accommodate, as the foregoing seems to suggest?

As preoperational children interact with their environment they begin to organize what they do—their actions—in each situation. Eventually, they generalize these actions and transfer them from one situation to another. For example, when children are first introduced to a tricycle, they learn that there are certain actions they must complete if they are to make it move. They will probably meet the next tricycle they encounter cautiously but will attempt those actions they found successful on the first tricycle. Eventually, they will generalize those actions to any vehicle analogous to a tricycle. Such generalizations Piaget called *schemes,* which he defined as "organization of actions as they are transferred or generalized by repetition in similar or analogous circumstances" (Piaget, 1969, p. 4). Notice that schemes have been built from actions; the preoperational child's schemes direct actions to be done. If, however, the child were asked to describe how to ride a tricycle, that explanation would not be forthcoming because it requires mental operations involving—at least—several reversals of thought and the ability to see states in a transformation. The presence of mental operations indicates that mental structures are present; preoperational children have only mental schemes available to them.

A young boy was using a rather large syringe to blow up a balloon. He would pull the plunger on the syringe out, put a balloon on the syringe's nozzle, push in the plunger, pinch the top of the balloon to keep the air from escaping, remove the syringe from the balloon, withdraw the plunger and start the process over. When the teacher asked him to explain how he did the process, he replied, "I don't know." He had developed the needed schemes by organizing his actions but did not have the mental operations either to mentally build the model which the experience had provided or to explain that model. Thus, the preoperational child adjusts his/her schemes as he/she repeats experiences or has an experience that closely resembles an earlier one. Eventually, the child begins to ask questions about the relationships between experiences; this child has now begun to perform mental operations and has begun to move into the concrete operational stage of development.

In summary, for anyone to learn, the content to be learned must match the intellectual level of the learner in order to enable the learner to build schemes—in the case of preoperational children—or to cause disequilibrium in concrete and formal operational students. But specifically, what from the content do students learn?

THE PRODUCTS OF LEARNING

Children experiencing a learning cycle in plant growth planted seeds in several different containers and placed some of the containers in the light and some in the dark. They gave each container the same amount of water. The number of seeds in the dark that produced plants was approximately the same as the number of those in the light that produced plants, but after a few weeks the plants in the dark died. What would children learn from this investigation?

Children learn how to conduct an investigation. They learn how to collect, process, and analyze data and how to make generalizations from their analyses. In addition, they can frequently state hypotheses after they have analyzed the data. In chapter 1, we said that the stating of hypotheses is a mark of formal operational thought. Concrete operational thinkers, however, can state *a type* of hypothesis that deals with what they believe will happen, based upon the experiences they have had. The data they use in making this type of hypothesis must come directly from those experiences and cannot be drawn from any abstract or hypothetical propositions. In the plant-growing experiment, for example, children will state what they believe "will happen"—their hypothesis—in terms of data they have collected. After stating their experience-based hypothesis, concrete operational thinkers can test those hypotheses and construct an understanding about what happened in the investigation. Such understanding represents the *content concepts* that the children carry away from the investigation with them.

(The young investigators also learn about the nature of science from an experience like the plant-growth investigation described here; we shall return to the nature-of-science topic in chapter 9). An elementary school science investigation, therefore, leads students to understand content by leading them to construct concepts. What is a concept? In chapter 2 we defined a concept as a major idea, and that's what it is. But students also learn facts, principles, and generalizations; how are those related to concepts?

CONCEPTS, FACTS, GENERALIZATIONS, AND PRINCIPLES

The atomic weight of sodium is 22.9898 atomic mass units. Wood comes from trees. Water will not dissolve oil. Oak trees have green leaves in the summer. In the winter the temperature of the water in a lake is warmer at the bottom than at the top. All of those statements are *facts*. A fact is something that actually exists. Because of their actual existence facts can be checked. You weigh a definite amount, you are a specific age and height—these are facts because they can be checked by someone else and similar results found. Facts do not *by themselves* lead to the construction of knowledge; they are end points. Do not interpret this last statement as being derogatory to facts; they are very much needed in the learning process. When we are learning something new, we probably assimilate facts or what we think are facts. That assimilation, however, does not represent learning. It is the accommodation our mental structures make to the assimilation, which then permits us to assimilate and transform data we could not have assimilated earlier, that represents learning. We believe, however, that the assimilation of facts starts the entire learning process, but learning

has not taken place if all students are asked to do is to "know" the facts.

A child places a bar magnet on a flat, paper-covered surface and slowly pushes small metal pieces toward it. The metal pieces reach a certain point where they no longer need to be pushed; they jump toward the magnet. The young investigator makes a pencil mark on the paper at the point where the metal piece jumped. After a time, there are many such marks surrounding the magnet, outlining an oval-shaped area. The child-investigator is asked to explain what the data from the investigation tell him/her. The young experimenter states that, if a small piece of the metal being used is placed in the space outlined around a magnet, the metal piece jumps toward the magnet. That statement is the concept. The child has obviously conducted an exploration, and the data from that exploration have led the child to invent a summarizing statement. *The child has just invented a concept.* To complete the conceptual invention, the teacher needs to explain that the space the child outlined with the pencil marks is called the *magnetic field.* Please remember, however, that stating the name of a concept is *not* stating the concept. In listing concepts to be taught, stating the names of the concepts is not sufficient. For an expansion-of-the-idea experience, the child could use other bar magnets or magnets of other shapes to outline magnetic fields.

The learning cycle just described tells how a concept is formed but does not explain what a concept is. Consider what the child in the magnetic-field investigation did. First, the child collected facts: (1) the metal piece jumps toward the magnet; (2) the metal piece jumps toward the magnet at a particular point; (3) farther from the magnet than those points, the metal piece has to be pushed toward the magnet. From these experiences, the child abstracts the idea that there is a specific space around the magnet in which the metal pieces jump toward the magnet. In other words, a concept is a specific idea abstracted from particular instances. How does that concept differ from a generalization? It probably doesn't, but spending the time necessary to pinpoint the specific similarities and differences, if any, hardly seems worthwhile. A concept is abstracted from experience, and a generalization can be a proposition which need not come from experience. This is the only meaningful difference we see, but even that is not too meaningful. Concepts are put together—abstracted—from data that came from experience by the *process* of generalization. Our belief is that *knowledge is constructed by abstracting concepts from some type of experience.*

Throughout the foregoing discussion, we have referred to the process of "abstracting" concepts. Do not confuse this use of abstract with abstract subject matter. Think of "to abstract" or "abstracting" as a process, and abstract subject matter as a body of content, such as higher mathematics and music theory.

Teachers frequently speak of "teaching concepts." This is not possible, since concepts are learned. The responsibility of the teacher is to provide the materials, the environment, and the guidance needed to assist students in constructing their own concepts about particular phenomena in science. In other words, concepts are what students carry away from a learning experience. A perfectly legitimate label for learning content is *conceptualization*.

The concepts on which the school's curriculum is based, therefore, are those we wish students to assimilate data about, and accommodate their mental structures to, in order to construct an understanding. These concepts represent the *only* content learned. We as teachers must state the concepts before constructing the curriculum. We must keep in mind, however, that they are *our* concepts, and we are assuming that our concepts are harmonious with the content being taught. We also hope that at the end of a learning experience, the concepts of the students match ours and the content. *Concepts,*

therefore, *are the ideas about a particular phenomenon students abstract from a learning experience.*

Consider this statement: *Every electric current has a magnetic field surrounding it.* Now this statement has meaning *only* if the person encountering it understands the concepts of electric current and magnetic field. The statement relating those two concepts is a *principle,* which the dictionary defines as the laws or facts of nature underlying the working of an artificial device. To understand how an "artificial device" works, one must understand the concepts on which it is based. It is such a statement of conceptual relationships that constitutes a principle.

W rite one science concept for each grade in elementary school—kindergarten through grade six—and defend why each statement you write is a concept.

TYPES OF CONCEPTS

Think back tc chapter 2 to the meaning of assimilation. During assimilation, learners take into their mental structures—absorb—the *essence* of the concept they are to learn. Now, we used the term "essence" purposely. The dictionary gives "fundamental nature" as one meaning for essence, and that is what learners must extract from a learning experience. But the learner extracts the fundamental nature of the concept to be learned only after that learner's mental structures have transformed (remember how mental structures were described) what has been assimilated. We postulate that complete assimilation occurs in two stages. First, students perceive and become aware of the learning task, and this awareness is what starts disequilibrium. The students' mental structures then begin to transform what has been assimilated into meaning, and at the conclusion of that transformation, accommodation has begun.

PLEASE do the following experiment. We are assuming you have not had such higher mathematics courses as advanced calculus, differential equations, or vector analysis. If you have, use a field with which you are not familiar. Select a textbook in a mathematics course above calculus. Open that book to a chapter beginning somewhere near the beginning. Read *four* pages. Write down what you did and did not understand. PLEASE do not read on until you have completed this experiment.

Our students tell us that in the foregoing experiment, three factors are evident. First, assimilation—most of the words are understood. Next, disequilibrium—the words do not have meaning when put together. Finally, accommodation—what happens when students really "put their mind" to understanding what they have read, or transform the data so it can be accommodated. Our students tell us that they cannot transform the data to meaning. The reason is that they do not have the necessary mental structures, which are the systems of transformation. In other words, learners cannot transform data to meaning and accommodate to it *if* they do not have the mental structures to make the transformation. This factor limits the concepts that can be taught to students in the several intellectual development levels. Consider the following examples:

In an exploration, fifth grade students 1) use a slingshot to propel a marble across the school yard, 2) apply heat to ice to make it melt, 3) send a golf ball down a ramp to strike a wooden block and make it slide, and 4) push each other up a ramp on a small cart. In each case, the students observed something happening: the marble flew across the school yard, the ice melted,

the wooden block moved, and they felt the exertion as they pushed each other up the ramp. They have absorbed that they had to do something to make something happen in three of the cases—stretch the slingshot, move the golf ball to the top of the ramp, and push a classmate up a ramp. In the third case, the heat caused the ice to melt. What the students have absorbed is the essence of the concept of energy—energy makes things happen. This concept and its language can now be invented for the students. Notice that the concept came from actual, concrete experiences the students had. They had gathered the data used to invent the concept. That level of understanding of the concept of energy can be accommodated by concrete operational learners because it comes from direct experience. When a concept can be learned from *direct* experience it is a *concrete concept*. The data assimilated in order to understand a concrete concept must be the result of student interaction with actual objects, events, and situations. These data can be treated in the step-by-step fashion needed by concrete operational learners, whose mental structures can transform data only in this linear fashion.

Suppose the fifth-grade students in the example were told that "energy is the ability or capacity to do work," and then watched demonstrations to prove that the given definition was correct. Or imagine that the experience with the materials occurred before the teacher introduced the foregoing definition. The description of energy at the beginning of this paragraph has meaning *only if* the learners understand the concepts of ability—or capacity—*and* work. In other words, the learners have to be intellectually able to consider each of the three elements—energy, ability, and work—simultaneously, and to consider each of them one at a time in relation to the other two. In chapter 1, we gave a description of formal thought: "each partial link is grouped in relation to the whole, . . . reasoning moves continually as a function of a 'structured whole' " (Inhelder and Piaget, 1958, p. 16). The concept of energy as it is presented at the beginning of this paragraph—and in most textbooks—requires formal thought to understand. The concept of energy presented in that manner is a *formal concept* and cannot be understood by concrete operational learners because they do not reason with the structured whole just referred to; those learners reason with direct experiences or experiences they have had.

A concrete concept, therefore, is one that can be invented from direct experience with concrete objects, events, or situations. So far, however, we have not made the description of a formal concept clear. To assist in developing that description, consider the definition of energy in the last paragraph. Two concepts in that definition need examination—ability and work. What is "ability"? The dictionary describes ability as the quality of being able; that doesn't help much. After due consideration, we concluded that ability is an axiom or a postulate—it is nonconcrete. Consider the concept of work. The physicist defines work as a force moved through a distance parallel to the force. In order to understand work, one must understand force and distance. These quantities are more concrete than ability, but when work is understood and then attached to the axiom of ability, the entire idea of energy becomes very abstract—a postulate. To comprehend a formal concept, each new idea that has been absorbed about it must be considered in light of assumptions, axioms, or postulates, and not just linearly in terms of what concrete ideas are already known. Formal thought is nonlinear. Earlier, we described formal thought as thinking with the structured whole. Another way to describe it is thinking with postulates, axioms, and assumptions. *Formal concepts, therefore, are those concepts that require reasoning with assumptions, postulates, or any other element of abstract thought.* Energy as defined in terms of ability and work is definitely a formal concept.

Consider each of the following concepts and, using what you have just read, label the concept as concrete or formal.

1. Mass is the amount of matter in a body.
2. Temperature is the reading you get on a thermometer.
3. Acceleration is the change of velocity with respect to time.
4. Molds, yeast, and other tiny organisms that cause food to rot are decomposers.
5. A physical change occurs when material that has been changed can be changed back to its original form.
6. The movement of heat energy along a metal rod is heat conduction.

FLEXIBLE CONCEPTS

In the last section you found out that the concept of energy could be a concrete concept (energy makes things happen) or a formal concept (energy is the capacity to do work). There is another class of concepts that can be either formal or concrete depending on both the exploration activities the students have encountered before the concept is invented and the language the teacher uses during the conceptual invention phase. In the concept of energy just discussed, language made the concept formal. Exploratory activities would let students absorb the essence of the concept, but whether or not concrete learners could understand the concept depends upon the language the teacher uses in the invention statement.

Consider the concept of temperature. Second-grade children—seven-year-olds—can develop the understanding that when something hot is brought in contact with a thermometer, the liquid in the thermometer rises. In other words, the "hotness" of an object is the reading on a thermometer. By fourth grade—nine-year-olds—children understand the concept that the *temperature* of an object is represented by the reading on a thermometer. This is a perfectly workable concept of temperature and certainly a concrete concept. Temperature, however, can also be thought of in terms of the kinetic-molecular theory of matter, which states that all molecules in an object are in motion as long as the temperature remains above absolute zero. The theory also states that as the temperature of an object rises, the object's molecules increase their motion. If temperature is considered in terms of the kinetic-molecular theory, it is a formal concept because understanding it requires reasoning according to this postulate.

Therefore, some concepts can be concrete or formal depending on how they are invented for the learners. The criterion for judging whether or not a concept is concrete is very direct. If a concept can be invented from data collected through *direct experience* with objects, events, or situations, the concept is concrete. If an assumption, postulate, or axiom is used to collect or interpret data leading to the conceptual invention, the concept is formal.

Some formal concepts cannot be made understandable at a concrete level. Consider the atom as an example. To understand the atom and its structure a student must understand many concepts—such as electrical charge—that he/she cannot experience. Even though much *indirect* evidence exists to support these concepts, they are really postulates. Furthermore, understanding the atom requires that each component in its structure be considered separately in relation to the entire atom. Such a process is "reasoning with the structured whole," which, as we have seen, represents formal thought.

Teachers frequently use models to help students understand difficult concepts. One model, and one of the most widely used, is the atomic model. Small spheres and sticks are frequently put together to represent not only the entire atom but its nucleus and the electrons in orbit around the nucleus. Do such models assist students learning formal concepts? Those models are extremely helpful in assisting *formal* stu-

dents to learn formal concepts because a model is really a postulate—in this case, a postulate or belief of what something looks like. Since formal thinkers can reason with postulates, models are helpful. But the concrete thinker cannot reason with postulates and therefore does not understand that the model is a representation of what we believe the atom looks like. Since concrete learners can deal only with reality, they *learn the model* but do not understand that it is only a model. They will not understand any questions asked of them or problems given them about what the model represents because these do not deal directly with the model. Models do not provide direct experience with the phenomena, so concrete learners do not learn formal concepts from them.

We know of one exception to the above statement about models. You have probably made a model (Figure 3-1) showing how we breathe using a coffee can, a one-holed rubber stopper, a glass tube, a small piece of rubber, and a balloon. The bottom is cut from the can and the rubber piece is stretched over the open bottom and held securely around the can's sides by a rubber band. A hole is made in the can's plastic top, and the rubber stopper, through which the glass tube has been passed, is sealed in the hole. A balloon is attached to the end of the glass

Figure 3-1   A Breathing Model

tube, which will be inside the can. The rubber piece is pinched at its middle and pulled outward. The pressure inside the can drops due to an increase of volume inside the can, and outside air pressure forces air into the balloon through the end of the glass tube exposed to the outside air. This model accurately depicts what happens when we breathe. When we expand our body cavity, the pressure inside drops. The outside air pressure forces air into our lungs through our nose and/or mouth. Now if children can watch the model work and at the same time place their hands on their ribs and feel their body expand, they will be provided with *direct experience*; the model only helps to explain that *experience*. When a model augments direct experience, it is useful to concrete operational thinkers.

Now it is your turn. Write down two concepts that are concrete and two that are formal. Do not write down concepts that can be taught as either concrete or formal. Explain why the concepts are concrete and formal. Now write down two concepts that can be invented as concrete or formal concepts. Explain how the concepts can be either concrete or formal.

MEASURING STUDENT UNDERSTANDING OF CONCRETE OR FORMAL CONCEPTS

Concrete operational students should not understand formal operational concepts, but formal operational students should understand both concrete and formal concepts. If groups of concrete and formal operational students are given examinations asking questions based on both formal and concrete concepts, the formal operational students should outscore the concrete operational students. This was the hypothesis

that guided our research into student achievement of concrete and formal concepts (Lawson and Renner, 1975).

In this research we used a student population containing both concrete and formal operational thinkers. Our earlier research (Renner et al., ch. 6) had shown that a sufficient number of students in grades ten, eleven, and twelve had entered the formal operational stage to allow us to use this student population in our research. We randomly selected fifty students from each biology and chemistry class in the cooperating high school. Since only thirty-three students were enrolled in physics, a random selection of fifty students was not possible.

With the assistance of the biology, chemistry, and physics teachers, we isolated the concepts that they would teach in those courses between the beginning of school and the following April. Multiple choice examinations to measure students' understanding of these concepts were prepared and their content validated. The examinations were administered to the students in late April. Earlier that month, we had interviewed each of the 133 participating students using tasks designed by Piaget and Inhelder (1958) (Renner et al., 1976, ch. 9). Three pieces of data, therefore, were available for each of the 133 participating students: an intellectual development score and scores measuring success on the questions measuring achievement on the concrete and formal concepts.

When we analyzed the data on the intellectual development levels of students, we identified and labeled seven categories: early concrete operational (Concrete IIA), transitional to complete concrete operational (Transitional concrete), concrete operational (concrete IIB), a category of students who were leaving the concrete period but not yet beginning formal operational (postconcrete), beginning formal operational (Formal IIIA), transitional to complete formal operational (Transitional formal), and formal operational (Formal IIIB).

The multiple-choice test format was used in

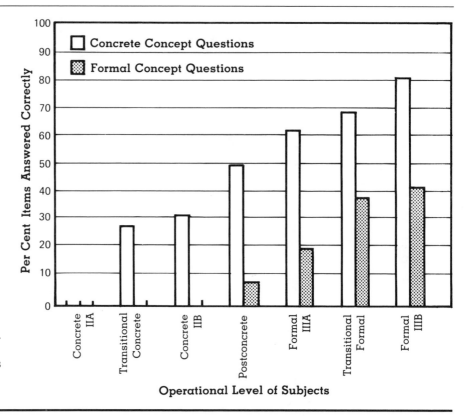

Figure 3-2 A comparison of success of concrete and formal operational students on concrete and formal concepts with chance eliminated.

the examination to measure student achievement in this research. Student scores on that examination format can be inflated due to chance success. To guard against that possibility we used the technique developed by Guilford (1936) in computing the students' individual scores on the concrete questions and on formal concept questions. A mean score was then computed for each of the seven intellectual development categories listed in the last paragraph on each type of question—concrete and formal—and that mean score was converted to a percentage. A bar graph was constructed from those data and is shown in Figure 3-2.

The data shown in Figure 3-2 confirm the hypothesis stated earlier and reveal an important finding: *Concrete operational students were unsuccessful in learning formal operational concepts.* Not until the postconcrete operational phase was any student success in learning formal operational concepts evident, and then the success rate was very low. The data in Figure 3-2 underscore the importance of the teacher's role in identifying concrete concepts for concrete operational students to learn. When concrete operational students are asked to learn formal operational concepts, they do not develop understanding. If they value grades and adult approval, they have only one option open to them—they must memorize enough of the language of the formal concepts to succeed on any test they are asked to complete. Using some of the language concerning a concept does not mean that the students understand the concept, but teachers often convince themselves that being able to use proper language means understanding.

What do the data presented in Figure 3-2 mean for you as a practicing teacher?

You will notice that student success on questions measuring understanding of formal concepts is not high. The classes in which the students were enrolled were taught in a traditional, expository fashion; learning cycles were not used. Perhaps even the formal operational students got bored. We have no other hypotheses to explain our finding but this one.

The conclusion we reached through the foregoing research, that concrete operational students do not learn formal concepts, is confirmed by Cantu and Herron in a statement based on their research: "Concrete-operational students did *not* learn any of the formal concepts very well" (1978). Purser and Renner (1983) report on research, described in chapter 10, done with tenth-grade biology students to ascertain, among other things, if the teaching procedures used influenced the understanding of formal concepts attained by concrete operational students. They conclude that "concrete operational students . . . do not learn formal content effectively regardless of the teaching procedure used." These two studies support the Lawson-Renner research conclusions that concrete operational students do not learn formal concepts.

THE RESULTS OF CONCEPT MISPLACEMENT IN THE SCHOOL

What do students learn when they are asked to learn concepts that are above their intellectual level? These students assimilate and accommodate as much information about what is to be learned as their mental structures will permit. Then they organize that accommodation with their existing knowledge, and a misunderstanding of the concept usually results.

A concept that is frequently found in elementary school science is dinosaurs and why those creatures are no longer found on the earth. The disappearance of the dinosaur is a formal concept because it involves stating hypotheses that cannot be tested. Obviously, concrete experience with the concept is impossible, and models are not helpful. To find out what senior high school students do understand about dinosaurs, we designed and carried out some research. Our results showed that only 4 percent of the students participating in our research demonstrated sound understanding of the concept. A common misunderstanding was that "human beings killed the dinosaurs either directly or indirectly, for example by destroying their food or habitat or by polluting their water." The research efforts just reported, we believe, generate an hypothesis about the results of requiring concrete students to study formal concepts, which can be stated: When concrete operational students are required to attempt to learn formal concepts, they develop misunderstandings. This hypothesis has not yet been tested. The reason for misunderstanding develops, we believe, principally during the accommodation and organization stages of the Piagetian functioning model. Remembering that concrete thought proceeds in a step-by-step fashion (Inhelder and Piaget, 1958, p. 16) we postulate the following model: only those parts of the concept that can be learned in a step-by-step manner are assimilated. Those parts of the concept that require the use of the structured whole are not assimilated. Accommodation is incomplete. When organization occurs, an incomplete—and probably erroneous—concept is combined both with concrete concepts that are understood *and* misunderstandings developed earlier. Little wonder that nonformal misunderstandings are developed.

CHARTING CONCEPTS

Shayer and Adey (1981, pp. v–vii) argue that there is a "massive mismatch in secondary schools between the expectations institutionalized in courses, textbooks, and examinations and the ability of children to assimilate the experiences they are given." This opinion emerged after they had spent many years studying the relationship between the content of science and the intellectual development patterns of children in England.

Now we can almost hear you reminding us that this book is about *elementary school*. In conducting their research, however, Shayer and Adey found that they had to analyze biology, chemistry, and physics to determine which levels of students—early concrete, IIA; concrete, IIB; early formal, IIIA; and formal, IIIB—could understand which parts of the principal concepts in those disciplines. That task required many years of work collecting and analyzing data from secondary school science classes. In the process, Shayer and Adey evolved a science-concept rating procedure (Shayer and Adey, chapters 8 and 9) useful to elementary school teachers because it clearly shows which aspects of concepts can be taught to elementary school children, who are concrete operational thinkers. We urge you to spend time with the Shayer and Adey text to understand their concept-rating procedure because you will find it a useful curriculum-construction tool.

Much has been said in this chapter about concepts. The next questions to ask are obvious:

What concepts from the several disciplines of science can be taught in elementary school? What do learning cycles for teaching these concepts look like? chapters 4, 5, 6, and 7 will be devoted to providing data to answer those questions.

References

Cantu, Luis L., and J. Dudley Herron. "Concrete and Formal Piagetian Stages and Science Concept Attainment." *Journal of Research in Science Teaching* 15(2): 135–43, 1978.

Guilford, J. P., "The Determination of Item Difficulty When Chance Success is a Factor." *Psychometrika* (1936): 259–64.

Inhelder, Barbel, and Jean Piaget. *The Growth of Logical Thinking.* New York: Basic Books, 1958.

Lawson, Anton E., and John W. Renner. "Relationships of Science Subject Matter and Developmental Levels of Learners." *Journal of Research in Science Teaching,* 12(4): 347–58, 1975.

Piaget, Jean. "Development and Learning," *Journal of Research in Science Teaching* 2(3): 176–86, 1964.

Piaget, Jean, and Barbel Inhelder. *The Psychology of the Child.* New York: Basic Books, 1969.

Purser, Roger K., and John W. Renner. "Results of Two Tenth-Grade Biology Teaching Procedures." *Science Education* 67(1): 85–98, 1983.

Renner, John W., Donald G. Stafford, Anton E. Lawson, Joe W. McKinnon, F. Elizabeth Friot and Donald H. Kellogg. *Research, Teaching and Learning with the Piaget Model.* Norman, Okla.: University of Oklahoma Press, 1976.

Shayer, Michael, and Philip Adey. *Towards a Science of Science Teaching.* London, England: Heinemann Educational Books, 1981.

II

CONCEPTUAL INVENTION

PROLOGUE TO THE LEARNING CYCLES FOR THE BIOLOGICAL, EARTH, AND PHYSICAL SCIENCES

Science content is usually divided into such disciplines as earth science, biology, chemistry, physics, astronomy, and geology. These disciplines represent organizing curricula. The learning cycles in the following chapters are drawn from three of these disciplines: biological sciences (chapter 4), earth sciences (chapter 5), and physical sciences (chapter 6). Each chapter contains learning cycles for each elementary school grade from one through six. Chapter 7 contains three learning cycles for kindergarten. Some of the materials in all of the learning cycles included here were taken from The Learning Science Program volumes, *Things, Changes, Systems, Variation, Action,* and *Models* by John W. Renner, Don G. Stafford, and Vivian Jensen Coulter (Encino, California: Benziger, Bruce and Glencoe, 1977). All twenty-one learning cycles reflect the language appropriate for the grade level for which it was written. Exploration is labeled GATHERING DATA; conceptual invention is labeled THE IDEA; and expansion is labeled EXPANDING THE IDEA. Each learning cycle is followed by TEACHING SUGGESTIONS.

Because this book is limited to six learning cycles for each of the biological, earth, and physical sciences, we were careful to develop a "sample" that would accurately represent each scientific discipline. To do this, we considered several questions when selecting the concepts from which learning cycles were developed: What concepts should be included in the biological, earth, and physical sciences? Are the concepts, principles, and topics of the learning cycles fundamental and central to the discipline? Can the investigations be conducted in elementary school classrooms?

Below are the concepts we have found usable in and appropriate for elementary school science. They are listed for the biological, earth and physical sciences for grades one through six. Concepts for the learning cycles in chapters 4, 5, and 6 were selected from these lists. The language of each concept does not necessarily reflect the grade level for which it is intended.

Concepts in the Biological Sciences

Grade one

1. An aquarium is a place for living things to grow.
2. Living objects in an aquarium are called organisms.
3. Seeds come from plants.
4. Seeds grow into plants.
5. Plants have roots.
6. Many seeds are edible, for example, pecans, peanuts, green beans.
7. All animals need food, water, and a place to live.
8. Animals have properties.
9. Properties tell us about the kinds of animals.
10. People have properties that make them different.
11. People use their senses to find out about objects.

Grade two

1. Seeds grow into plants and plants grow and change; that sequence is called the plant's life cycle.
2. Every animal goes through a life cycle.
3. Some plants change with the time of year.
4. Plants grown in the light are different from plants grown in the dark.
5. Animals change as they grow older.
6. An animal's home is its habitat.

7. Plants have roots that help hold them in the earth and grow.
8. Living things in the aquarium grow and change.
9. People change as they grow older.
10. Babies grow teeth and these teeth change as people grow.

Grade three

1. If a seed has light, water, and warmth, it will germinate, or begin to grow.
2. A plant gets minerals from the soil.
3. Plants use light and water to make food.
4. Seeds are often moved in many different ways to a place where they can grow.
5. Organisms of the same kind that live in the same place are known as a population.
6. Animals cannot make their own food so they eat plants or other animals.
7. Organisms eat one another in a sequence called a food chain. For example, a rabbit eats grass, and a fox eats the rabbit.
8. A food web is formed when several food chains or parts of food chains are combined.
9. The bones in your body form a system called a skeleton, or skeletal system, which serves as a framework for your body.

10. The bones in your body are fastened together at places called joints.
11. Bones have special properties such as size and shape, which determine their special uses.
12. The human backbone is known as the spine, and it is made up of small separate bones called vertebrae.
13. The muscles in your body make up a part of your body known as the muscular system, which helps move your body.

Grade four

1. The properties of a population have great variation.
2. Organisms in the same population can have many variations; for example, there is no other person in the world exactly like you.
3. Part of your breathing system is called the lungs.
4. A person's activities influence breathing rates.
5. Blood is pumped through the body in regular beats called a pulse, which varies with age.
6. The dark spot in the eye, the pupil, is affected by the amount of light present.
7. The surroundings in which organisms live are called the environment.
8. Temperature, chemicals, and the amount of water present influence the environment and are called environmental factors.
9. People are able to live in varied environments in the world by controlling some factors of the environment.
10. Adaptations are special properties that help an animal survive in certain environments.
11. Animals can be grouped according to the kind of food they eat.
12. Foods are placed together because of the food elements they contain.
13. To be well nourished you should eat food from each food group every day.
14. Foods selected each day from each group provide a balanced diet.

Grade five

1. When exact numbers of particular objects or traits are not needed or available, it is useful to make an estimate.
2. All organisms living in an area must have a source of food.
3. Mold is a fungus and may be made up of tiny organisms.
4. Organisms that cause organic material to decay are called decomposers.
5. Yeast, like mold, feeds on organic material and like mold and bacteria, is a decomposer.
6. Food producers, food consumers, and decomposers make up a food cycle.
7. Organisms in an area interacting in this kind of food cycle relationship are called a community.
8. The process of converting food into a state the body can use is called digestion. The many organs that carry out this process are called the digestive system.
9. Food gives off energy when it is used by the body. This energy is measured in a unit called a calorie.
10. Calories of energy can be stored by the body.
11. Any substance essential to body functioning can be called a nutrient.
12. Your diet should be balanced between energy foods and foods your body needs for growing and for repairing damaged parts.

Grade six

1. Seeing with two eyes is called binocular vision.
2. The hole in the eye that lets the light in is called the pupil.
3. Images focus on the retina, which is on the back of the eye.
4. The eye has a changeable convex lens that focuses images on the retina.
5. Your heart has valves and pushes blood through your body.

6. The rate of the heart beat is affected by body activity.
7. Breathing is controlled by the changeable volume inside the chest cavity.
8. The populations of organisms within an area interact with one another and are called a biotic community.
9. A biotic community interacting with environmental factors is an ecosystem.
10. Humans and other animals add carbon dioxide to the air.
11. The movement and use of gases in the environment are sometimes referred to as the oxygen-carbon dioxide cycle.
12. Any substance that in quantity has a bad effect on any organism can be called a pollutant.

Concepts in Earth Science

Grade one

1. The sun gives light and heat, which warms the earth.
2. The moon is an object like the earth, but it is different too.
3. Air is an object and has properties.
4. Clouds are objects.
5. Thunder is sound caused by lightning.
6. A rainbow is made of light of many colors.
7. Water is a liquid.
8. Water can be a solid called ice.
9. Rain and snow are made of water and come from clouds.
10. Mountains and land are made of rocks and soil.

Grade two

1. The sun appears each morning, and this is called sunrise.
2. The sun disappears each evening, and this is called sunset.
3. Objects can stop some light, making a darker place called a shadow.
4. Light from the sun bounces off objects, and this is called reflected light.
5. The moon changes in shape, color, and position in the sky.
6. The sun and moon do the same things over and over again. Things repeated are called cycles.
7. Moving air is called wind.
8. The wind is described by how fast it is blowing and from which direction it is moving.
9. Clouds are different sized and shaped objects that move in the sky.
10. Temperature tells how hot or cold an object is. Some places on earth are cold, some are hot, and some are in between.
11. A year has twelve months each consisting of about thirty days, and the months make four groups called seasons.
12. The earth has a layer of air around it and a layer of water on it.

Grade three

1. Evaporation is changing from a liquid to a gas; water can evaporate.
2. Condensing is changing from a gas to a liquid; water vapor can condense.
3. The water vapor in a cloud that condenses and falls to the earth is called precipitation.
4. How well things can be seen through the air is called visibility.
5. The air around us is known as the atmosphere, and it can have many conditions such as wind, moisture, and temperature.
6. Weather is the result of the conditions of the atmosphere.

7. The kind of weather in a place over a long period of time is known as climate. Climate is the average weather in a place, and there are different kinds of climate.
8. Weathering is the action of wind and water on the earth's surface and on its landforms.
9. When a forest fire destroys the trees, there is an open space on the land.
10. A volcano is a vent in the earth's crust where steam and molten rock shoot out when the volcano is active and the cooled molten rock builds up into a mountain.
11. When the ground at the surface shakes and trembles an earthquake is occurring.
12. The four seasons during a year—spring, summer, fall, and winter—each has its own kind of weather.
13. Plants and animals of long ago left their imprints, which are called fossils, in the rocks.
14. Dinosaurs, the largest land animals to live on earth, have become extinct, but we know a great deal about them from fossil evidence.

Grade four

1. Water evaporates, and that vapor mixes with air causing humidity.
2. Air can hold only a certain amount of water vapor at one temperature. If the air temperature gets higher, it can hold more, and if the temperature gets lower, it can hold less.
3. Atmospheric pressure is measured with an instrument called a barometer.
4. The amount of precipitation can be measured in inches or centimeters with a rain gauge.
5. Moving air is wind, and its direction can be measured with a weather vane.
6. Temperature, humidity, wind direction and speed, visibility, clouds, and precipitation are used to describe the conditions of the air which are called weather.

7. Weather conditions over a long time are called the climate.
8. Moving water and wind interact with objects such as rocks or soil and cause erosion.
9. Plants and animals decompose to produce humus, which, when mixed with sand, clay, and other minerals, makes soil.
10. Streams or rivers make up the drainage system of land.
11. A lake is an inland body of standing water in a depression or basin in the earth.
12. An ocean is a continuous body of salty water; oceans cover most of the surface of the earth.
13. Rocks are the materials of which the crust of the earth is made and form the mountains.
14. Minerals are the materials of which rocks are made.
15. Traces of animal and plant life preserved in rocks are called fossils.

Grade five

1. The direction in which the numeral 12 on a clock is pointed when used to find objects is called reference direction.
2. A compass can be used to describe the location of an object.
3. The pair of numbers that tell where two lines cross are called the rectangular coordinates of that point.
4. An object that can be used to identify a particular place is called a landmark.
5. A map is a kind of drawing that shows the location of objects and places on the earth.
6. Rectangular coordinates can be used with maps.
7. The position of an object or a place can be described as a certain number of degrees from a reference direction called a polar coordinate.
8. The location of an object or a place can be found if polar coordinates from two different positions are known. This is called triangulation.

9. Almost any solid piece of matter near the surface of the earth can be called a rock and is made up of one or more pure substances called minerals.
10. The different characteristics of the earth's surface are called surface features.
11. The general shape of the land is called a land form.
12. The materials supplied by the earth are called natural resources.
13. Natural resources that can be used again and again are renewable resources.
14. The most abundant fossil fuel in the United States is coal, and enough coal reserves exist to last hundreds of years.
15. Saving and protecting our natural resources is known as conservation.

Grade six

1. The properties of air especially interesting to weather scientists are called weather elements or elements of weather.
2. An air mass on earth is a huge body of air that can be hundreds of miles wide and many miles high and has the same temperature and humidity throughout.
3. An air mass with a lower temperature than the surrounding air is called a cold air mass, and an air mass with higher temperatures than the surrounding air is called a warm air mass.
4. When two air masses meet, the boundary between the two is called a front.
5. The model of the earth that best explains what people observe is a sphere.
6. The sun cycle changes position in the sky with respect to the earth from one part of the year to another.
7. There are four periods of the year called seasons, which can be differentiated from the earth-sun system model.
8. The sun is a star and gives light and heat to the earth.
9. The earth revolves around the sun.
10. The earth has a large spherical mass that revolves around it called the moon.
11. An object that revolves in an orbit around a larger object is called a satellite.
12. Some objects in the sky are called planets and are satellites of the sun.

Concepts in the Physical Sciences

Grade one

1. All things are objects.
2. Color, shape, size, feel, and smell are properties of objects.
3. Objects are made of material.
4. Material is matter.
5. All matter takes up space.
6. Objects have their own sounds.
7. Sound moves in the air.
8. Moving air makes sound.
9. Music sounds have a pattern while noise sounds have no pattern.
10. The clock tells the time things happen.
11. A minute and a second measure time. A minute is longer than a second and there are sixty minutes in an hour.
12. Machines make doing work easy.
13. The lever and the wheel are machines.

Grade two

1. Temperature tells us how hot or cold an object is.
2. A thermometer may be a glass object containing liquid; heat makes the liquid move.

3. Pushing and pulling are forces.
4. Water digging up dirt and stones is erosion.
5. Windstorms are air moving with a lot of force.
6. All meter sticks have a balance point in the middle of the stick called the center of balance.
7. The longer the string of a pendulum, the slower the pendulum swings.
8. Magnets are special objects that stick to or attract iron.
9. One end of a suspended magnet points north.
10. A compass is a magnet.
11. Vibrating objects make sounds that travel through the air.
12. Strings vibrate to make sound.

Grade three

1. The three states of matter are solid, liquid, and gas.
2. An electrical circuit provides a pathway for electricity, which lights a light bulb.
3. The evidence of interaction among the elements in an electrical circuit can be the brightness of a light bulb.
4. When electrical objects are put together and the bulb does not light, an open circuit is present.
5. Material that closes an open circuit is an electrical conductor.
6. When a magnet and an object pull toward each other, this pulling is called magnetic attraction.
7. Iron filings are tightly held to a magnet's poles.
8. Alike poles on magnets repel and opposite poles attract.
9. Electricity can cause magnetism.
10. Adding heat can make objects get hot and taking heat away lets objects get cool.
11. Heat can make other things happen in a system.
12. When talking about how hot or cold an object is, you are talking about its temperature.

Grade four

1. What is seen in a mirror is called a mirror image.
2. A line of symmetry divides a shape into two like parts.
3. Different kinds of matter having different properties are called substances.
4. Matter that has variable properties is called a mixture.
5. If water and another material form a clear mixture when put together, the mixture is called a solution.
6. When a solvent has dissolved all of the solute it can hold, the mixture is called a saturated solution.
7. The transfer of heat energy through a material such as a metal rod is called conduction, and the material which allows the energy to be transferred through it is called a conductor.
8. Heat travels through air by convection.
9. There is an advantage to using the machine called a lever because the lever multiplies force.
10. A ramp, or inclined plane, multiplies force and is called a machine.

Grade five

1. Energy is something that causes objects to do things they would not do without it.
2. One object or system giving energy to another object or system is evidence of energy transfer. The object or system giving the energy is the energy source, and the object or system receiving the energy is an energy receiver.
3. Heat is a kind of energy.
4. Stored energy is potential energy.
5. Rubbing an object gives it an electrical charge, which is called static electricity.
6. Energy from dry cells is moving electrical energy and is called an electric current.
7. Energy produced when chemicals interact is called chemical energy.
8. Energy can cause things to vibrate, which produces sound.

9. When liquids of different temperatures are put together the resulting temperature—equilibrium temperature—is greater than the colder one and less than the warmer one.
10. Machines can multiply force.
11. Energy can be changed from one form to another.
12. Motion is a change of position.
13. The push given to an object is called action, and the push the object gives back is called reaction.
14. Gravity attracts objects, often causing them to fall down.
15. The movement of an object both horizontally and falling toward the earth at the same time is called projectile motion.

Grade six

1. The smallest particle of a pure substance is called a molecule.
2. When an object increases in volume or size, the object expands, and when an object gets smaller or decreases in volume, the object contracts.
3. When an image is clear and sharp, it is said to be in focus.
4. When an object is far away, the distance from the lens to its image is the focal length of the lens.
5. The angle of a light ray going into a mirror is the same as the angle of the light ray reflected from the mirror.
6. The bending of light by glass (or any material) is called refraction.
7. One kind of matter moving through another kind of matter is known as diffusion.
8. Electricity is a form of energy because it can cause something to be done.
9. A wire, a dry cell, and a light bulb can be arranged in a system that causes an interaction—the light bulb lights. Such an arrangement is called an electrical circuit.
10. The interaction of the wire, the dry cell, and the light bulb causes electrical current in the circuit.
11. Objects hooked together in a circuit in a way that allows the same amount of current to flow through each of them form a series circuit.
12. Objects in a circuit can be connected so that the energy source—the battery—affects them the same way, but the current in each is different. Such a circuit is a parallel circuit.
13. The accuracy of a model depends upon the quality and quantity of information given the person building the model.

CHAPTER FOUR

LEARNING CYCLES FOR THE BIOLOGICAL SCIENCES

Six concepts from the biological science concepts identified in the prologue have been selected for the conceptual invention phase of the six learning cycles that follow. These concepts are:

Grade 1: An aquarium is a place for living things to grow (biology concept #1).

Grade 2: Seeds grow into plants, and plants grow and change; this sequence is called the plant's life cycle (biology concept #1).

Grade 3: Organisms eat one another in a sequence called a food chain. For example, a rabbit eats grass and a fox eats the rabbit (biology concept #7).

Grade 4: Part of your breathing system is called the lungs (biology concept #3).

Grade 5: Organisms that cause organic material to decay are called decomposers (biology concept #4).

Grade 6: Your heart has valves and pushes blood through your body (biology concept #5).

LEARNING CYCLE FOR FIRST GRADE

Building an Aquarium

Today you will work with some living objects.

You will make a place for the objects to live.

Gathering data

Here are pictures of some of the objects.

Name the objects.

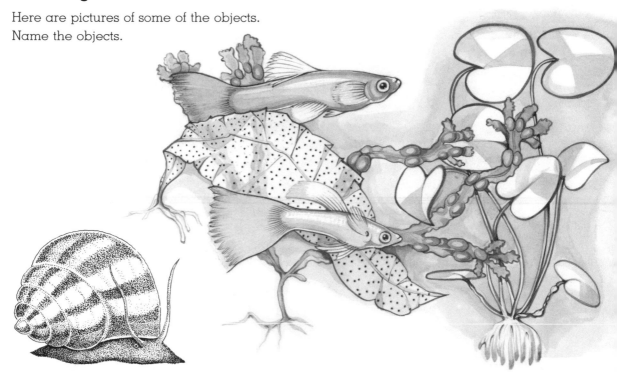

Make a place for the objects to live.

You will need a jar.

You will need some water.

You will need some sand.

Wash the sand.

Put the sand in the jar.

Put water in the jar.

The idea

You have made an aquarium. It is a place for living things to grow.

Expanding the idea

Fish can live in an aquarium.
Plants and snails live there too.
You can watch the aquarium.
You can see what happens.
Put your living things in the aquarium.
Put in the water plants.
Plant them in the sand.

Put fish in the aquarium.
Put snails in, too.
Take care of your aquarium.
Watch the fish.
Watch the snails and plants.
Tell what happens.

CHECKING UP

1. Name some things in the aquarium.
2. How must you care for the things in the aquarium?

TEACHING SUGGESTIONS

Here is a list of the materials you will need to set up aquariums. There should be an aquarium for every three or four children:

Aged water

Fish food

Fish net

Guppies

Sand

Snails

Water plants

Half gallon jars

Be sure to "age" the water by letting it stand in an open container for twenty-four hours. The aging allows harmful gases to escape from the water and permits the temperature of the water to approach that of the room.

Among the water plants that are suitable for an aquarium are the vallisneria, elodea, sagittaria, and cabomba. You can obtain these plants from a pet store.

Put the fish in the aquarium after the plants. Guppies are excellent aquarium fish, but any other fish that are easily maintained may be substituted. Put from two to four guppies in each jar, both females and males. Male guppies are usually smaller and more colorful than the females. Add several snails to the aquarium. Permit the children to put the aquariums in several different places around the room. If the aquariums are in different places, they will develop in different ways. (The amount of sunlight is one condition which makes a difference.)

It is important that each group keep a record of what was put in their aquarium and the date it was done. A picture record is useful if the children are careful to show the exact number of organisms in the aquarium.

Fish in the aquarium may die. If this happens, *do not remove the dead organism.* Allow the children to observe and discuss the event. A snail may eat the dead fish. The children then can make inferences about the snail's sources of food. If a number of organisms die at the same time, this may be an indication of a badly polluted aquarium. Cloudiness of water usually indicates a concentration of bacteria resulting from the decay of excess food or dead organisms.

In building an aquarium and observing the interactions within the aquarium environment, the children will be developing concepts relating to living organisms. Their learning will depend to a large extent upon your willingness to provide time for observation, discussion, and simple experimentation.

A teacher may be tempted at times to skimp on materials and to avoid child participation when dealing with living things in the classroom. But the obvious interest of the children and the ongoing opportunity for concrete learning make the value of these experiences apparent.

| LEARNING CYCLE FOR SECOND GRADE | Plants Grow And Change |

A plant is a living thing.
Let's find out about plants.
Let's see how they live.
Let's see how they grow.
Let's see how they change.

Gathering data

Plant some pea seeds.
When does the plant come up?
How long does it take?
Plant some bean seeds.
When does the plant come up?
How long does it take?

You planted a pea seed.
A pea plant grew.
The plant has pods.
What is inside the pea pods?

You planted a bean seed.
A bean plant grew.
The bean plant has bean pods.

The idea

**Seeds grow into plants and plants grow and change; this
sequence is called the plant's life cycle.**

Expanding the idea

We plant a seed.
It grows into a plant.
The plant grows more seeds.
The new seeds can grow more plants.

A tomato plant grows and changes.
It grows from little seeds.
Look at the tomato seeds.

Tomato seeds change into tomato plants.
What do the tomato plants make?

CHECKING UP

1. How many days did it take before your seed grew a plant?
2. What is inside a bean pod?
3. What do we call the changes in seeds and plants?

TEACHING SUGGESTIONS

Beans, peas and corn seeds

Potting soil

Planting containers

Spoons or small hand trowels

Pea and bean pods

Support sticks for plants

Twist'ems or other fasteners for plants.

Plan regular observations of the plants. Continue to encourage the children to draw the plants as they develop. Continue to save at least some of the drawings so you can later use them to illustrate the changes that took place during the plants' life cycle. You may wish to provide sticks to use as props when the plants get tall enough. "Twist'ems" work well for fastening plants to support sticks.

After the plants mature, flowers will appear. From the flowers, pods will develop. Open pods from the class pea and bean plants. By comparing seeds, the children can state that some are called pea pods because they contain pea seeds that grow into pea plants, and some are called bean pods for similar reasons.

Be sure to water the plants regularly and keep the plants near a light source.

This learning cycle leads the children through an exploration of change in the plants they have been growing. It introduces them to the concept of life cycle. It also helps them to realize that certain seeds produce certain plants, that is, a tomato plant does not grow from an orange seed.

**LEARNING CYCLE
FOR THIRD GRADE**

Getting Food

Do you have a pet? If so, you must feed your pet. You must give it food. You must give it the food it needs. Animals in their natural habitats must find their own food. There is no one around to feed them. What food do animals eat? How do animals find their food?

Gathering data

Fill a two-liter jar with clear water. Let the water stand for two days. Then put six guppies in the jar. Do not feed the guppies for three days.

Next, fill a small jar with water. Take one guppy from the two-liter jar and put it in the small jar. Then put several daphnia into the small jar. What happens?

Daphnia eat algae, which are plants. Daphnia are animals. Animals eat plants. Guppies eat daphnia. Guppies are animals, too. One animal eats another animal. What has happened can be shown in this way:

Algae→daphnia→guppies.

The arrow means "eaten by."

Now, read these diagrams:

1. Grass ⟶ rabbit ⟶ fox.
2. Corn ⟶ cow ⟶ people.
3. Seeds ⟶ sparrow ⟶ cat.
4. Leaves ⟶ caterpillar ⟶ robin.
5. Acorn ⟶ squirrel ⟶ coyote.

The idea

Organisms eat one another. This is a sequence called a *food chain.* **For example, a rabbit eats grass and a fox eats the rabbit.**

Expanding the idea

Algae and daphnia make up populations. Guppies are another population. As you have observed, one population eats another population. Which population eats which? Food chains tell you.

Complete each of these food chains. Replace the question marks with the names of organisms. Make a record of each in your science notebook:

1. ? ⟶ cricket ⟶ frog.
2. ? ⟶ sheep ⟶ wolf.
3. ? ⟶ chicken ⟶ people.
4. ? ⟶ mouse ⟶ cat.
5. ? ⟶ deer ⟶ mountain lion.

What goes in place of each question mark? After you decide, write it down. How are the words you used for the question marks alike? The words you used for the question marks tell you something. What do they tell you?

The beginning of a food chain is always a green plant. Green plants make their own food. They do not have to eat other organisms. Green plants combine water and carbon dioxide to make food. They do this with the help of light.

Each food chain has at least two animals in it. (A long food chain may have more than two animals.) One animal is eaten. The other animal does the eating. An animal that eats another animal is a *predator.* The animal which is eaten is the *prey.*

Read this diagram:

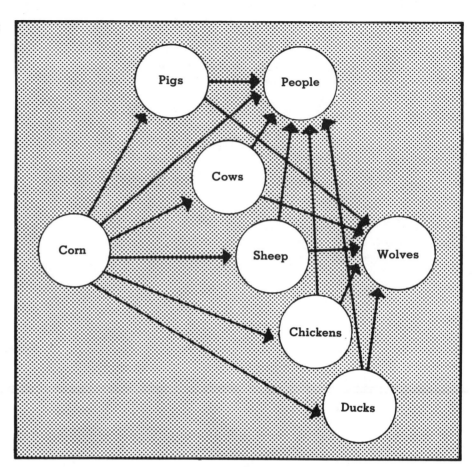

Which are the predators? Which are the prey?

Look at the list of organisms in the chart.

Make a food chain diagram. Which animal is the predator and which is the prey?

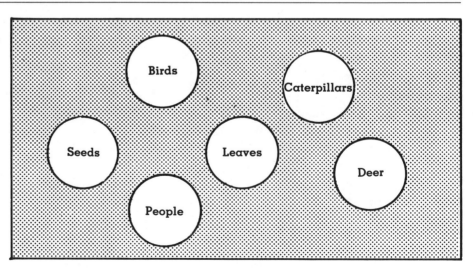

CHECKING UP

1. A daphnia is part of a food chain. What other organisms are you likely to find in the same food chain?
2. What kind of organism is always at one end of a food chain?
3. Which of the animals listed below are predators?

| frog | sheep | cat | wolf |
| mouse | chicken | owl | cricket |

4. Make a food chain for these three organisms: eagle, grass, gopher.
5. From where does a green plant get its food?

TEACHING SUGGESTIONS

Daphnia
Guppies
Jars
Paper towels
Eye droppers

You can obtain daphnia from a supply house, or you can find some daphnia in a pond. Daphnia is commonly known as a "water flea," and it can be found in great numbers around ponds and streams. Once you have a few daphnia, you can easily culture a large colony.

Instruct each group to put only one guppy into each jar with the daphnia. The guppies may possibly be hungry enough to eat all the daphnia within two or three days.

The children have observed a food chain. (Do not use the name yet.) Daphnia are eaten by guppies. Introduce the arrow. Explain to the class that the arrow is a symbol that means "is eaten by." The diagrams represent three food chains. Algae are eaten by daphnia, and daphnia are eaten by guppies. Grass is eaten by a rabbit, and the rabbit is eaten by a fox. Corn is eaten by a cow, and the cow is eaten by people. Call to your students' attention that each food chain begins with a plant.

The children will carry out experiments that lead to the invention of a food web by interpreting diagrams. The children should think this exercise through carefully, and each child should be allowed to pick out predators and prey. Allow each child to take an animal through a particular sequence and find out when it is a predator and when it is prey.

The untangling of the food webs to distinguish predator and prey is a revealing exercise. The children must do this in order to become aware that a particular organism does not always stay in the same food chain.

**LEARNING CYCLE
FOR FOURTH GRADE**

Lungs

As a human organism, you are made up of many systems. There are many systems in your body. Your eyes, heart, and lungs are all parts of body systems.

Gathering data

Count the number of times you breathe in one minute. Make a record of that number. Now, repeat the measurement. Find out how many times you breathe in five minutes. Make a record of that number. How many times will you record that you breathe each minute?

Use the records of every one in this class to make a class histogram. Choose a title for the histogram. Ask your teacher to explain what "rate" means. What is the range of the rates? What is the rate for the greatest number of people in your class?

Put your hand on your ribs. Take a deep breath. Feel your chest expand. Your lungs are expanding as they fill with air.

Your lungs are made of a spongy tissue. This spongy tissue expands when you take in air. Then, when you breathe the air out, your lungs squeeze together, or *contract*.

Run hard in place for several minutes. Stop running. Have a friend count the number of times you breathe in one minute. Compare that rate with the rate you found earlier. What do these two pieces of quantitative data tell you? Make a record of how your breathing is different after running. (Build model that is described in the Teaching Suggestions.)

The idea

Part of your breathing system is called the lungs.

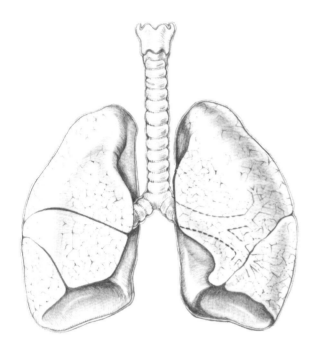

Expanding the idea

The human lungs are located in the chest cavity. One lung is on each side. Their function is to furnish oxygen to the blood and to remove carbon dioxide.

Air enters through the nose and travels down the windpipe to the two branches of the lungs. The tubes leading to the lungs divide into smaller and smaller branches, ending in millions of tiny air sacs.

Tiny blood vessels surround these air sacs. It is here that the blood picks up oxygen and releases carbon dioxide. The carbon dioxide is breathed out of the body. The blood with a fresh supply of oxygen is returned to the heart to be pumped around the body.

Lung tissue is soft, light, and spongy. A thin membrane covers each lung. Breathing is done largely by a muscle called the diaphragm.

Children's lungs are usually pink, depending on the cleanness of air they breathe. The color of lung tissue varies with the environment. Some dust and dirt particles from the air remain trapped in the air sacs and cause a change in the appearance of lung tissue.

Lung tissue from people who smoke or who work in dusty places is found to be dark and less able to provide oxygen. These people are thought to be more likely to suffer from certain diseases.

When we breathe quietly, each breath contains about a pint of air. Great activity causes a change of this amount. We may take in as much as six times more air to provide enough oxygen.

Take as deep a breath as you can. Use that breath to blow up a balloon. Be sure you have blown as much as you can in one breath into the balloon. Tie the open end of the balloon securely. Tie it with a string.

Tie a nylon cord with two plastic rings as shown. Tape the rings to the balloon. Study the picture. Make sure the balloon moves freely along the cord.

Now, cut the balloon open. Cut off the end that is tied with a string. Use a pair of sharp scissors. What does the balloon do when you cut it open?

How does this experiment give you quantitative data? What do the quantitative data tell you? Why is nylon cord used in the experiment? Fishing line does nicely.

Repeat the experiment until you find out the lung size of everyone in the class. Use your data to make a histogram. What is the variation in your classmates' lung sizes?

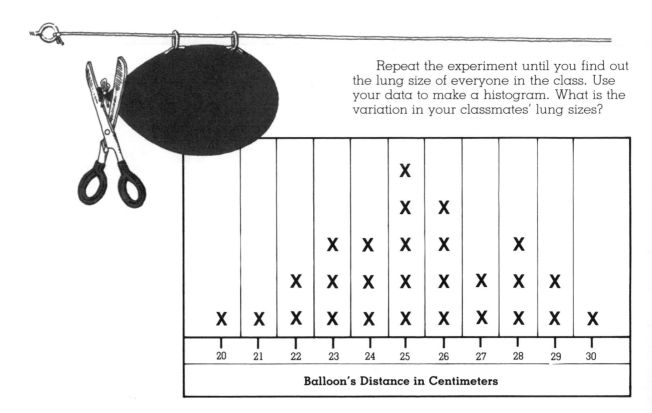

					X					
					X	X				
			X	X	X	X		X		
		X	X	X	X	X	X	X	X	
X	X	X	X	X	X	X	X	X	X	X
20	21	22	23	24	25	26	27	28	29	30

Balloon's Distance in Centimeters

Lung size is often called *lung capacity*. Why is "capacity" a better word to use than "size"? Refer to a dictionary.

You now have a set of data about lung capacity. You can use your data to find out something else. First, measure the height of everyone in the class. Record these data.

Combine the data about height with your data on lung capacity. Arrange all the data in a table. The picture shows a plan for a table. Your table will show two pieces of quantitative data for each member of the class. Height and lung capacity are recorded in the table.

Look at the quantitative data you have found for the two variables. Compare everyone's height with lung capacity. What do you see that might be important?

Student	Height	Lung Capacity

CHECKING UP

1. What happens to your chest when you take a deep breath?
2. What happens to your lungs when you breathe air in?
3. What happens to your lungs when you breathe air out?
4. Name something that might change your breathing rate.
5. Give some evidence about variation in lung capacity.

TEACHING SUGGESTIONS

One pound coffee can (with clear plastic lid and metal ends removed)

Thin rubber sheet about 15 cm square

No. 1, one-hole stopper

Glass tube about 9 cm long

Balloon

Large rubber band

Candles

The model is a simple apparatus. An inflated balloon (a lung) is sealed inside the can (the chest cavity). The mouth of the balloon is fixed to a glass tube (the trachea) which opens into the atmosphere, but not into the can. On the bottom of the can is a movable rubber covering (the diaphragm). When this covering is stretched, the interior volume of the can expands. When the rubber covering is pushed in, the can's volume is reduced.

Be sure your students understand these properties of the model:

1. The air can get into the inside of the balloon from the outside, but it cannot get into the inside of the can.

2. When the rubber piece on the bottom of the can is stretched, the area inside of the can becomes bigger.
3. When the rubber piece on the bottom of the can is pushed in, the area inside of the can gets smaller. (The "inside" of the can is the volume of the can.)

The ideas you need on pressure are very simple. If the air pressure on the inside of a container is lessened, air quickly moves in and raises the pressure back to normal. If the air pressure on the inside of a container is increased, air moves out and returns the pressure to normal. Be sure that the children understand that pressure always moves in order to remain as normal as possible (that is, a high pressure area will tend to reduce its pressure and a low pressure area will tend to have its pressure raised).

Students will develop a concept of breathing by interpreting the model. As the children will learn, air pressure and the movement of the chest make it possible for a person to breathe.

LEARNING CYCLE
FOR FIFTH GRADE

Decomposition

On what things is mold likely to grow? Will mold appear on leather? What about paper? Will a plastic cup grow mold? Does mold grow on wood? Will mold grow on butter, meat, and celery?

Gathering data

You will need a mold terrarium to carry out this investigation. You can easily make the terrarium. Use any clear container with a tightly fitting lid. A gallon jar works well. Put in several inches of sand or dirt. Pour in enough water so the sand is damp. Choose the things you want to test. Then put them in the mold terrarium.

Keep a class record of all the materials placed in the mold terrarium. Be sure to record the date on which you placed each material in the terrarium. On which materials do you believe mold will grow? Make a prediction. Watch for the appearance of any growth and record the date. Keep the lid on the terrarium.

Your record of this experiment should look like this:

GROWTH IN MOLD TERRARIUM

Object	Date Put In	Prediction	Results	Date
Bread	March 4	Yes	Mold grew	March 9

Keep your mold terrarium growing for as long as you observe interesting action. What finally happens to the things inside the container? Check your predictions about the different materials.

Now, it's time to open the terrariums. Dump the materials out and take a good look at what is going on. Carefully observe the condition of the materials. Spread out the contents on a paper towel. Observe the materials with a hand lens. Compare the contents of your terrarium with the contents of other terrariums.

The idea

Organisms that cause organic material to decay are called decomposers.

Expanding the idea

To compose something means "to put together." The prefix "de" means "the opposite of." So the word decompose means "to take apart." When mold grows on something it uses that material for food. It takes what it needs for its own growth. In doing so, the material is taken apart, or is said to decompose.

Decomposition is an ongoing process. Mold spores are present all around. If environmental factors are favorable, the spores grow and decompose whatever organic material they contact.

Molds grow in varied shapes and colors. Bread mold is usually seen as a black, cottony growth. It can obtain food from living or nonliving materials. It is one of the most active decomposers.

Some molds can be called parasites. A parasite is an organism that lives on living material. These parasite molds are the cause of much decomposition in fruit and vegetables. Plant molds destroy large amounts of farm crops.

Certain molds are present in soil and water. Water molds live on the bodies of fish and insects. Greenhouses and fish hatcheries are interested in the control of these fungi.

One of the most destructive fungi is the one that attacks potato plants. It grows on the leaves of the plant and can destroy an entire crop.

When decomposers are not controlled they can be harmful. Remember, however, their part in decomposing unwanted materials. Decomposition is a process necessary to the well-being of every environment.

CHECKING UP

1. Describe what happened in your model terrarium.
2. What materials molded first?
3. What does decompose mean?
4. In what way is mold a decomposer?
5. In your opinion, is mold a helpful or a harmful organism?
   Explain your answer.

TEACHING SUGGESTIONS

Gallon jar with lid

Sand or dirt

Water

Materials to test (paper, plastic, foods, leather piece)

Students are usually familiar with terrariums as containers in which plants grow. Explain that they now will build a mold terrarium. Decide how many terrariums you would like to have in the classroom. One would be adequate, but, if your class is large, you may need two to accommodate all the things which the students will want to test. Be sure the container has a lid. Wide-mouthed gallon jars work well and are inexpensive.

Discuss what to put inside the terrarium for a base. Soil or sand is fine. The terrarium should be damp and it should be set in a warm place. Question the children about what materials should be placed inside. The stu-

dents may suggest items on which they know mold will grow. They will test the items by putting them in the terrarium. Instruct the children to keep a record of the materials they test. Refer to the chart under Gathering Data in the learning cycle as a means of keeping records. Call attention to the Prediction column on the chart.

Students may wish to keep adding items to the mold terrarium. Allow them to do this only until a good growth of mold in occurs. Once there is considerable mold in the jar, discourage your students from taking off the lid. Discuss the changes that occur.

As a final activity with mold, have the children open the terrarium and examine the contents. The organic material should now be in a state of decomposition. The observation leads you directly into the students' conceptual invention of decomposition and into their perception of mold as a decomposer.

**LEARNING CYCLE
FOR SIXTH GRADE**

How the Heart Works

Put the finger of your left hand on the thumb side of your right wrist. You will feel a thump, thump, thump. You probably know that you have just felt your pulse. Your pulse, as you know, has something to do with blood and the heart.

You know more about your body than people in the year A.D. 150 knew. In those days everyone felt that the thump on the wrist had something to do with air. A physician named Galen then found out that blood causes the pulse, not air.

Galen wrote many books. He studied how the human body works. Galen had many good ideas, but he did get some things wrong. For one thing, he gave a wrong explanation of how blood moves through the body.

An English physician, William Harvey (1578–1657) provided a better explanation.

Galen was a famous man, and many people went along with his ideas instead of Harvey's. Still Harvey's explanation proved to be right.

For many years, Harvey had studied how blood moves around the body. In 1628, he wrote a book showing Galen to be wrong. Just imagine! More than 1,400 years had passed since Galen's ideas! Sometimes, even when ideas are wrong, they last a long while.

But what did William Harvey find out? What were his ideas? What kind of model did he build for blood moving throughout bodies? Harvey first suggested the model we use today. There have been some small changes, but the model is basically like the one that Harvey proposed. Let's find out about Harvey's famous model.

Gathering data

You need to build equipment to use in the following experiment. There are some special things you will need. Here is a list of what you will need for the experiment.

1. Get a plastic bottle like the one pictured below. Be sure the bottle is soft enough to squeeze.
2. You will need two rubber stoppers, each with one hole.
3. Get two pieces of glass tubing, each about 8 cm long.
4. You will need two pieces of rubber or plastic tubing, each about 20 cm long.
5. Get two jars. Each one should hold about 300 cubic cm.
6. You will need a third piece of rubber tubing about 50 cm long.

Now, put your equipment together. Follow these directions:

1. Hold a rubber stopper and a piece of glass tubing under water. Gently twist the glass tube through the hole in the stopper. Then do the same with the other rubber stopper and glass tube.
2. Cut a hole in the bottom of the plastic bottle. Fit one of the rubber stoppers into the hole.
3. Take the cover off the bottle. Fit the second rubber stopper into the hole in the top of the bottle.
4. Now, attach a piece of rubber tubing to each glass tube. Your equipment should look like this:

Next, half fill one of the jars with water. Call this *jar 1*. Leave the other jar empty. Call this *jar 2*. Put one of the pieces of tubing hanging from the bottle into jar 1. Put the tubing on the other end of the bottle into jar 2. Call the tube in jar 1 tube A. Call the other tube B.

Now you are ready to use your model. You will need a partner.

Put water into the bottle until it is about half full. To do this, you can remove the stopper at the top of the bottle. Squeeze tube B tightly so that the water does not leave the bottle while it is being filled. Hold the bottle on its side. Squeeze tube A with your fingers.

Now, give the bottle a quick, hard squeeze. Do not release the bottle. Observe what happens. Hold the end of tube B above jar 2. Now, release the bottle. Repeat this until the water in the bottle is about half gone.

Tightly squeeze tube B. Squeeze the bottle and release it. What happens to the water in jar 1? Repeat this several times. Make a careful record of what happens when each of the tubes is squeezed tightly.

You also have a piece of rubber tubing about 50 cm long. Put one end of that tubing into the jar tube B has been emptying into. Suck the air out of the long tubing. Start the water running from jar 2 to jar 1. You may have to practice a few times. Practice as much as you need to. Keep the water running between the jars.

Now your equipment is working. Water is moving from jar 1 to jar 2 through the bottle. You know how to squeeze the bottle and the tubes to do this. Practice until you can keep the amounts of water in jars 1 and 2 the same.

Describe how the water goes from jar 1 to jar 2. Compare how the water reaches jar 2 with how it goes from jar 2 to jar 1. Be sure to compare the way the water flows in both cases. Make accurate records about the differences in the flow from jar 1 to jar 2 and from jar 2 to jar 1.

Again, feel your pulse. What in your experiment could be compared with the thump of your pulse? What caused the short burst of water that entered jar 2? Use your data to answer these questions.

What in your body causes the thump of your pulse? Use the data you have gathered to make a model of how your heart pushes blood though your body. How does your model allow you to explain heart beat?

Your fingers were an important aid in moving water form jar 1 to jar 2. Explain their purpose in the experiment.

The idea

Your heart has valves and pushes blood through your body.

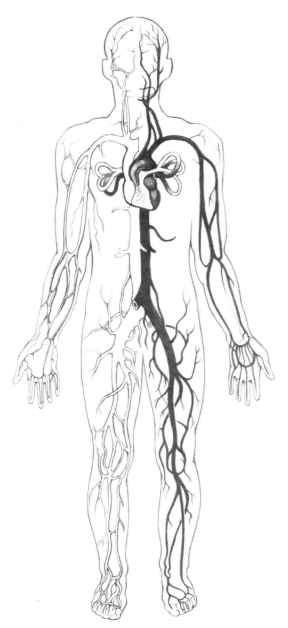

Expanding the idea

The valves in your heart keep blood in its proper part. Your fingers worked as valves in your experiment. Your heart delivers blood to the *arteries* in your body. It delivers blood to the arteries in spurts.

The heart is a pump. It is an organ that pumps blood through the body. As a pump, the heart is also a muscle. It is a muscle that keeps working automatically.

The human heart is made up of four separate parts. All mammals have hearts consisting of four parts. The heart has a right side and a left side. A wall known as the *septum* lies between the two sides.

The blood leaves the heart through the aorta. The *aorta* is the principal blood-distributing *artery* in the body. Smaller arteries branch from the aorta. They carry blood to the head, arms, legs, intestines, liver, kidneys, and stomach.

In all parts of the body, there are small blood vessels called capillaries. The blood flows from the arteries into the capillaries. From the capillaries the blood flows into the *veins*. The veins carry the blood back to the heart.

The blood flows from the veins into the right atrium, an upper part of the heart. The blood then begins its flow through the heart itself. From the right atrium it drops into the right ventricle. The *ventricle* is a lower part of the heart. The blood flows from the right atrium to the right ventricle through the *tricuspid valve*.

All the blood flows into the right ventricle, and the tricuspid valve closes. The blood then flows through the *semilunar valve* into the *pulmonary artery*. The *pulmonary artery* carries the blood to the lungs.

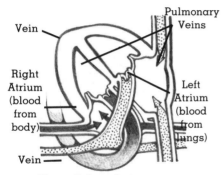

Vein

Pulmonary Veins

Right Atrium (blood from body)

Left Atrium (blood from lungs)

Vein

1   Heart Relaxed: blood enters atria

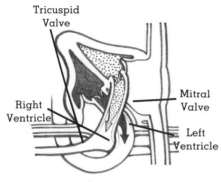

Tricuspid Valve

Right Ventricle

Mitral Valve

Left Ventricle

2   Atria Contract: blood enters ventricles

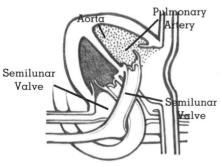

Aorta

Pulmonary Artery

Semilunar Valve

Semilunar Valve

3   Ventricles Contract: blood enters system

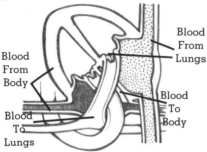

Blood From Body

Blood From Lungs

Blood To Lungs

Blood To Body

4   Heart Relaxed: blood enters atria

The lungs remove carbon dioxide from the blood. The blood has picked up the carbon dioxide as a waste product from the body. The carbon dioxide is exchanged for oxygen. With a fresh supply of oxygen for the body, the blood then flows from the lungs into the *pulmonary veins*.

The blood returns to the heart through the pulmonary veins. It flows from the pulmonary veins into the left atrium. The *mitral valve* opens. The blood then flows into the left ventricle.

The mitral valve closes. The left semilunar valve then opens, and the blood is pushed into the aorta. The process starts over. You must remember that both sides of the heart work at the same time. You have been led through the circulation here one stage at a time.

In the capillaries, the blood picks up waste products including carbon dioxide. The kidneys remove much waste from the blood. The lungs remove carbon dioxide and put oxygen into the blood.

CHECKING UP

1. What can you feel when you put your finger on the thumb side of your right wrist?
2. Where does the blood go when it leaves the heart?
3. To what part of the body do the veins deliver blood?
4. What purpose do the heart valves serve?
5. Explain the difference between veins and arteries.

TEACHING SUGGESTIONS

Glass tubing (2 pieces, 8 cm long)

2 jars (300 cubic cm capacity)

Plastic bottle

2 rubber stoppers (one-hole)

Rubber tubing (or plastic tubing; 2 pieces, 20 cm long)

Rubber tubing (1 piece, 50 cm long)

The boys and girls in your class will construct a model of the circulatory system. With this model, they will do an experiment that shows how the heart functions. The students will learn about the valves of the heart and how the valves control the flow of blood. The chapter is largely an investigation of pulse rates.

The model is actually a siphon, which causes water to flow from one jar to another, just as the heart pumps blood to the body and back to the heart. The children must be sure that the water is started properly. To assure a smooth flow, they must constantly compress and release the plastic bottle. This compression and release corresponds to the heart beat. The water flowing through the bottle from one jar to the other is the "blood," and it moves in spurts.

It will probably take at least two periods for the children to get their apparatus constructed and functioning properly. Children of this age will have the temptation to shoot water at one another and to engage in water fights. Be aware of this possibility.

The children are inventing the concept of heart valves based on their concrete experience. Their fingers acted as valves when they removed them from one side of the plastic bottle and placed them on the other side in order to stop the flow of water in one place or to start it in another place.

Call the children's attention to the fact that they have constructed a model of the circulatory system and the heart. The tube through which the water flows from one jar to another represents the veins. Jar 1, tube A, and the plastic bottle are the heart. Jar 2 is the body. Thus, we have "blood" flowing from the heart to the body and back to the heart.

CHAPTER FIVE

LEARNING CYCLES FOR THE EARTH SCIENCES

Six concepts from the earth science concepts identified in the prologue have been selected for the conceptual invention phase of the six learning cycles that follow. These concepts are:

Grade 1: Mountains and land are made of rocks and soil (earth science concept #10).

Grade 2: A year has twelve months each consisting of about thirty days, and the months make four groups called seasons (earth science concept #11).

Grade 3: A volcano is a vent in the earth's crust where steam and molten rock shoot out when the volcano is active and the cooled molten rock builds up into a mountain (earth science concept #10).

Grade 4: Traces of animal and plant life preserved in rocks are called fossils (earth science concept #15).

Grade 5: A map is a kind of drawing that shows the location of objects and places on the earth (earth science concept #5).

Grade 6: When two air masses meet, the boundary between the two is called a front (earth science concept #4).

**LEARNING CYCLE
FOR FIRST GRADE**

Soil and Rocks

Above the earth is air.
There are clouds too.
On the earth there is water.
But the earth is made of something else.
It is made of rocks.
It is made of soil.

Gathering data

Look around you.
What is the earth made of?
What do you walk on?
What holds trees?
What do flowers and grass grow in?
What are houses built on?
What is at the bottom of a river?
What is a mountain made of?

Find some rocks.
Find rocks of different colors.
Find rocks of different sizes.

Look for a very small rock.
Look for a very big rock.
Tell where you saw them.

Look at a rock.
Use a hand lens.
Tell what you see.

Feel some rocks.
Tell how they feel.
Make a group of smooth rocks.
Make a group of rough rocks.

Get a pan of water.
Drop a rock in the water.
Tell what happens.
Will a little rock float?
What do you think?
Try it and see.

The idea

Mountains and land are made of rocks and soil.

Expanding the idea

Rocks are hard chunks of matter.
Some rocks are very large.
Mountains are mostly rock.
Some rocks are very small.
A tiny grain of sand is a rock.

There are different kinds of rock.
There is hard rock like granite.
There is soft rock like talc.
There is light rock like pumice.
But most rock is heavy.

Rocks are found in many colors.
Some like quartz are clear.
Some like lava are black.
There are green, red, blue, and yellow
rocks too.

Soil is called "dirt."
It is what plants live in.
Soil also has many colors.
Soil can be red or yellow.
Soil can be black or orange.
Soil has tiny rocks in it.
They are like grains of sand.
Look at these pictures of animals.
Some live in soil.
Some live in rock caves.
What other animals live in soil?
What other animals live in rocks?

Farmers use soil.
They plant crops.
They grow wheat and corn.

They grow vegetables.
People use the crops for food.

CHECKING UP

1. Name two properties of rocks.
2. What colors are rocks?
3. Name an animal that lives in soil.
4. How do farmers use soil?
5. How are rocks different?

TEACHING SUGGESTIONS

Hand lens

Pan

Rocks (variety of colors and textures)

Rock kits (optional) available from supply house

Sand

Much of the learning cycle can be conducted outside around the school or in a nearby field. The children can collect rocks and soil and make many of their observations. Their collections can be supplemented with pictures of rocks, fields, and landforms (mountains, canyons, hills, and volcanoes).

Some of the children may already have a variety of rocks they've collected. You may want to use their rocks or purchase rock kits, which are available through science supply organizations. Excellent rock and mineral samples are provided in these kits—granite, talc, pumice, and mica. It is not important that the children identify these rocks and minerals but that they experience the properties of the samples—color, texture, and feel, for example.

LEARNING CYCLE FOR SECOND GRADE

The Year

Some changes on earth happen every day.
The sun rises and sets.
The day gets light.
Then, it gets dark.

Some changes happen each month.
The moon is full.

Then it changes shapes.
It becomes full again.

The daily change is a cycle.
The monthly change is a cycle.
The earth has another cycle too.

Gathering data

Look at a calendar.
Count the number of pages.
Each page is one month.
Look at each page.
Count the days.
How many days are on each page?
How many days make one month?
Do all months have the same number of days?
Write the names of the months on cards.
Make groups of the months.
Group them by how many days they have.
Each month has a name.
We use the name to tell about things.
Christmas comes in December.
Valentine's Day comes in February.
Thanksgiving is in November.
What happens in other months?
Tell something.
What month were you born?

Put the cards into groups.
Put January and February and March together.
They make one group.

Put April and May and June together.

Make a group of July, August, and September.

Make another group of October, November, and December.

Each group of three months makes a season.

What happens in the spring?

What happens in the summer, fall, and winter?

January	April
February	May
March	June
WINTER	**SPRING**
July	October
August	November
September	December
SUMMER	**FALL**

The idea

A year has twelve months. Each month has about thirty days, and the months make four groups called seasons.

Expanding the idea

Each year begins the first day in January.
We call this New Year's Day.
It is in Winter season.

It is usually cold in the Winter.
People wear coats to keep warm.
The wind blows.
Sometimes it snows.

Then comes Spring.
Puffy clouds fill the sky.
Rains come.
The temperature is warmer each day.
People plant seeds.
Soon the seeds will sprout and begin to grow.

The Summer season is often hot.
Sometimes there is not enough rain.
But it is a fun time of year.

Fall is harvest time.
Wheat and corn are ripe.
The air begins to cool.
Soon Winter will come again.

The seasons happen over and over.
They are a cycle.
The whole cycle is one year.

Find out more about the seasons.
What things happen in Spring?
What things happen in Fall?
What things happen in Summer and Winter?

You name them.
Let the teacher make a list.
Make it on the chalkboard.

Spring Things	Summer Things	Fall Things	Winter Things

CHECKING UP

1. How many months are in one year?
2. Name the four seasons.
3. What months are in the Spring? Fall?
4. What happens in the Spring? Fall? Winter?
5. How many days are in the longest months?

TEACHING SUGGESTIONS

Calendars
Cards (4" × 6")

Time is a concept, but it is hard to define. Probably the best definition of time is the space between any two events. But you will immediately recognize great inadequacies in that definition. A second definition might be the period during which something happens. The Christmas season is an example.

Part of the trouble of defining time is that the definition of time must almost inevitably employ "space" or "period" or a similar word. In effect, we are defining time with examples using time. This process is illogical and improper. By now, you have probably concluded that there is no way in which time can be succinctly defined, and that all the definitions available are unsuitable for concrete operational thinkers. This leaves one alternative for you and your second-graders: they must experience time.

In this learning cycle, you will be using the students' experience of the different events that occur in the different seasons. Changes in temperature during the year are a good example. Ask the children what temperatures characterize the seasons. Have them correlate the seasons and the seasonal temperatures. You might like to show it graphically on the board (e.g., a picture of a girl and boy perspiring next to a blazing sun). Sports activities and holidays are also useful to develop and stress the correlation.

LEARNING CYCLE
FOR THIRD GRADE

Volcanoes

Weathering and erosion wear down the earth. With constant weathering and erosion, landforms change. The earth changes. Other forces build up the earth. Sometimes these forces work slowly. At other times, these forces act quickly. What builds up the earth?

Gathering data

Get a plastic squeeze bottle. Fill the bottle with a mixture of dirt and water. Put a square of cardboard on your desk top. Now, gently squeeze the bottle over the cardboard. Observe the mud that comes out. Observe how the mud spreads over the cardboard.

Let the mud on the cardboard dry. Then squeeze the bottle again. Squeeze more mud out of the bottle onto the cardboard. Let this mud dry. Then squeeze more mud onto the cardboard.

Keep squeezing mud onto the cardboard. Let the mud dry each time you squeeze. What is happening? What is the shape of the "landform" which is building up? What shape is the mud forming?

The idea

A volcano is a vent in the earth's crust where steam and molten rock shoot out when the volcano is active, and the cooled molten rock builds up into a mountain.

Expanding the idea

The inside of the earth is hot. At a depth of fifty kilometers, the temperature is 700°C. The extreme heat melts rock deep below the surface of the earth. The hot, molten rock is called *magma*. Magma seeps into the underground cracks and fissures of the earth.

Sometimes a deep crack forms in the earth. Magma flows into the crack and pushes its way up to the surface of the earth. When the magma shoots out, it is called *lava*. The place where it comes out is a volcano. Lava spews from an erupting volcano.

Lava, smoke, steam, and ashes shoot into the air. As more and more lava streams out, a mountain begins to form. When the lava cools, it becomes solid rock again. In a short time, a volcano can grow to a height of many meters.

Volcanoes formed the land that is now the state of Hawaii. Nearly all the volcanoes in Hawaii have been inactive for many years. But one of them still *erupts*, or pours out lava, from time to time. The name of the active volcano is *Mauna Loa*. Mauna Loa builds up the land each time it erupts. It is more than 4,600 meters high.

CHECKING UP

1. What is the difference between magma and lava?
2. What happens when a volcano erupts?
3. How does a volcano change the land?

TEACHING SUGGESTIONS

Cardboard

Dirt

Plastic squeeze bottle

Water

Building a model of a volcano can be a messy investigation. You may want to collect an ample supply of newspaper to cover the floor. The children will be making mud and must be cautioned against making it too moist. The wetter the mud, the longer the drying time.

The teacher could demonstrate a "working" volcano after the children have built their own volcanoes. Directions to construct a variety of different "working" volcanoes can be found in most earth science textbooks or laboratory manuals.

Most areas do not have volcanoes (either active or extinct), so the children may not be able to see a volcano. Mt. St. Helens is an active volcano in Washington and an extinct volcano (Pilots Knob) exists in central Texas.

LEARNING CYCLE
FOR FOURTH GRADE

Fossils

People learn about the earth from rocks. That is why geologists study them. They look for information about the earth's surface. They look for *evidence* of changes in the surface. They look for *evidence* of changes in the climate. And they look for *evidence* of things that lived long ago. Rocks tell the history of the earth.

Gathering data

Look at this stack of playing cards. Suppose each card was laid down one at a time. What is the order from first to last?

Look at these layers of rock. Which of these layers were laid down first? The study of layers of rock is called stratigraphy.

Some geologists study the rocks themselves. This is called *petrology*. Every rock can tell a story. Look at these pictures of rocks. What story does each tell?

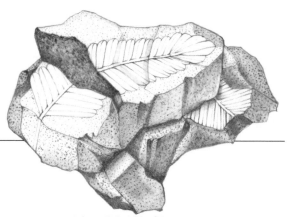

Work together in a group of three or four persons. Mix some plaster of paris with water. Make it like thick pancake batter. Make about one cup. When plaster of paris dries, it hardens like a rock. Pour the plaster of paris into a flat container. Smooth the surface. Then push some object into the plaster of paris. Make an imprint. Take the object out and let the plaster of paris dry. Let others try to figure out from the imprint what the object was. Let each person tell about the object from the imprint.

Geologists use rocks to tell what has happened on the earth. Layers of rocks tell the order in which things happened. The types of rocks tell about what kinds of things happened.

The idea

Traces of animal and plant life preserved in rocks are called fossils.

Expanding the idea

People can learn a great deal about the earth by studying sedimentary rock. Fossils, evidence of plants and animals, are almost always found in sedimentary rock. Paleontologists study fossils to see what kinds of animals and plants lived while the rock was being formed. They can tell the size and shape of the animals. They can even tell the climate during a certain period of time. In some cases, geologists find evidence for an ancient ocean where land is now. A layer of sedimentary rock with sea shells in it is evidence. Rocks show that even the tops of some mountains were once under the sea.

Go on a fossil hunt. Look in the same places you looked for rocks. Make a collection of fossils. Remember, anything that gives evidence of ancient life is called a fossil. A fossil can be just the tracks of an animal

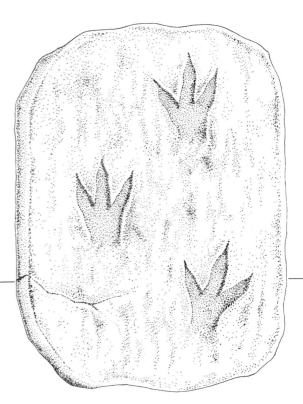

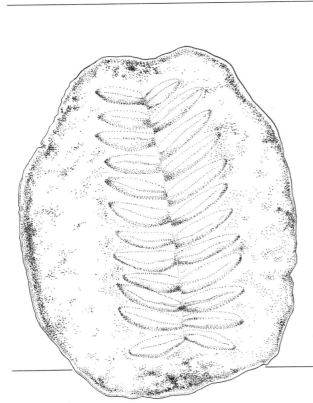

or the imprint of the organism.

A fossil can be a piece of skin or a shell.

Or a bone.

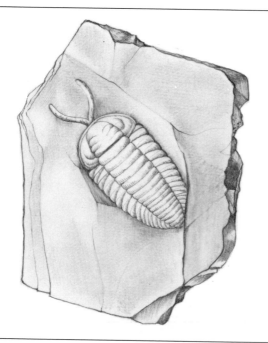

A fossil can be the whole animal.

Or just some evidence that an animal has
been there.

CHECKING UP

1. What is a fossil?
2. Give three examples of types of fossils.
3. What kind of rock is a fossil usually found in?
4. Tell how a fossil might be formed.
5. What does a petrologist do?

TEACHING SUGGESTIONS

Paper cups (small)

Plaster of paris

Stirring sticks

Variety of small objects (coin, screw, whistle, washer, pencil)

The plaster mixture must not be too wet because, in addition to taking a very long time to dry, the imprints will not form. Tell the children to keep their imprinting objects a secret from their classmates. After the imprints dry, the children will remove the mold from the paper cup and let their classmates try to identify the object from the imprint.

You will want to check around your community to see if fossil beds are nearby. (A fossil hunt can be an exciting field trip.) Several sources may provide directions to fossil beds: the local/state geological survey, geologists and petrologists at a university, local earth science teachers.

Most fossils are found in sedimentary rock. Recall that there are three main rock groups: Igneous, Sedimentary, and Metamorphic. Rocks are classified by the way they are formed.

Igneous rocks are formed from melted rock that cools and hardens. During the cooling process, crystals (grains) of different minerals "grow." The size of the mineral grains depends on how fast the molten rock cools. Rocks with larger crystals cool more slowly than those with smaller crystals.

Sedimentary rocks are formed 1) from previously existing rocks that have been broken up into small fragments or 2) by the accumulation of the remains of living things or 3) by chemical precipitates (dissolved material that comes out of solution). These rocks appear as fragments of materials cemented together. The fragments can be large like pebbles or as fine as mud-sized particles.

Metamorphic rocks are formed from previously existing rocks that have been subjected to heat, pressure, or hot fluids, but never melted. Pressure on these rocks produce a flattening of the rock's minerals. Sometimes these rocks are heated by nearby molten rock. This heating can produce larger minerals in the rock formation.

LEARNING CYCLE
FOR FIFTH GRADE

Reading a Map

You can give directions to an object or a place in many ways. Using the numbers on a clock face is one way. Or, you can use a compass and tell the direction to an object or place in degrees. Rectangular coordinates on a grid help to locate position. Landmarks help locate a particular place. In this investigation, you are going to put these ways together with other ways to determine location.

Gathering data

Look at the map of Yellowstone National Park. Study the map closely. Where are the rectangular coordinates on the map? Where is the compass rose? Which direction is north on the map? What are some of the landmarks on the map?

Find these places on the map:
Yellowstone Lake
Old Faithful Geyser
Fishing Bridge
Mammoth Hot Springs
Pyramid Peak
West Entrance

Tell another person how to locate each of these places. Describe the location of each place using the rectangular coordinates.

The numbers above the compass rose show the *scale* of the map. On this map, 1 cm represents 6 km. How far is it from the west entrance to Old Faithful Geyser? Use a ruler to find the answer.

The idea

A map is a kind of drawing that shows the location of objects and places on the earth.

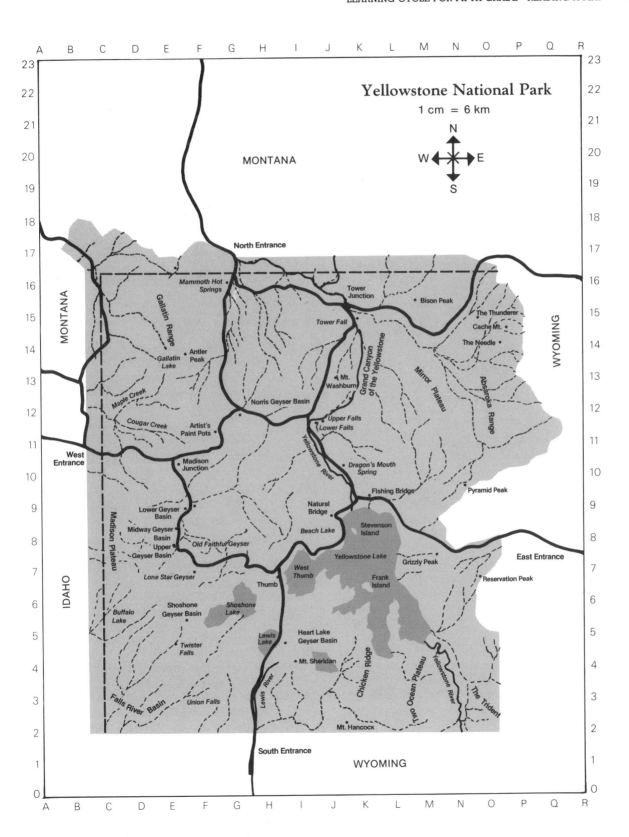

Yellowstone National Park

1 cm = 6 km

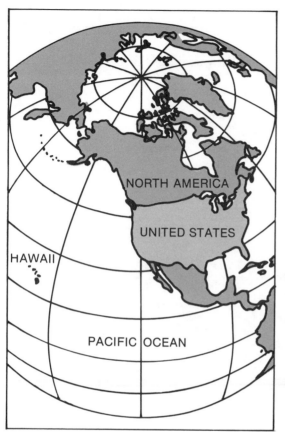

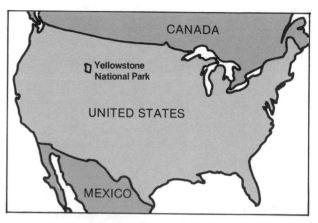

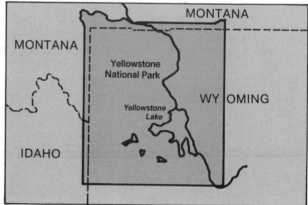

Expanding the idea

The scale of a map is very important. The larger the scale, the more area is shown on the map. Look at the three maps shown here. The map on the left has the largest scale. It shows all of North America, parts of Asia, Europe, and South America.

The map on the top right is a smaller scale map. It is still a very large scale map, however. This map shows all of the United States. The third map has the smallest scale. It shows the location of Yellowstone National Park in the western United States.

Compare each of these maps with the map of Yellowstone National Park. This map has the smallest scale. The smaller the scale of the map, the less area is shown on the map. A small scale map shows much more detail, however.

Maps use symbols to show different kinds of objects. A *symbol* is a kind of simple picture. For example, the symbol for an airport is a picture of an airplane. Different kinds of maps use different symbols.

A *road map* is designed for people who wish to travel by automobile. It has symbols for the different kinds of roads, highways, freeways, and streets in an area. There are also symbols for points of interest, such as historical spots, and symbols for state parks, campsites, and other objects or places.

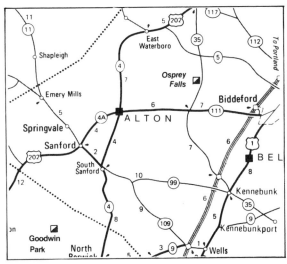

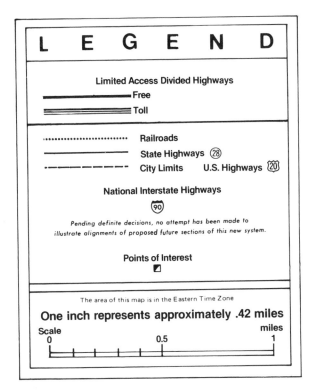

The symbols used on a map are explained in one corner of the map. All the symbols and what each one means are in a box called a *legend*. The legend for a road map is shown here.

Maps also show the natural features of an area. Lakes, rivers, mountains, and other natural features are shown. Each natural feature is labeled. Sometimes the height of the taller mountains is also given.

Symbols are used to show the size of cities and towns. A small town may be shown as a colored dot. A city may be shown as a colored circle. On large-scale maps of the United States, the state boundaries are also shown.

Get a road map of your state. Examine the map closely. Find the legend. What

symbols are used on this map? What is the scale of the map? What kind of coordinates are used?

Find the location of your city or town on the map. Then choose a city or place in another part of the state. Choose a city or place you would like to visit. How many people live in this place? Check the legend to find out.

How far away is this place? Check the scale on the map. Then measure the distance from your home to this place. Use a ruler.

In which direction from your home is the place you would like to visit? Does more than one road go from your home to this place? If so, which road would you use to travel to this place? Why would you use this road?

What kinds of natural features would you pass on your way to this place? Would you cross any rivers or mountains? What points of interest are there along the way?

Write a report on how you would travel to this place. Be sure to tell how long you think the trip would take.

Examine different scale maps that show the location of the city or town where you live.

First, examine a large scale map showing the entire country. Compare this map with a map of your state. What is the scale of each map?

Now, get a street map of your city or town. Compare the scale of this map with the scales of the other maps. Which map shows the greatest area? Which map shows the most detail? Which map would be best for finding the location of a particular street? Would this map be good for helping you plan a trip to a city in another state?

CHECKING UP

1. How does a map help you to find a position?
2. How can the scale on a map be used to tell distance?
3. What is the legend on a map used for?
4. What is a symbol?
5. How are natural features shown on maps?

TEACHING SUGGESTIONS

Ruler (metric)

State map

Street map of your city

String, around 1 meter

Map of the nation

After the children become acquainted with Yellowstone National Park, they will proceed with investigations relating to map-reading and to finding the positions of landmarks and cities in their own state and elsewhere in the country.

Perhaps some of the children have been to Yellowstone National Park. If some of the stu-dents have visited the park, ask them to tell about their experiences. Discuss the pictures and the references to various sites and land-forms in the park.

In teaching the idea of scale, do not intro-duce the notion that one inch, for example, equals so many miles or kilometers. Such an understanding of scale is probably beyond the concept level of the fifth-grade child. Instead of actually defining a scale, have the children use a string. They can determine the length of string which covers the distance from one city to another. Then they can put the string over the scale. They will be able to see how many sections of the scale the string covers.

LEARNING CYCLE
FOR SIXTH GRADE

Weather Fronts

You can describe the atmosphere as you can any other object. But there are special properties of the atmosphere that weather scientists consider important: barometric pressure, humidity, temperature, wind velocity and direction, cloud cover, and precipitation. These are elements of weather. There is another aspect of the atmosphere that is like other parts of the universe. It is continuously changing. Sometimes the changes take place slowly. Sometimes they are very fast. Weather scientists look for patterns in weather changes. They also seek to explain the patterns with models. In this lesson you will learn about one of the models used by weather scientists or meteorologists.

Gathering data

Place three birthday candles on a metal tray. Place them ten centimeters apart. The base of each candle can be supported by a small piece of clay. Next, set the tray on the floor in front of a refrigerator door. Light the candles. Then open the refrigerator door. Observe the flames of the candles. What evidence can you give that cool air moves downward? Record your observations. A body of cool air such as the one that moved out of the refrigerator is called an air mass. In this case, it is called a cool air mass.

To do the next experiment, you will need a small metal can, a thermometer, and some chipped ice. Fill the metal can with warm tap water. Record the temperature. Then slowly add chips of ice to cool the water. Stir the ice-water mixture. Record the temperature of the water when water first begins to condense on the outside of the metal can. This temperature is called the dew point of the air surrounding the can. The temperature of the air is such that the relative humidity is 100 percent. That means that the air is holding all of the moisture it can at that temperature.

An air mass on earth is a huge body of air. An air mass can be hundreds of miles wide and many miles high. An air mass has a temperature and humidity that is the same throughout. An air mass with a temperature lower than the surrounding air mass is called a **cold air mass.** If the air is warmer than the existing air, it is called a **warm air mass.**

The idea

When two air masses meet, the boundary between the two is called a front.

Expanding the idea

There are two common kinds of fronts. If warm air is pushing colder air ahead of it, the front is called a warm front. If cold air is pushing warm air ahead of it, the front is called a cold front.

When a warm front advances, the warm air (or light air) moves up over the retreating cold air.

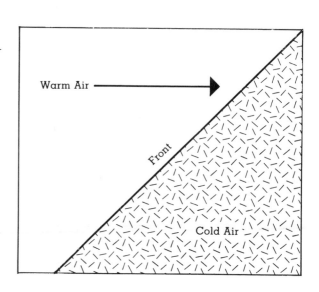

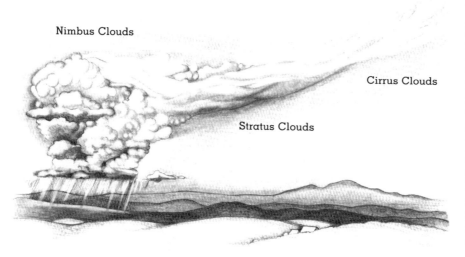

When the warm air is pushed upward by the cool air, it becomes cool. The air reaches its dew point and the moisture condenses to form large masses of clouds along the warm front. Where the level of air is highest, cirrus clouds form. Behind the cirrus clouds, stratus clouds form, with nimbus stratus or rain clouds last and nearest to the ground.

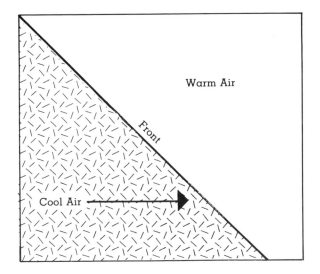

Warm Air

Front

Cool Air

When a cold front advances, the cold air pushes under the retreating warm air. This lifts up the warm air. A cold front usually moves faster than a warm front. The heavy cold air can move the light warm air easily. As the warm air is lifted up quickly, the water vapor condenses to form different kinds of clouds, especially cumulonimbus (thundershower) clouds. The rains produced by a cold front are rather violent and last only a short time. These are called thunderstorms. Sometimes the masses of cold and warm air stop moving. The boundary between the two air masses stays in the same place. This is called a *stationary front.*

Clouds are grouped by their shape and by the height at which they are formed.

Name	
Cirrus	(Latin: curls), "horse tails," thin halos
Stratus	(Latin: spread out), layered
Cumulus	(Latin: piled up), cottonlike

Prefix	Height or Altitude
Cirro-	6–12 kilometers (high)
Alto-	2.4–6 kilometers (middle)
Strato-	below 2.4 kilometers (low)
Cumulo-	large vertical development

Another prefix that can be used is "nimbo" meaning *rain.*

Names of clouds can be formed by combining a prefix and a name. For example, a strato cumulus cloud is a fluffy, cottonlike cloud at low altitude. Observe cloud formations during the next few weeks. Keep a record of your observations. Discuss the name you would give to different clouds you observe.

Two things that are often observed along the boundary of a front are thunder and lightning. Lightning is an electrical discharge. It can happen between clouds or within a single cloud. When lightning occurs, it heats the air, making it expand rapidly. The rapid expansion produces thunder. Observe clouds to see lightning. Is all lightning alike? Describe the different appearances of lightning. What types of clouds often produce lightning?

CHECKING UP

1. Describe a cold front.
2. Describe a warm front.
3. What causes clouds to form as a warm front advances?
4. What is lightning?

TEACHING SUGGESTIONS

Birthday candles

Clay

Ice

Metal can

Metal tray

Thermometer

The children will be doing experiments to observe the interaction of air masses on a small scale. Two such experiments are presented in this learning cycle. These experiments will provide the children with data that will allow them to experience models of weather fronts. For accurate results, it is important that there are no "room" air currents. If fans are operating or windows are open, the flame movement on the candles may be affected.

Take the opportunity to go outside and observe fronts and cloud types. This investigation may be conducted over a several week period. The fall and spring season will provide a continuous variety of weather fronts and cloud formations.

CHAPTER SIX

LEARNING CYCLES FOR THE PHYSICAL SCIENCES

Six concepts from the physical science concepts identified in the prologue have been selected for the conceptual invention phase of the six learning cycles that follow. These concepts are:

Grade 1: Color, shape, size, feel, and smell are properties of objects (physical science concept #2).

Grade 2: Magnets are special objects that stick to or attract iron (physical science concept #8).

Grade 3: The three states of matter are solid, liquid, and gas (physical science concept #1).

Grade 4: Matter that has variable properties is called a mixture (physical science concept #4).

Grade 5: Energy is something that causes objects to do things they would not do without it (physical science concept #1).

Grade 6: The interaction of the wire, the dry cell, and the light bulb causes electrical current in the circuit (physical science concept #10).

**LEARNING CYCLE
FOR FIRST GRADE**

Properties

Name all the objects.
How are the objects different?
We can find out.

Gathering data

Name the color of the top. (The objects
should be different colors when student
sheets are prepared.)

Name the color of the whistle.

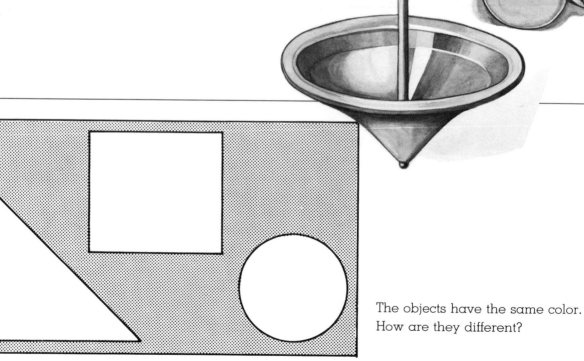

The objects have the same color.
How are they different?

Name all the objects.
Each object has a shape.
What shapes do you see?

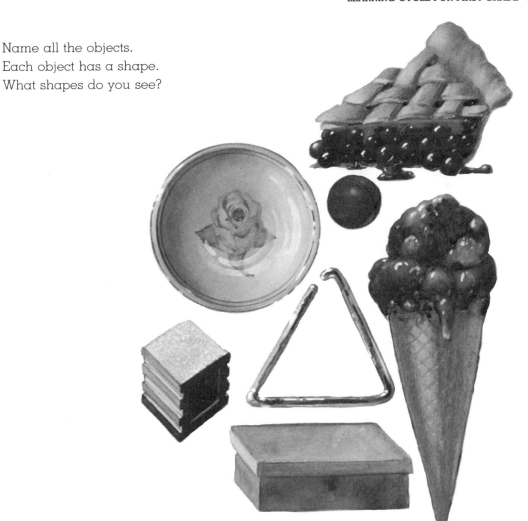

Look at the mother hen.
See the baby chicks.
The mother hen is big.
The baby chicks are small.
Look at the mother dog.
See the little puppy.
The mother dog is big.
The puppy is small.

Roll some clay into a ball.
Make a big, round ball.
Make another ball of clay.
Make a little ball.

Go to the window.
Rub the glass.
Rub it with your hand.
How does the glass feel?

Get a piece of sandpaper.
Rub the sandpaper.
Rub it with your hand.
How does the sandpaper feel?

Get a piece of wool.
Rub the piece of wool.
How does the wool feel?

The idea

Color, shape, size, feel, and smell are properties of objects.

Expanding the idea

The objects have properties.
Each has two of the same properties.
Name the two same properties.

CHECKING UP

1. Here are things in rows.
2. What objects do you see?
3. What do you see in each row?
4. Which object does not belong?

TEACHING SUGGESTIONS

Numerous objects of various colors

2 or 3 colored tops

2 or 3 colored whistles

Construction paper of various colors

Classroom objects of various shapes

Cardboard shapes (triangles, squares, circles, rectangles)

Cotton balls

Numerous small hard objects

Numerous small soft objects

Pieces of cloth

Pieces of wood

Sandpaper

In this learning cycle, you will be conceptually inventing property for the children. (Property is the most basic concept of all science.) Explain that color is a property, shape is a property, size is a property, and feel (texture) is a property. Stress that properties tell about an object.

Pick up one object and ask a boy or girl to identify its properties. Do not accept as properties the name of the object or what it does. Explain that a name or what the object can do does not tell anything about the object. Property is the thing that tells about an object. Property tells what an object is like.

Point out that an investigator can determine color, shape, and approximate size by looking at an object. But to know about texture, he/she must feel the object. Explain that words such as "hard," "soft," "rough," "smooth," "sharp," "dull," and "bumpy" can be used to describe texture.

You might reinforce the idea that *name* and *use* are not properties by first talking about the name of an object and discussing its use. For example, you could talk about a pencil. Ask the children to give the name of the pencil and tell about its use. Listen to their responses. Then say, "Now, what are the pencil's properties?"

LEARNING CYCLE
FOR SECOND GRADE

Magnetism

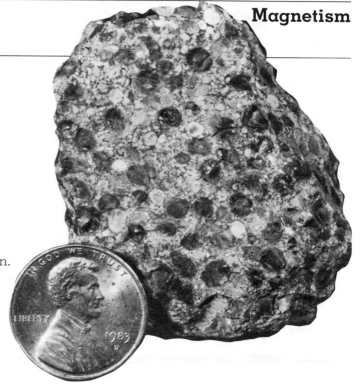

There are many metals in the world.
Gold is a metal.
Steel is a metal.
Silver is a metal.
Iron is a metal.
Metals help us.
Steel is used in cars.
Gold is used as money.
So is silver.
Iron is used in many objects.
You are going to experiment with iron.

Gathering data

You need iron nails.
You need two other iron objects.
Touch one iron object to another.
What happens?
Try to make the iron objects stick together.
What happens?
What do the iron objects do to each other?

Get a special iron object.
It is shaped like a bar.
Get it from your teacher.
Use the bar-shaped object.
Use it with other iron objects.
Tell what happens.
Use objects not made of iron.
Use the bar-shaped iron object.
What happens?

Here is a different object.

Get one like it.

Use the new object with iron objects.

Tell what happens.

Use the bar-shaped object from the last experiment.

Use it with your new object.

Tell what happens.

How is the new object like the bar-shaped object?

How are the objects different?

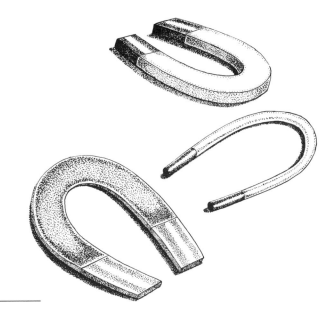

The idea

Magnets are special objects that stick to or attract iron.

Expanding the idea

Get a magnet.

Be sure it is a good one.

Test it.

Attract iron paper clips with it.

Use many other objects.

Which ones does the magnet attract?

What materials are the objects made of?

Which ones does it not attract?

What materials are the objects made of?

What materials do magnets attract?

What materials do magnets not attract?

CHECKING UP

1. What does a magnet do?
2. What were the shapes of the magnets you experimented with?
3. Magnets attract each other. What does that mean?
4. Magnets attract iron objects. What does that mean?
5. What materials do magnets not attract?

TEACHING SUGGESTIONS

Various types of magnets

Objects for the class to test magnetic attraction, e.g., chalk, a marble, nail, coat hanger, eraser, nuts, bolts, etc.

Your students will be investigating the properties of a magnet. They will be developing the concept of magnetic attraction. Try to have various kinds of magnets on hand for the class.

During *THE IDEA* phase, use the term "magnetic attraction" and continue to use it as appropriate. Proceed by telling the students that they will be finding out what other objects show magnetic attraction. Among objects they might test are a pencil, an eraser, a marble, a paper clip, a metric ruler, a crayon, a piece of chalk, a ball point pen, a nail, a nail file, a paint box, and a coat hanger.

Explain to the class that they need to keep a record of what does and what does not show magnetic attraction. Encourage the children to test many objects and to make a record of each test.

You might put a list of the objects the children test on the chalkboard. The class can discuss the list after the students have completed their testing. In the discussion, ask the students to explain how the items which showed magnetic attraction seem to be alike. What property do they have in common?

If the children are uncertain, spend some time naming some of the properties of the objects. Be sure the children name the materials that have been tested. If the term "metal" does not come up, introduce the term yourself. Lead the children to note that all the objects that showed magnetic attraction are made of some kind of metal.

LEARNING CYCLE
FOR THIRD GRADE

States of Matter

Suppose you throw a glass of water on a window. The water will splash and run down the window. Try it and see. Suppose water is frozen into ice. Suppose you threw the chunk of ice against the window. What would happen? Don't try it!

Water is a *liquid*. A liquid can be poured. When you pour it into a cup, it takes the shape of the cup. Frozen water is a *solid*. You cannot pour a solid. A solid has its own shape. To change the shape, you must break it apart.

Water can be a solid or a liquid. It can be a *gas*, too. But what is a gas? How can water be changed into a gas? You can find out by doing an experiment.

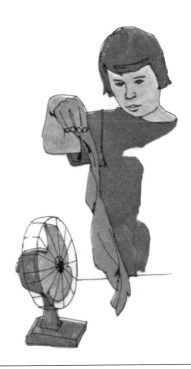

Gathering data

Wet a piece of cloth in water. Squeeze the cloth to get most of the water out. Put the wet cloth in front of a fan. Observe carefully as the cloth dries. Where does the water go? Write down what you believe.

Water is boiling in a pan. Steam rises from the pan. Observe the steam. Your teacher holds a cool spoon above the pan. What collects on the spoon? How is this like the fan and the wet paper towel? Write down an answer to this question.

Put water in a jar. Fill the jar almost to the top. Then put ice in the water. Put a lid on the jar. Next, wipe the outside of the jar. Wipe it dry with a paper towel. Observe the outside of the jar for several minutes. What collects on the sides of the jar? Explain what happens. Make a record of the experiment. How is this like the steam and the spoon experiment? How is it like the fan and the paper towel experiment? Write down what you think.

Place an ice cube on a plate. Set it on a window sill. Put it in the sun if you can. What happens to the ice? Write down what you found.

Put some water in a pan. Put the pan in a freezer. Leave it for a day. What happened to it? Make a record of what you found.

As you have observed, a liquid can be frozen. Water freezes into ice, a solid. When water freezes, there is a change in it. There is a change in how it looks and feels, or in the way it is. This is called a change in *state*.

The idea

The three states of matter are solid, liquid, and gas.

Expanding the idea

To *evaporate* is to change to a vapor. This happens when water turns to a gas. A solid can change to liquid. This happens when ice melts. Water is matter. It can be three states. Water can be a solid, a liquid, or a gas.

Water vapor condenses on a cool surface. To condense is to change from the gas state to the liquid state. There is water vapor in the air all the time. Usually you cannot see it. But you can see water vapor when it condenses because it turns into water.

Maybe you have gone for a walk early in the morning. When you walked through grass, your feet or shoes got wet. The grass had water on it. It was wet. There had been no rain. Still, the grass was wet.

When night comes, the earth gets cool. Plants on the earth get cool, too. Water vapor in the air turns into drops of dew on the plants. The water vapor *condenses* and turns into liquid water. The water goes from the gas state to the liquid state.

There is dew on the grass early in the morning. Then the sun comes up. It shines down on the plants and the dew. The sun warms them. The dew changes from the liq-uid state to the gas state. It rises into the air as water vapor. The dew *evaporates*, or changes into a vapor. The process is known as *evaporation*. Matter goes from the liquid state to the gas state.

Fill an aquarium tank with water. Then lower a glass into the water. Put the glass in the water with the open end down. Observe what happens. What happens to the air in the glass? What two states of matter are here?

Now, tip the glass. Explain what happens. What did one state of matter do to the other?

Now, let us investigate air. First, catch some air in a plastic bag. Fill the bag with air. Close the bag by twisting the open end. Keep the air from escaping. Observe the air carefully.

How does air differ from water, a liquid? What state of matter is air? How does air differ from ice, a solid? Make a record of the differences. List some properties of air.

CHECKING UP

1. Look for the three states of matter in your classroom. Name them.
2. How is the gas state of matter different from the liquid state?
3. Drops of water collect on a glass filled with ice. What change of state of matter was observed?
4. How can you change the state of matter of water?
5. How is the liquid state of matter different from the solid state?

TEACHING SUGGESTIONS

Aquarium tank or any large container with water in it

Wiping cloths

Drinking glass

Fan

Ice

Jar with lid

Plastic sandwich bag

Spoon

Hot plate

Container to boil water

The first experiment in the Gathering Data section enables the children to observe evaporation. You might prefer to do this experiment as a demonstration. The fan will hasten the evaporation of the water in the cloth. Have your students examine the cloth when it has dried out. Explain that the water in the cloth evaporated, or changed into a gas.

An experiment with boiling water provides another example of evaporation. Use a hot plate to boil some water in a beaker or in a teakettle. Explain to the class that, when it boils, water changes into water vapor, a gas. Call attention to the steam. Point out that the visible steam is not water vapor. The steam consists of water droplets which condensed from the water vapor. The cool surface of the spoon caused the water vapor to condense.

The next experiment provides another example of condensation. It is a good idea to do this experiment during the same period in which you boiled the water and observed evaporation. The two experiments go together.

Have the children work in groups of three or four to do the experiment with the ice water. Let each group fill a jar with ice and water. Instruct the children to seal the lid on the jar tightly. Tell them to be sure to wipe the outside at the beginning of the experiment. Have them form a circle around the jar to observe the results of the experiment.

In time, the water in the air will condense on the cool surface of the jar. Have the children discuss the experiment. In all likelihood, most of the students will conclude that the water which collects on the jar came out of the air. If some of the children have the notion that water seeped through the jar, repeat the experiment using warm water. Let the children discuss the experiment.

In the experiment with air, the children will observe that air takes up space. Air is matter. They also will observe that air takes up space when they put a drinking glass into the water in an aquarium tank.

The students' experiments and observations have made it clear to them that matter exists in states. Introduce the term "states of matter." In your discussion, call upon students to explain the difference between a liquid and a solid and between a liquid and a gas.

LEARNING CYCLE
FOR FOURTH GRADE

Mixtures

A substance is matter that has definite properties. Substances can be elements, such as copper, oxygen, gold, or mercury. Compounds such as salt, water and sugar are also substances. Each piece of matter just named has definite properties. It is a substance. You will now investigate another kind of matter.

Gathering data

In this experiment you will mix one substance with another. You will stir them together. In each part of the experiment you will control the amount of one substance. You will vary the amount of the other substance.

Use five glasses of tap water filled to the same mark. Fill each glass almost full. To each glass add the following amounts of table salt and stir:

Glass 1: one small crystal.

Glass 2: ¼ teaspoon.

Glass 3: ½ teaspoon.

Glass 4: 1 teaspoon.

Glass 5: 1 tablespoon.

Stir the salt and water until all of the salt disappears. Then look at the salt-water systems. Observe each salt-water system. If the salt-water systems look different, record that difference.

Next, taste each salt-water system. Compare the taste of each system. What variation do you notice? What was the controlled variable in this experiment?

Repeat the experiment you just completed. In repeating the experiment, use food coloring instead of salt. Put one drop of food coloring in one glass. Put two drops of food coloring in another. Put three, four, and five drops in the other glasses. Stir the water and the food coloring. Describe the variation in color from one glass to another.

Stir some solids together. Put table salt and colored sand together. Stir them well. Make several combinations of salt and sand. Vary the amount of one of the substances in each of your combinations. Observe the systems with a hand lens. Describe the variation in the system.

You can put together different amounts of salt in water. That is, you can vary the amount of salt. The salt-water systems look very much alike. But there is a variable. Their taste is variable.

When food coloring is mixed with water, the color of the systems varies. You mixed sand and salt. Again, you observed a variation in properties.

The idea

Matter that has variable properties is called a mixture.

Expanding the idea

Most of the materials you use are mixtures. Many foods are mixtures. Soft drinks are mixtures. Some of the materials you find in the kitchen are pure substances, such as sugar, salt, and baking soda. But you almost always mix these together with other materials before you sit down and eat. Cooking can change a mixture to one or more compounds. But then the new compounds make up a mixture.

Air is a mixture. It has elements mixed together in it. Those elements are oxygen, argon, and nitrogen. Carbon dioxide is also in the mixture called air. Carbon dioxide is made of two elements, carbon and oxygen. It is a compound.

There are also substances in the air mixture. All air has some dirt in it. Most furnaces have objects that take out most of the dirt. Those objects are called filters. Breathing a dirt and air mixture can be unhealthy.

The properties of a clean air mixture make air healthy to breathe. Remember that the properties of a mixture depend upon the amount of each substance in it. Too much dirt in the air mixture makes it unhealthy. There are many other substances in air. Automobiles give off a compound called carbon monoxide. This compound is poisonous. Breathing too much of it can cause sickness or death. In cities where there are many automobiles, the properties of the air mixture change. The properties of the air mixture become more and more like carbon monoxide. As more salt is added to water, the mixture tastes less like water and more like salt. That is what happens to air. The air mixture becomes *polluted*.

Not all air pollution comes from automobiles. Many factories also let harmful materials escape into the air. When that happens, the properties of the air mixture change. They become less like a clean air mixture. The properties of the air mixture become more and more like the harmful substance entering it. Air pollution must be stopped. If it is not, we won't have a clean, healthy air mixture to breathe.

Mixtures can be separated into substances. One way to separate a mixture of water and another substance is by heating. Water evaporates, or changes to a gas. The gaseous water can then be condensed, or changed back into a liquid.

Water that is evaporated and then condensed to a liquid again is called distilled water. Almost pure water can be obtained by distilling water. When the water is distilled, the dissolved material is left behind.

Make a simple distilling apparatus. Set up a flask, a beaker, a hot plate, and some glass tubing. Separate the salt and water from a salt-water mixture.

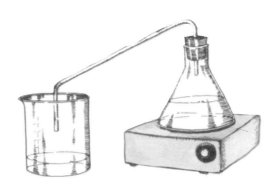

Mix a teaspoon of salt with a teaspoon of clean white sand. Use a hand lens to observe the mixture. Then place the mixture in an empty tea bag and staple it closed. Place the tea bag on the side of a glass. Put water in the glass. Put enough water in the glass to cover about half of the tea bag.

Observe the interaction. When no more of the mixture dissolves, remove the tea bag. Dry the material left in the tea bag and examine it. Explain why some material is left in the tea bag. How did the properties of the water change? What is the water now?

What property does salt have that the sand does not have? Tell how this variation in property allows you to separate salt and sand.

Try separating another mixture. This mixture is chalk and salt. First, mix together a teaspoon each of chalk and salt. Put some of the mixture in an empty tea bag and staple it closed. Put the tea bag in a glass and add water. Observe carefully and describe the results.

Add 1 cubic centimeter of white vinegar to a glass that contains a mixture of water and bromothymol blue (BTB). Observe any change you see in the mixture. Add another cubic centimeter of vinegar and observe any change in the mixture. Keep adding BTB one cubic centimeter at a time. Compare the properties of the BTB-water mixture with the properties of the BTB-water-vinegar mixture. Record your comparisons.

CHECKING UP

1. What is a mixture?
2. Tell why the vinegar, BTB, and water you put together form a mixture.
3. When a person washes dishes or clothes, a mixture is used. How is the mixture made?
4. Lemonade is a mixture. How does one lemonade mixture vary from another?
5. How could you separate a mixture of sand and iron fillings?
6. How can you change the properties of a mixture?
7. How is air pollution caused by a mixture?

TEACHING SUGGESTIONS

Beaker

Bromothymol blue (BTB)

Chalk dust

Flask with rubber stopper for glass tubing

Food coloring

Funnel

Glasses

Glass tubing approximately 35 cm long

Hand lens

Hot plate

Ice or cold water

Measuring spoons

Medicine dropper

Paper plates

Salt

Sand (colored and white)

Stoppers (one-hole)

Sugar

Tea bags

Vinegar

The first three experiments in this learning cycle established a key idea: You can vary the amount of the substances that are put together to form mixtures. In a mixture, the substances that are mixed together retain their own properties. There is no chemical change in any of the substances when they are combined. Be sure the children understand that a mixture consists of two or more substances.

Distillation is the process commonly used to separate mixtures in a laboratory. You can refer to the illustration in the learning cycle as a guideline for setting up the apparatus. First, bend the ends of a length of glass tubing. You can do this by heating the glass over a flame.

Insert one end through the hole in a one-hole rubber stopper. Add a portion of your salt solution to a flask. Put the rubber stopper with the glass tubing into the mouth of the flask. Place the other end of the glass tubing in a beaker.

Put the flask on a hot plate. As the solution boils, water vapor will escape through the glass tubing. The beaker should be set in a pan of ice or cold water. The water will condense as it drains into the beaker. Liquid water will be collected in the beaker. Salt crystals will remain in the flask as a precipitate. Since you will be boiling water, you might do this experiment as a demonstration.

Expect the following to occur in the EXPANDING THE IDEA experiments: The salt in the tea bag dissolves in the water that soaks through the tea bag. The dissolved salt then diffuses through the tea bag into the glass containing water. The sand remains in the tea bag. Salt has the property of solubility. Sand does not dissolve. The fact that salt dissolves makes it possible to separate the salt from a salt-sand mixture.

Salt can also be separated from chalk by filtering the solution. The liquid that passes through the filter is called the filtrate. The solid that remains on the filter paper is called the residue. The solid is chalk; chalk is the residue. Salt passes through the filter along with the water. The salt could be recovered by distilling the water.

In the experiment with vinegar, the baking soda will fizz. The vinegar contains acetic acid. The acetic acid reacts with the baking soda, causing carbon dioxide to be released.

Materials can also be tested with bromothymol blue (BTB). The BTB causes a change in color. As the children will observe, a solution of BTB and white vinegar is yellow. A solution of BTB and ammonia water is blue.

LEARNING CYCLE
FOR FIFTH GRADE

Energy

A car speeds along the freeway. The traffic lanes are jammed. The rush-hour traffic slows to a crawl now and then. But in the open spaces, the cars are moving at the legal speed. The cars have motion.

A speeding train has motion, too. A waterfall and a whistling teakettle have motion. A roller skater and a bicycle rider have motion.

The car, the train, the waterfall, the teakettle, the roller skater, and the bicycle rider all have something in common. True, they all have motion. But what else do they have in common? What causes them to have motion?

Gathering data

Build a ramp like the one shown in the picture. Be sure one end is at least ten centimeters higher than the other end.

Place a paper cup at the bottom of the ramp. The open end of the cup must be toward the ramp. You now need a large sphere. A golf ball will work nicely.

Place the golf ball at the top of the ramp. Let it roll down the ramp. Be sure it rolls into the cup. Record what you see.

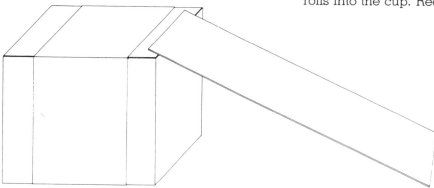

You need a large metal washer. Tie a string around it and make a pendulum. Set the paper cup on the table. Hold the string in one hand so the washer hangs straight down. Use your other hand to pull the washer back as far as you can. Let the washer go and strike the cup. Watch the cup. Record what happens.

The idea

Energy is something that causes objects to do things they would not do without it.

Expanding the idea

When moving objects strike objects at rest something always happens. If you ride a bicycle into a large cardboard box, you know something will happen. If you throw a ball into a catching net, you can see something happen.

When water falls and strikes the earth something happens. The earth is eventually worn away. If a glass object is held above your head and dropped, something happens. The glass object is probably broken. Imagine that a rubber ball is held above your head and dropped to the floor. Something happens. The ball bounces back up. All of these events happen because of energy. *Energy is something that causes objects to do things they would not have done without it.*

When a ball is thrown at a batter it can go right past. If the ball does not pass the batter, energy must be used. The batter must use energy to swing the bat. Suppose the moving bat strikes the ball. The ball goes back toward the pitcher. The ball would not have done that if the bat had not hit it. In order for the bat to hit the ball, the batter must use energy. Energy causes something to happen that does not happen without it.

Suppose you have been told to wash a car. The soapy water will just stay in the pail and the dirt will stay on the car. But you can use energy to scrub the dirty car with the soapy water. The car then becomes clean. In order for that to happen you had to use energy.

You will use the ramp that you built earlier to do another experiment. You will need three different size spheres. A baseball, a golf ball, and a marble will do.

Place the paper cup at the bottom of the ramp as you did before. Then let one of the spheres roll down the ramp into the cup. Measure the distance the cup moved. Repeat this for the other two spheres. Which sphere pushed the cup farthest? Which sphere had the most energy?

Again, use the ramp that you built earlier. This time use only the golf ball. First, set the box on the table as you did for the other experiments. Roll the golf ball down the ramp into the paper cup. Measure how far the cup moved. Now, raise the higher end of the ramp. You can do this by placing books under the box. Again, roll the golf ball down the ramp. Be sure to start the ball at the same place as before. Which time did the cup move farther? Which time did the ball have more energy?

Use the pendulum with one washer that you used earlier. Set your cup on the table and swing the washer toward it. Measure how far the cup moved.

Now put three washers on the string and repeat the experiment. How far did the cup move? Which pendulum provided the most energy?

CHECKING UP

1. What is energy?
2. You guide a power lawn mower to mow the lawn. Where does the lawn mower get its energy?
3. A golf ball travels down the fairway. Where does it get its energy?
4. What makes it possible for a bowling ball to knock over bowling pins?
5. Look at the pictures below. Where do the ping pong ball, the frisbee and the wagon get energy?

TEACHING SUGGESTIONS

Baseball

Boards (ramps)

Chalkboard eraser

Cups (or beakers)

Golf ball

Spheres (metal, marble-sized)

String

Weights (or bolt nuts)

The children will begin by doing an experiment with an inclined plane. The sphere pushes the eraser. The children may also observe that, the higher the ramp, the greater the distance the eraser is pushed.

Refer to **THE IDEA:** *The experiments you have done produced the results they did because of energy.* This is the most significant invention, or concept, that the children will encounter in their study of fifth-grade science. *Energy* is what makes things go. For your students, this is a much better definition of energy than the conventional definition, which is: energy is the ability to do work. To understand the formal definition, the student must know the meaning of the word "ability" and must be able to explain the term "work." Without such prerequisites, the child can develop a concept of energy merely by understanding that *energy is what makes things go.* Teach this definition to your class.

LEARNING CYCLE
FOR SIXTH GRADE

Electricity

Electricity is energy. A special system is needed to use electrical energy. No matter what is using electrical energy, that special system is there. That special system follows certain rules. In this lesson you will find out about some of those rules.

Gathering data

You will need a wire, a dry cell, and a light bulb. The objects are shown in the picture. Put the three objects together. What evidence do you find that the objects will interact? After you find evidence of interaction, draw a picture of how you connected the wire, the dry cell, and the light bulb.

First, use one wire to produce interaction. Then use two wires. Draw a picture of how the two wires, the dry cell, and the light bulb were connected when you saw evidence of interaction.

Compare the two pictures you have drawn. How are they alike? How are they different?

At how many *different* points did you have to touch the dry cell before you observed evidence of interaction? At how many places did you touch the light bulb before you saw evidence of interaction?

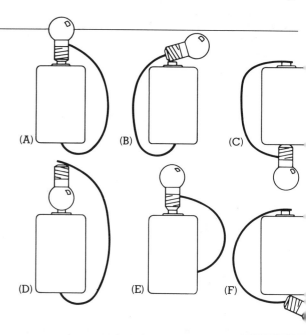

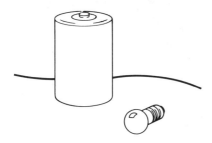

Each of the six pictures on this page shows a system made up of a wire, a dry cell, and a light bulb. The objects are connected differently in each picture. Predict in which of the systems the bulb will light. Record your predictions in a table like the one shown here. Write "yes" or "no" in the "Prediction" column.

Picture	Prediction (Yes or No)	Experiment (Yes or No)
A		
B		
C		
D		
E		
F		

From now on, do not change any of your predictions. You are going to use a wire, a dry cell, and a light bulb to test your predictions. Arrange the objects just as they are shown in pictures A, B, C, D, E, and F. Record in your table whether or not you found evidence of interaction by writing "yes" or "no."

A wire, a dry cell, and a light bulb can be arranged in a system that does something. There is evidence of interaction. The light bulb lights.

With the lighting of the light bulb, energy is being used. The dry cell supplies the electrical energy. But in order to see evidence of interaction, you had to arrange the wire, the dry cell, and the light bulb in a certain way. With that arrangement, you observed evidence of interaction. Such an arrangement is called an *electrical circuit*.

The idea

The interaction of the wire, the dry cell, and the light bulb causes electrical current in the circuit.

Expanding the idea

The word "current" means anything that is running or flowing. Maybe you have watched a large crowd from a tall building. The entire crowd seems to stand still but the people in it move or flow through the crowd. This is a current of people. The people flow along through the crowd.

You are probably familiar with a current of water. Suppose it's a river. The river seems to stand still but the water moves. Water moves along a certain path. That movement is often said to be a "swift current" or a "slow current." Persons using these phrases are using the true meaning of the word current. The water is flowing along.

When giving weather reports, weather forecasters often talk about currents. They discuss air currents. Differences in temperature cause air currents. These currents can affect the type of weather we have. When air currents get moving too rapidly, we call them wind.

You know that the dry cell or battery of cells in a circuit is the energy source. The light bulb or some other object is the energy user. But in order for a light bulb to use energy from a dry cell, the energy must get to it. The wires are the connectors in an electrical circuit. The light bulb does not light until wires connect it and the dry cell.

When the bulb lights you have evidence that the bulb, wire, and dry cell are interacting. The evidence of the bulb lighting can be thought of as showing something additional. The light in the bulb suggests that the wires are carrying energy from the dry cell to the bulb. The wires are actually transferring the energy.

When you think of the evidence in that way, seeing why the name current was used is not hard. The electricity flows just as people flow through a crowd. The flow of electricity is like the flow of water in a river or in air. So the flow of electrical current is used to discuss what happens in the wires. But remember, it is a model. No one has ever seen it happen.

To make the model more clear, some people call the electricity "juice." This model says that something that flows like juice is present in the wires. Just remember that the flow of electrical current is a model. This model explains how the electrical energy gets from the energy source to the energy user.

You need a dry cell, a light bulb, two brass clips, three pieces of wire, a holder for the dry cell, and a socket for the light bulb.

Put the objects together as shown in the drawing. As you will observe, the light bulb gives no evidence of interaction. Next, touch wire A and wire B together. What happens?

Put different kinds of objects between wire A and wire B. Touch the two wires to the objects. Which objects cause the light bulb to light?

When the light bulb lights, the circuit is a *complete circuit*. Make a record of the kinds of materials you used in your circuit. Indicate which materials made a complete circuit.

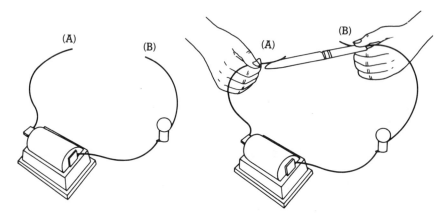

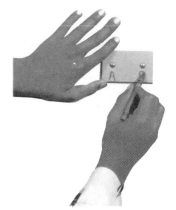

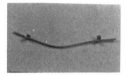

Refer to the photograph above. When a system of electrical objects is arranged like the system in the first photograph, the arrangement is called an *open circuit*. The circuit is a *closed circuit* when something is put between wire A and wire B and the light bulb lights.

The system you just worked with is a circuit tester. A circuit tester quickly tells you when you have a complete circuit. You now can do an experiment with a circuit tester.

Push two brass paper fasteners through a piece of cardboard. Put them five centimeters apart. Connect the two brass fasteners with a piece of wire. Connect them on the back of the card.

Now, use your circuit tester. Put wire A of the circuit tester and wire B of the circuit tester on the paper fasteners labeled A and B. What happens?

Remove the wire from between the paper fasteners. Then put wires A and B of the circuit tester on the paper fasteners. What happens?

What was the purpose of the wire between paper fasteners A and B? Make a record of your answer.

The picture shows a circuit board. There are six paper fasteners on it. Some of the fasteners are connected with wires. Some are not. The back of the circuit board is covered, and the edges are sealed.

Your teacher will pass out some circuit boards like the one in the picture. *Do not take the back covers off the circuit boards.*

Test the circuit boards to find out which of the paper fasteners are connected with wires. Use your circuit tester. Draw a model of the back of each circuit board you test. Design a way to record your data before drawing the model. You should test at least four different circuit boards.

Design a way to close the circuit tester. Put a device between wire A and wire B that can be used to open and close the circuit. You will be making a *switch*.

If you finish your circuit boards before the others, try this experiment:

Get two circuit boards. Tie one wire from the top of any brass fastener to any other fastener on the other board. Then use your circuit tester. Find out how adding that wire changed the circuits in the board.

Now, add another wire that joins the two boards. What happens to the number of circuits in the two boards after the two wires are added?

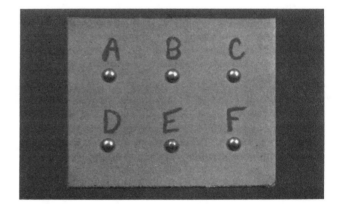

CHECKING UP

1. What are the parts of an electrical circuit?
2. What happens to an electrical circuit when the energy source is removed?
3. What is the difference between a closed circuit and an open circuit?
4. What happens to a closed circuit when you move a switch?
5. Why is the moving of energy from a dry cell to a light bulb called an electrical current?

TEACHING SUGGESTIONS

Brass clips
Dry cell
Dry cell holder
Light bulbs
Light bulb socket
Wires

The children will be observing the interaction between a dry cell and a light bulb in order to produce a light. The boys and girls will assemble a circuit for the first time, but do not use the word "circuit" at this point. Provide ample time for the children to assemble the circuit. Insist that each child draw a picture of how the wire, dry cell, and light bulb are connected. To make the light bulb light, they had to touch the dry cell at its top and bottom. They had to touch the light bulb at its side and at the metal tip on the bottom. Both the dry cell and the light bulb had to be touched in two places. When this is done, the light bulb lights.

Before you continue, be sure that each child knows how to make the bulb light. Insist that the children refer to the dry cell as a dry cell and not as a battery. A battery is a collection of dry cells. The children are likely to use the term "battery." Point out that what they actually are using is a dry cell, not a battery.

The electrical current is the interaction of the wire, the dry cell, and the light bulb. Something happens to the circuit, and that interaction causes electrical current. Do not try to define an electrical current as a flow of electrons or something like water moving along the wires. It is simply the interaction that occurs among the objects in the circuit.

The circuit-board testing will take some time, and you should allow the children to work at their own pace. The students need only to follow the directions in the learning cycle. Allow as much social interaction as possible. Permit the children to share data, exchange ideas, and help each other. This activity is excellent for developing a laboratory spirit—an attitude, that is, which assumes that everyone is doing many experiments and is helping everyone else.

CHAPTER SEVEN

LEARNING CYCLES FOR THE KINDERGARTEN CHILD

The kindergarten science learning cycles achieve a twofold objective. The program (1) develops the children's early understanding of science and also (2) introduces the process skills that the boys and girls will be applying to their learning in all the disciplines throughout their years in school.

As a kindergarten teacher, you are aware of your pupils' uniqueness. Your pupils have learning characteristics that are wholly unlike those of older children. Most certainly in your classroom you will have many preoperational children. In fact, there is a great probability that all the children in your classroom are preoperational. What do preoperational children do?

The preoperational child learns about the environment through *action*. The concept of action means exactly what the word conveys—the child does something physical to the object, event, or situation in the environment. Suppose, for example, that the concept of "rough" was to be taught to kindergarten children. The exploration phase of the learning cycle would consist of letting the children explore all types of rough materials—walls, wood, metal, sandpaper, and other familiar objects. Next, the teacher would intervene and tell the children that all the objects they had experienced were alike in one way; all the objects were rough.

The newly invented concept (the con ept of roughness) can be applied to further activities (Expanding the Idea). The children can feel other objects that are rough (bark, a stone, a nail file). They can observe the difference between a rough board and rough sandpaper. The learning cycle has moved through its three phases, but exploration (Gathering Data) and expansion (Expanding the Idea) are conducted at the action level.

The child develops the concept; he/she acquires a knowledge of roughness by acting upon the objects being studied. The learning cycle is appropriate for teaching kindergarten children, but it must be implemented on the action level. Preoperational children—remember, the majority of kindergarten children are preoperational—cannot yet internalize action and perform mental operations.

LEARNING CYCLE
FOR KINDERGARTEN

Summer and Fall

Gathering data

Lead the children in a discussion of how their summer days were different from the days they are now experiencing. Now they are in school, and their days are different from their summer days. Center on the things they were doing during the summer that they are not doing now (going to the beach, playing outdoor games, going on vacations, etc.).

Explain that the class will be making a chart. The chart will tell about the things the children were doing before school started. Have available some pictures that can be placed on the chart. The pictures should depict activities such as swimming, picnicking, gardening, sightseeing, vacationing, playing baseball, and celebrating the Fourth of July. Place the pictures on the chart or bulletin board. Ask the children to discuss the pictures and to relate them to their summertime activities. Work up a lively discussion.

The idea

Explain to the children that they have been talking about a time of the year called *summer*. Write the word "summer" at the top of the chart. You need not assume that the children will learn to read the word "summer," but, in all probability, some of them will be developing reading skills.

Expanding the idea

Expand the idea by having the children look in magazines for additional pictures that remind them of summer. Give them some suggestions. Suggest that they look for pictures of yards, gardens, trees, and summertime events (baseball games, water skiing, etc.). Bring up the idea that the clothes we wear in summer are different from the clothes we wear during other seasons of the year. Sunsuits, swim trunks, sheer dresses, thin suits—these are the clothes of summer. Turn your chart into a collage of summertime things and summertime events.

Develop your summer chart fully. Then bring out a second piece of chart paper. Explain that the class will now be developing a chart that depicts the events occurring right now. You might first put up a picture of a classroom scene. The children are in school. Instruct the boys and girls to look in magazines and newspapers for additional pictures of fall scenes.

Name your second chart "Fall." Make a collage of the things and events that are typical of the fall season in your community. Do not suggest that the chart be completed immediately. Instruct the children to watch for changes. They can add pictures as the events occur. Among the changes the children might observe are the colorful fall leaves, brown grass, bird migration, and cooler temperatures.

Leave the collages up and continue to discuss and expand them. As the year progresses, you will develop the other two seasons in a similar manner. The children will be comparing one season with the other seasons. In time, they will have made a study of all the seasons—fall, winter, spring, summer.

Instructions to the children: Color the pictures that make you think of summer.

**LEARNING CYCLE
FOR KINDERGARTEN**

The Shape of Things

Gathering data

Give each child a pencil and a piece of paper. Explain that you are going to do something on the chalkboard and that the children are to do the same thing by using their paper and pencil. Place your left hand, with the fingers separated, on the chalkboard and draw around it with a piece of chalk.

Help the children to do the same thing, using paper and pencil. When the outlines are drawn, instruct the children to color them with a crayon. The outlines will show up clearly when colored.

The idea

Here the children will be inventing the concept of a shape. Instruct the boys and girls to observe their drawings. Then explain that they have drawn a "shape." Each has drawn the shape of his or her hand. Apply this idea by drawing the outlines of other objects on the chalkboard. Put freehand drawings of a cup, a foot, a chair, and an ice cream cone on the chalkboard. Ask the children to identify the objects you have drawn. Emphasize that they are looking at the shapes of things.

Expanding the idea

Show a large paper circle to your class. Say, "Here is another shape." If the children cannot identify the shape, explain to them that it is a "circle." Tell the children that they can make circle shapes on pieces of paper. Distribute round jar lids and have the children draw around them. Have them color the circles they draw.

Use a similar procedure to introduce the square. Draw a square on the chalkboard by tracing the sides of a square block. Then have the children trace a square block. Discuss sides and corners. Use the words "shape," "circle," and "square" as you discuss once again the outlines you have put on the chalkboard.

Have a "shape hunt" in the classroom or on the playground. Ask the children to find objects that have the shape of a circle and the shape of a square. If rectangular objects are identified as squares, call attention to the difference in sides. Say that there is a special name for shapes like these—the name "rectangle." You need not push this idea at this point. The rectangle can be invented later.

Show the class a large piece of paper cut into the shape of a triangle. Draw a triangle on the chalkboard. Ask the children to draw the same shape on pieces of paper. (Without a triangle to trace, their drawings will be crude, but the children should have little difficulty in conceptualizing the shape.) Have your pupils compare the sides of a square with the sides of the figure they have drawn. Make sure they conclude that the new shape has three sides, whereas a square has four sides. Explain to the class that the shape they have drawn is known as a "triangle."

Take the children outside and ask them to arrange themselves to form a circle. Holding hands and standing in a circle is fairly easy. But talk with the children about any "bumps" or "dents" that distort the roundness of their circle. Stress that a circle is round. A true circle has no "bumps" or "dents" in its side.

Next, have the children form a square. Have the boys and girls discuss how they should make a square. Place one of your large paper shapes on the ground as a model for the arrangement. Point out that all the sides of a square are the same in length. Equal numbers of children on each side make an acceptable formation. Discuss how the sides join.

Use the word "corner" and let the children arrange their lines to form the corners. This is a good time to demonstrate straight line and crooked line. Talk about the straight line on the sides of a square. Ask the children if their lines are straight or crooked.

Do not expect anything near perfection in the children's formations. From their positions, the boys and girls cannot get a good view of the shape they are making. Suggest that the children squat down. Then permit one or two children at a time to stand up and observe the shape which they have made.

Strengthen the feel for shapes by having the children draw shapes in sand. Show how a shape can be drawn in the sand in a sandbox. Ask the children to draw shapes with their fingers. Or use round cans and square boxes to make imprints in the sand. Alternate the shapes and discuss how the repeated shapes make a pattern.

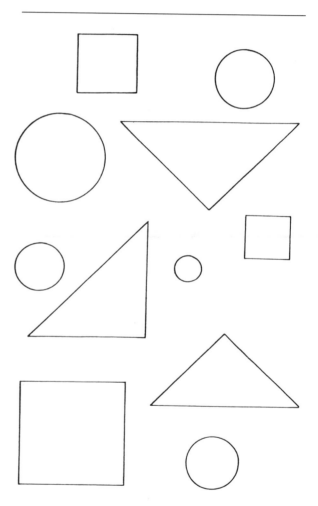

Instructions to the children: Look at the shapes. Look at the squares, the circles, and the triangles. Color the squares blue. Color the circles red. Color the triangles yellow.

LEARNING CYCLE
FOR KINDERGARTEN

Animals at Home

Gathering data

Begin by talking with the children about the
houses in which they live. Some people live
in houses and others live in apartments. A
family may live in a small house or apartment or a large house or apartment. But, no
matter how big or small, the place where
people live is called a "home." What about
other animals? Where do they go when they
go home? What do their homes look like?
What are they called?

The children probably know about a
bird nest, a fish bowl, a spider web, and an
ant hill, or colony. They probably know
about a stable, a pig pen, and chicken
coop. But do they know about a gopher's
burrow or a squirrel's hollow log? Refer to
the animals listed below. Tell where each
animal lives and give the name of its home.

Animal	Home
Pig	Pen
Dog	Kennel
Fox	Den/Lair
Cow	Barn
Horse	Stable
Chicken	Coop
Lion	Den
Gopher	Burrow
Ant	Hill/Colony
Bee	Hive
Hornet	Nest
Beaver	Dam
Squirrel	Hole/Hollow Log
Bird	Nest
Spider	Web
Bear	Cave/Den
Goldfish	Bowl
Sheep	Fold
Hermit Crab	Shell

The idea

Do not expect the children to remember the names of all the animal homes. The important idea is that there are many different kinds of animal homes. Along with this idea, the children should develop the understanding that animals of the same kind live in homes that are alike. For example, all bees live in hives.

Expanding the idea

Have the children work through the following exercise. Give them plenty of time to cut out the pictures and paste them alongside the pictures of the animals. Then ask several children to display the work they have done. Evaluate the children's work and make sure that each child has matched the pictures correctly.

You might also make a class collage from pictures that the children bring to school. Have the children paste their pictures of animals and their homes on a piece of white butcher paper about six or eight feet long. The children can work on the project at the same time, trimming and pasting their pictures.

Instructions to the children: Cut out the pictures on the next page. Each picture is a picture of an animal's home. Now, look at the pictures on this page. Each picture is a picture of an animal. There is a space beside each picture. Put a picture you have cut from the next page in the space. Match the picture of each animal with a picture of its home.

III

EXPANSION OF
THE IDEA

CHAPTER EIGHT

PREPARING LEARNING CYCLES

You have just experienced learning cycles prepared by other people. The question we must ask next is: how does a teacher go about preparing a learning cycle? There is no single, simple answer to this question, and no doubt the answers you get depend upon whom you ask. The profession of science education has not agreed on how learning cycles can or should be prepared. What follows is a description of how we prepare learning cycles.

FINDING WHAT IS TO BE TAUGHT

The first guideline, which must be adhered to, is that elementary school students in grades two through six are *concrete operational*. Students in kindergarten and most of first grade are pre-operational, which means they can make observations and report what they *believe* they saw. This guideline is perhaps the most difficult for parents, teachers, and school administrators to accept, because young, concrete operational thinkers have such excellent memories. These learners can repeat what we want them to understand and can frequently fool adults into believing that they do understand. In chapter 1 we quoted Piaget (Piaget, 1972), who said his research had revealed that formal operational thought was found in secondary school students between the ages of eleven and fifteen years; but when he made this finding, he took students "from the better schools in Geneva." We do not know what criteria Piaget used to identify the "better schools." We did our research to test when students *enter* the formal thought period in the public schools. We administered the conservation of volume task to approximately twenty-five sixth graders at three different times. Only 15 percent of these students were successful with the conservation of volume task. This finding corroborates the first guideline, that elementary school students—beyond the first grade—need to be treated as though they reason with concrete operational logic, and leads to a second guideline: *Only concrete concepts can be taught in an elementary school science program.*

The two foregoing guidelines demand that a content-selection question be answered: What standards need to be used in selecting concrete concepts? *Concrete operational students learn only through direct experience with the phenomenon to be learned.* If the concept that plants need light to survive—as opposed to grow—is to be learned, concrete operational students must grow plants in light and in darkness and collect data from this concrete experience. These data are then used to invent the concept.

To teach science to concrete operational learners, materials and supplies are necessary to provide direct experience. This need leads to an important question: How are concrete concepts isolated from formal concepts? If materials can provide *direct* experience with a concept, that concept is concrete. This axiom can also be used to distinguish which parts of formal concepts can be taught to concrete operational students. If any part of a formal concept can be taught using materials, *that part* is concrete. For example, diffusion can be taught concretely by having students put several drops of colored dye in a glass container of clear water, observe the results, and verbalize the phenomenon. This is a concrete concept learned through concrete experience. But the concept—diffusion—is formal if taught as the random movement of molecules

from a place of higher concentration to a place of lower concentration. Random movement of individual molecules cannot be observed or experienced; it requires formal operational thought to be understood.

This third guideline does not mean that a formal concept can be made understandable by teaching any part of it that is concrete. The only part that students will understand is the part they directly experience. Furthermore, if the understanding of a concrete portion of the concept depends on first understanding a formal portion, neither portion will be understood. Concrete operational children need to learn science from concrete operational concepts. Preoperational children need to experience science through observation and then discussion.

DECIDING WHAT TO DO

The exploration

Assume that at this point, you have identified the concept to be taught and the materials to teach it. Remember that elementary school students must have concrete *experiences* with materials to learn concrete science concepts. What does that mean? The children must do experiments and gather data. But before they can do so the teacher must decide what activities the children will engage in to find the needed data and what records they should keep. In other words, the teacher must prepare instructions to give to the children to assist them in collecting their information. These instructions need to direct the students' activities, suggest what records students should keep, and neither tell nor explain the concept. The following fourth-grade learning cycle (Renner, Stafford, and Coulter, 1977) illustrates how to present the concept of the *standard unit of measure.*

Gathering data
Tape two sheets of notebook paper together end to end. Place your arm on the sheet with your

fingers straight out. Make one pencil mark on the paper at your elbow. Make a second mark at the tip of your middle finger. Use a meter stick and draw a straight line between the two pencil marks.

The line you just drew is the oldest unit of measurement we know about. The Babylonians and Egyptians used this unit many centuries ago. The length of the line you just drew is a *cubit*.

Do not be misled into believing that the introduction of the word "cubit" constitutes a conceptual invention; it is not. "Cubit" is not a concept. Rather, the word "cubit" is the name of an object, which is the line just drawn. The exploration phase of the learning cycle continues.

Measure the length of the longest chalkboard in your classroom. Record that measurement. How many cubits long did your classmates find the chalkboard to be? Compare your measurements with the measurement others made. How much do the measurements vary? You and your classmates figure out a way to make a record of those variations. What do you think causes the variations? Make a record of reasons you and your classmates give.

Notice that the directions given are specific; there is no doubt about how to proceed. No hint is given, however, about what the concept being assimilated is. After the exploration experience, some children make comments such as, "We all need to use the same cubit. That will cut down the variation." These children have assimilated the essence of the concept of a standard measuring unit. This is an example, not of *free* assimilation but of *guided* assimilation. We believe that this type of assimilation is appropriate to the constraints on the teaching of science in the elementary school.

A deficiency sometimes found in learning cycles is a lack of experience in the exploration phase. Those preparing learning cycles must remember that the assimilation process requires time, and that time also needs to be spent with the materials and activities that will lead to the concept. A good exploration provides opportu-

nities for students to assimilate the concept from more than one activity. The following illustrates this point for the standard measuring unit.

The Roman empire lasted from 753 B.C. to A.D. 476. During that period the Romans used the length measure called the foot. That measure is based upon the length of the human foot.

Get a piece of cardboard a little longer than your foot. Remove one shoe and stocking. Place your foot on the cardboard and stand up. Have a friend place a pencil mark at the end of your big toe and at your heel. Use a meter stick to draw a straight line between those marks. The distance between those markers is *one foot*.

Measure the length of your classroom with your foot ruler. Record the data from that measurement. Compare your measurement with the measurements of five classmates. Why do you think those measurements varied? Make a record of the reasons you and your classmates gave for the variations found.

The inch had two beginnings. At one time the inch equaled the length of the first joint of the thumb. At another time three barley seeds laid end to end were called an inch. Use the first joint of your thumb. Measure the length of a book. Record your measurement. Compare your measurement with the measurements of the same book taken by five others. Make a record of why you think you found variation in the six measurements.

While the exploration phase must provide adequate time for assimilation, it must not go on so long that students get weary. *No one can judge that except the teacher in the classroom with the children, and that judgment is crucial.* The learning cycle should contain an "extra activity" to be used if, in the teacher's judgment, it is needed. Such an activity could include the following:

Use beans to measure the length of a book. Make a record of the number of beans you need. Record the numbers of beans used by four others in your class. Compare the number of beans you used with the numbers others used. Discuss with your classmates why the numbers varied. Make a record of why you think variations were found. What could you do to make those variations as small as possible? Make a plan and try it.

These directions are representative of the kind of instructions that need to be provided to children during the exploration phase of the learning cycle. Do the children need to be given these instructions in writing or can they be given orally? Only the teacher can make that judgment. We have had success with both. But written instructions can provide children with practice in reading and following directions, and probably reduce the misunderstandings that can result from oral directions.

The conceptual invention

As you are aware, this phase of the learning cycle is not student-centered as in the exploration phase but teacher-centered. The principal purpose of the conceptual invention phase is to lead to accommodation. Students must center on the primary findings of the exploration and accommodate to them. Furthermore, the teacher must introduce the language the students will use to refer to their conceptual understandings in the future; students will also need to accommodate to this language.

While preparing the learning cycle, the teacher can decide to do the invention orally or present it in writing. Regardless of which method is used, four factors must be included in a conceptual invention:

1. The findings of the exploration need to be reviewed and summarized.
2. *All* findings used must be the students'.
3. The concept must be stated in proper language.
4. Some reason(s) for the importance of the concept need(s) to be given.

Here is an example of a written conceptual invention:

Getting the idea
You measured the length of the classroom chalkboard with *your* cubit. The number of cubits long you found it to be was different from your classmates. You measured the length of the classroom in feet. You used the length of your foot. You measured the length of a book in thumb joints. You used your thumb. In each case your measurements were different from your classmates. Comparing the measurements of the classroom's length and the book was difficult. Those comparisons were difficult because the length of arms, feet and thumbs are different.

All objects you measure with need to be the same. All cubits need to be the same. The length of the foot needs to be the same. So does the length of an inch. When all units are the same people can talk to each other about them. When someone says, "A foot long," we know what is meant.

Making all cubits or inches or feet the same is making a

standard unit.

A group of standard units is a

measuring system.

There is nothing magic about a measuring system. To be helpful, everyone must know about it and use it.

Even if the teacher decides to use an oral technique for the invention, writing out something like this the first time really helps. It forces the teacher to state what he/she really believes the students should accommodate to, and helps crystallize the teacher's thinking. If a written conceptual invention is used, the reading experience—probably aloud—profits the children. A discussion following the invention, regardless of the form it takes, is essential.

The expansion of the idea

The purpose of this phase of the learning cycle is to provide the students with the opportunity to *organize* the concept they have just learned with other ideas that relate to it. For preoperational and concrete operational children, such organization requires that they have direct experiences with the concept and the ideas related to it. Of special significance and importance is the principle that *the language of the concept must be used during the expansion-of-the-idea phase.* Such use requires the students to continue to accommodate to both the concept *and* the language because the language leads them to recall the experiences they have had in establishing the concept. The same general guidelines about directions for the students to follow—written or oral—developed for the exploration phase apply equally well to the expansion phase. In fact, our research in secondary school chemistry (Abraham and Renner, 1983) has shown that investigatory activities used in the exploration and expansion phase are interchangeable if the language used in the expansion phase is deleted and introduced as usual in the conceptual invention phase. If you are unsure about the kind of directions students need to conduct an investigation, please reread the discussion on preparation of the exploration phase earlier in this chapter. What follows are several activities suggested for use in the expansion phase of the learning cycle on the standard unit of measure. Notice that the use of the language related to the concept in these expansion activities differs from that used in the exploration activities.

Expanding the idea

Make a standard cubit for your classroom. Each student should now measure the chalkboard's length with the standard cubit. Make a record of your measurement results. Compare your results with five classmates. The six of you should write a description of how your results compare.

In the first part of this investigation you measured the chalkboard with your cubit. Compare those results to the results you got when you used the standard cubit. How did the variations in the two sets of measurements change?

Early measuring systems came from non-standard objects. Grain kernels and body parts were often used. A group of standard units came from those early attempts to measure. Those standard units are the English Measuring system. Standard units in the English system are:

12 inches = 1 foot
3 feet = 1 yard
5,280 feet = 1 mile
2 pints = 1 quart
16 ounces = 1 pound

Tape pieces of notebook paper together. Use a foot ruler. On the paper, make a square one foot long on each side. You just drew a square foot. Make a square that is one yard on each side.

What would you call that? How many square feet are in it? Design a way to find out. How many square feet are in your classroom? Using the standard-unit square foot, how could you find out? What other way could you find out?

Get six squares of cardboard. Make each square one standard foot on each side. Make a box by taping the squares together. Each edge of the box should be one standard foot long. You just made a cube. The space inside the box is its *volume*. Your cube has a volume of one standard cubic foot. Explain why that is true. Make a record of your explanation.

The foregoing represents a perfectly adequate expansion of the concept invented and most learning cycles could end here. All disciplines contain content that can be called *culturally imperative*—that is, the content must be taught, not necessarily for the experience provided by the discipline, but because the culture in which we live demands it. Special learning cycles can often be prepared to teach such content, but frequently, the expansion-of-the-idea in a specific learning cycle phase can be used.

The content-topic of measurement contains content representing a cultural imperative for United States students—the metric system. Students must become literate in using the standard units in the metric system. After experiencing the learning cycle through the English system, they are ready to become functional with the culturally-imperative content of the metric system. Only a few of the possible activities will be included here to demonstrate how the expansion phase of the learning cycle can be used to teach culturally imperative content.

Suppose you want to change pounds to ounces. You must multiply the number of pounds by 16. Changing yards to feet means multiplying by 3. Changing feet to inches tells you to multiply by 12. All of those numbers 16, 3, and 12, are different. Then the hard one is changing miles to feet. You have to use 5280.

Now think about the number 10. If you multiply 10×1, what do you get? Next, multiply 10×10. What's the answer? Multiplying by 10 is easier than multiplying by 16, 3, 12, and 5,280!

The next measuring system uses the number 10. That system is called the *metric system.* That system has been adopted in Canada, England, and Australia. Only the United States and a few small countries still use the English system.

Get a meter stick. The meter is the standard unit of length in the metric system. Notice that the meter stick has 100 numbers on it. Place one thumb on the number 50. Place your other thumb on the number 51. Notice the distance between your thumbs. That distance is *one centimeter.* There are 100 centimeters in one meter. Study your meter stick. Make a record of why you believe there are 100 centimeters in one meter.

Make a cardboard cube. Make your cube one centimeter wide on each side. The volume of your cube is one *cubic centimeter.* The standard unit of volume in the metric system is one cubic centimeter.

Now imagine that your cubic centimeter is full of water. That much water weighs one gram. The gram is the standard unit of weight in the metric system. Food is often sold by the kilogram. One kilogram contains 1,000 grams.

Expansion activities emphasizing the metric system of measurement could continue. We have done very little with weighing in metric units and have not mentioned the liter as a measure of volume in the activities included here. The original source for the measurement learning cycle does contain such activities (Renner, Stafford, and Coulter, 1977), but whether these activities are used or not is—as we said earlier— a decision the teacher must make. As long as students' interest remains genuine, the activities should continue. If their interest declines, further learning in the metric system will depend on students' using *only* the metric system every time they measure length, weight, or volume. The only way children will develop metric understanding and eventually "think metric" is through constant use of the metric system.

In review

Making a neat, compact list of steps to guide you in writing a learning cycle isn't really possible because too much depends on the preferences of the individual teacher. In planning learning cycles we urge you to outline them in writing when you first begin preparing them. We find that the longer we teach using the learning cycle the briefer our outlines become. Principally, we note the concept and the activities in all the phases and prepare written materials for the students. A major decision the teacher must make is whether student instructions will be written or oral. You have no doubt concluded from what we have said here that we prefer providing written data-collection and concept-expansion directions to the students. In our judgment, providing such written directions reduces children's confusion about what they are to do and makes them more independent of the teacher in collecting their data. We have, however, observed many excellent science classes based on a learning cycle in which teachers used *only* oral directions. You, the teacher, must make that decision.

While it is not possible to provide a precise summary of the guidelines to use in writing a learning cycle, there are some rather broad criteria which can guide learning cycle preparation:

1. Select the concept students are to learn and write out a concise statement of it.
2. Choose the activities students will use to collect data for the concept invention.
3. Prepare instructions to give to students for collecting the data. If written instructions are to be provided to students, prepare them. If oral student instructions are to be used, prepare a teacher's outline to follow in doing it.
4. Be certain that the instructions direct students *only* in the collection of data and *do not* permit them to ascertain the concept *only* from the instructions.
5. Prepare teacher guidelines for use during the conceptual invention phase.
6. Select the activities to use during the expansion-of-the-idea phase. Be sure these activities use the concept *and its language* freely.

7. Prepare any evaluation materials that are to be used. (We shall return to this point later.)

ADDITIONAL TOPICS TO CONSIDER IN PREPARING A LEARNING CYCLE

The teacher demonstration

You are well aware that no one can assimilate for learners; they must do it for themselves. Students need to interact with the materials of the concept being taught, to do the experiments, make the observations and measurements, and record the data themselves. Maximum assimilation takes place when the students *directly* interact with the materials. This last sentence really represents an hypothesis, which we have had the opportunity to test.

We selected a twelfth-grade physics class (Renner, Abraham, and Birnie, 1983) because at this level, the students are more verbal in explaining how they feel about learning; probably because many of them have entered the formal-operational thought period. The students participating in our research had already experienced learning about twenty physics concepts through learning cycles. We made a videotape of a teacher doing an experiment in the exploration and expansion phases that gave the students exactly the same data they would have gotten had they done the experiment themselves. Following a viewing of the videotape, we interviewed six of the students to ascertain their beliefs about how it affected their learning.

Student JG:	Watching the videotape was all right—you see the same results.
Interviewer (I):	Do you like it as well as doing it yourself?
JG:	Yeah, you get as much out of it but it sure would be easy not to.
I:	What do you mean?
JG:	You remember the details better if you do it yourself. Not doing it

yourself those details can go in one ear and out the other. If you find out things for yourself you remember them better. There is the possibility the tape is not as good as far as knowing what goes on.

JG has neatly summarized why students need to interact with materials. Notice that JG began by stating that students get as much out of a videotape as they do from doing the investigation themselves. After JG "thought out loud" about it for a while, however, he concluded that there "is the possibility" that doing the investigation is better than watching a videotape. Notice JG's reason for feeling that way: "If you find out things for yourself you remember them better." In other words, no one can assimilate for JG, he must do it himself.

A second twelfth-grade physics class received data during the exploration and expansion phases by watching a teacher do the experiment. PK was asked to review how she normally got her data in physics experiments just to give her a basis for discussing the teacher demonstration. Here is what she said:

PK:	We collect data and have a discussion over it. Actually we get what we learn from our experiment—what we did. [PK is saying that she learns what is learned from the assimilation—collecting data—and the accommodation—the conceptual invention made during the discussion.] Next we do the problems and questions and have more class discussion. Sometimes we go back to the lab.
I:	How do you feel about learning like that?
PK:	I like it, it's more fun. The class doesn't go slow [sic]. You are doing something instead of just listening to somebody talk. [We consider this to be an extremely important point in the explanation of the success of the learning cycle with students. They are *constructing* their own knowledge—"doing something"—instead of experiencing instruction—"listening to somebody talk."]
I:	In this investigation the teacher did a demonstration. How do you feel about that?
PK:	I'd rather get it [the data] myself. We pay more attention if we do it ourselves.

PK's remark about paying more attention is really her way of stating that assimilation is an individual matter.

Both JG and PK have made clear that assimilating science concepts through watching a demonstration—whether "live" or on videotape—is inferior to assimilating through interaction with the materials of the concept. Does this finding mean that teachers should not use demonstrations or films and videotapes? Certainly not. There are at least two specific times when a demonstration should be used. The first is when student safety is involved. There are materials that are a potential danger to the students if handled—acids, boiling water, active chemicals such as sodium. When data are to be collected from investigations involving such materials, the teacher should probably let the students observe a demonstration. But the data collected must be carefully reviewed at the end of the demonstration, because as both JG and PK emphasized, student attention is not always completely on the demonstration. Also, when sufficient apparatus and materials are not available to permit every student to do the experiments in an investigation, the teacher has no choice but to do a demonstration.

Watching a demonstration is better than reading about it from a book, being told about it orally, or not having an opportunity to learn the concept through a demonstration. But attempting to assimilate a concept through a demonstration is always inferior to assimilating that concept through interacting with materials. A good rule of thumb is: use a demonstration *only* when the safety of the children is involved or when materials for the children to gather their own data are not available. Remember, however, *demonstrations are inferior to having students interact with materials.*

What has been said thus far about teacher demonstrations, films, and videotapes applies to providing students with the data for conceptual invention or experiences during the expansion-of-the-idea phase of the learning cycle. There is still another reason for using demonstrations, films, and videotapes that has nothing to do with the learning cycle. Sometimes there is something the teacher wants students to see, hear, feel or whatever. The thrill of a space walk, the horror of a nuclear detonation, the excitement of seeing images from an electron microscope are all examples of what can be seen on film and videotape that cannot be experienced otherwise. Not infrequently, such notions can be incorporated into the expansion phase of a learning cycle. No teacher, however, should hesitate to provide any such experience when available. There is nothing wrong with walking into the classroom and announcing that today the students will see a special film on monkeys or any other topic and showing it when the *professional* judgment of the teacher tells him/her it should be. In our interview with JG, we asked about watching videotapes—remember that tape was used *within* the learning cycle—and he said: "Watching a tape one or two times just gives a little variety." And variety is important even in a course taught with learning cycles.

Evaluation

The educational system in which we work stresses the importance of student evaluation. Student grades are important, and in the present and evolving educational climate, grades are assuming even greater importance. How, then, can students who have studied science through learning cycles be evaluated?

First, we recommend that all students keep some kind of records and that teachers evaluate these records. First-grade children can draw pictures of an investigation such as planting beans, counting the number of beans that were produced from one seed, or mixing certain liquids to discover what colors occur. Second graders can begin to augment their drawings with simple sentences and so on. Children *must* learn to keep records in science, and the process must begin in the first grade. Students' records provide a source of student evaluation.

The second form of evaluation we recommend is a list of questions that can be answered in writing—as soon as children can write—during and at the end of a learning cycle. Earlier in this chapter we used the activities from a learning cycle on measurement as examples. The following questions can be used for evaluation *after* students have experienced the English system of measurement:

1. How much does a pint of water weigh?
2. How many standard measuring cupfuls are in a pint?
3. How many square inches are in one square foot?
4. How many tablespoonfuls are in one standard measuring cup?
5. How much does your favorite kind of candy bar weigh?
6. How many bottles of pop make a quart?

Before answering these questions the children must do the activities; then they can construct reasonable answers. Not only do these questions demand the "right answers," they also evaluate if the children know *how* to find out. This latter objective is extremely important, and we will returned to it in chapter 9.

The following questions would be used for evaluation after students have studied the metric system and have done the activities suggested:

1. Use a balance and weigh some water in grams. Weigh 20, 30, 50 and 100 milliliters. How much does one milliliter of water weigh?
2. Which is the longest distance, three meters or three yards? What is your evidence?
3. Ten members of a fourth-grade class each measured the length of a chalkboard with a 10 centimeter ruler. Ten other members of the same class each measured the length of the same chalkboard with a meter stick. Which group's data do you think would vary the most? Explain why you think so.
4. How many square centimeters are there in a square meter. Be sure to explain how you figured out your answer.
5. Look at labels on cans of food at home.

Write down how many ounces and grams each can contains. How many grams are in one ounce? How many grams in one pound?
6. Get a meter stick. How many centimeters are there in a meter?
7. Go back to the meter stick. How many millimeters are there in a centimeter? Now, how many millimeters are there in a meter?

We recommend the foregoing kinds of activities and questions for nonexamination evaluation. But what about examinations? What kinds of examinations—or tests—should be given? Our position is that *students should be tested as they were taught.* The learning cycle does not focus students' attention on learning facts. In examining children, therefore, strictly factual questions are out of place. By "strictly factual questions" we mean such questions as:

1. How many inches are in a yard?
2. How many grams are in a pound?
3. Joe walked two miles. How many feet did he walk?

Questions such as these emphasize that the students should have memorized facts and should be able to repeat them when called upon. They are nonscience questions because all they emphasize are the products science has produced and not the search for knowledge.

Examination questions that evaluate students taught with the learning cycle should require them to use data and base all their responses on those data. Objective questions are rarely suitable for the evaluation of concepts learned through the learning cycle. Instead, we recommend questions such as these:

1. You measured a cubit using your arm. The class then agreed upon a standard cubit. Why is the standard cubit probably different from your cubit?
2. Why isn't the length of three barley seeds a good standard unit for the inch?

3. Why is a standard unit of length important in a measuring system?

The evaluation of students' learning is a very important teacher responsibility. Students' periodic written work, records, and examinations are important sources of data for responsible evaluation. There is one axiom that must be paramount in evaluating students: *students must be evaluated using the same procedures used in teaching them.*

Science is a unique discipline and is taught in an educational environment. As yet, we have said nothing about the discipline of science or what education should lead students to achieve. These topics will be dealt with in chapter 9.

References

Abraham, M. R., and J. W. Renner. *Sequencing Language and Activities in Teaching High School Chemistry*. A Report to the National Science Foundation. Norman, OK: Science Education Center, University of Oklahoma, 1983.

Fischer, L., T. Campbell, L. Graham, and J. Folks. *Safety Precautions for Science*. Oklahoma City: Oklahoma State Department of Education, 1982.

Piaget, Jean, "Intellectual Evolution from Adolescence to Adulthood." *Human Development* 15: 1–12, 1972.

Renner, J. W., M. R. Abraham, and H. H. Birnie. *Sequencing Language and Activities in Teaching High School Physics*. A Report to the National Science Foundation. Norman, OK: Science Education Center, University of Oklahoma, 1983.

Renner, J. W., D. G. Stafford, and V. J. Coulter. *Variation*. Encino, Calif.: Benzinger, Bruce and Glencoe, 1977. The example quoted is based upon a learning cycle found on pages 140–60.

CHAPTER NINE

THE EDUCATIONAL SIGNIFICANCE OF THE LEARNING CYCLE

The purpose which runs through and strengthens all other educational purposes—the common thread of education—is the development of the ability to think. This is the central purpose to which the school must be oriented if it is to accomplish either its traditional tasks or those newly accentuated by recent changes in the world. . . . Many agencies contribute to achieving educational objectives, but this particular objective will not be generally attained unless the school focuses on it. (Educational Policies Commission, 1961, p. 12)

A thorough understanding of the Educational Policies Commission statement of educational purpose must focus on the word "central." Those writing the document from which the statement is taken wished readers to attribute to it its precise meaning, "the center of." The central purpose of every school activity should be encouraging activities that will lead students to develop their thinking abilities. *According to the E.P.C., the school is an intellectual institution, and developing the intellect of the students is its central business.*

But what is thinking? What does having the ability to think enable one to do? If the thinking abilities of students are to be improved, what do schools have them do? What does a teacher who wishes to encourage students to develop thinking abilities do in the classroom? Such operational questions as these must be answered before the E.P.C. statement on educational purpose has practical value.

THE LOGIC OF THE EPC STATEMENT

This nation was founded on the premise that all persons are entitled to their individual freedoms. Freedom, however, requires certain factors for its establishment and survival, and these include "the social institutions which protect freedom and the personal commitment which gives it force" (E.P.C., 1961). But social institutions will neither be free nor advocate freedom if those governing them do not so demand, and these individuals will not demand freedom if they are not committed to it. In order to demand and practice responsible freedom, individuals must have what the E.P.C called "freedom of the mind," "a condition which each individual must develop for himself. In this sense, no man is born free. A free society has the obligation to create circumstances in which all individuals may have the opportunity and encouragement to attain freedom of the mind" (E.P.C., 1961).

Now, freedom of the mind entails many factors. Most certainly the way we function is influenced by "the aesthetic, the moral and the religious." The E.P.C. insists, however, that in developing a free mind there is "a unique central role for the rational powers of an individual," and it states that those powers involve the processes of recalling, imagining, classifying, generalizing, comparing, evaluating, analyzing, synthesizing, deducing, and inferring. According to the E.P.C., the rational powers enable individuals to apply logic and the available evidence to their ideas, attitudes, and actions and to pursue their individual goals. The rational powers are not "all of life or all of the mind, but they are the essence of the ability to think" (E.P.C., 1961).

Let's recapitulate: Schools are supported by our free society to perpetuate the principles upon which society is founded. In order to perpetuate a *free* society, however, the individuals making it up must have freedom of mind. To have freedom of mind students must be led to develop the ten rational powers that are the essence of the ability to think. So operationally, if schools are to achieve their *central* purpose, the experiences they provide students must lead them to develop their rational powers. Students must have experiences that demand analysis, synthesis, deduction, inference, and so on.

CONTENT AND THE RATIONAL POWERS

Schools teach content, that is, subject matter. Teachers must possess a thorough knowledge of content because it is what they use to lead students to develop their rational powers. But just the study of subject matter does not "in and of itself . . . necessarily enhance the rational powers" (E.P.C., 1961). That students know the facts, concepts, principles, and laws of science does not *necessarily* ensure that they have developed their rational powers. Students, who are, for example, "perceiving and recognizing pattern in a mass of . . . data," are learning to analyze, deduce, and infer. That, of course, is science, but the E.P.C. also said:

No particular body of knowledge will of itself develop the ability to think clearly. The development of this ability depends instead on methods that encourage the transfer of learning from one context to another and the reorganization of things learned. (p. 18)

It is *how* the content is used and not necessarily the content itself that leads to rational power development. Our discipline is science and, according to the E.P.C., the teaching procedure we use in science must facilitate both the transfer of knowledge from context to context and the reorganization of knowledge if that teaching procedure is to lead students to develop their rational powers. The question we must then ask is: **Does the learning cycle lead students to develop their rational powers?**

THE LEARNING CYCLE AND THE ABILITY TO THINK

In the discussion that follows, we will equate the "ability to think" with students' development and use of the rational powers. We feel justified in making this equation because the E.P.C. has said that the rational powers are the *essence* of thinking ability.

Consider the exploration phase of the learning cycle. In the learning cycles in chapters 4 through 7 this phase played a unique role. It is, of course, the time during which the major assimilation that leads to conceptual understanding takes place. In making this assimilation students classify the results they receive, which means that they compare them, and comparing results requires at least a minor evaluation. Students use several of the rational powers, therefore, in just the act of exploring. Before conceptual invention students must make a thorough analysis of the data resulting from their exploration. The conceptual invention is obviously a synthesis incorporating the use of imagination. Classifying, comparing, evaluating, and inferring are necessary in formulating the invented concept. All these activities lead to transference of the data received through the context of exploration to the context of knowledge construction. Such activities also make evident why accommodation takes place during the conceptual invention phase.

In the expansion-of-the-idea phase the transfer of knowledge from one context to another reaches its zenith. The newly acquired knowledge—the new concept—is immediately put to use in a new context and with new materials. This causes students to reorganize their fresh understanding of the concept and, of course, generalize about it. Most certainly, students are using deduction throughout this entire learning-cycle phase.

The evidence we have presented here clearly leads to the inference that providing experiences with all the phases of the learning cycle leads students to develop their rational powers, making it an appropriate teaching procedure to use in the classroom. Before this teaching procedure can be used the content the students are to study must be organized into learning cycles, as we described in chapter 8. Thus, the combination of curriculum organization and classroom teaching procedures using the learning cycle leads students to achieve the *central* purpose of education.

Write a paragraph—more if you need it— that describes why the learning cycle is an appropriate teaching procedure to use in leading students to develop the ability to think.

SCIENCE AND THE LEARNING CYCLE

In chapter 3 we described a plant-growth investigation and said that children learn about the "nature of science" from such investigations. By the "nature of science" we mean what science is. Science is usually thought of as disciplines—biology, chemistry, geology, meteorology, and physics—that is, content to be taught. Certainly, content from disciplines such as those listed must be taught for the teaching activity to be recognized as *natural* science—that is, the *science of nature*. These disciplines are concerned with explaining nature. But what does the "science of nature" mean? In other words, what is science?

Albert Einstein stated that "The object of all science is to coordinate our experiences and bring them into a logical system" (Holton and Roller, p. 214). How does one learn science by coordinating experiences? First, learners must be allowed to have experiences and to coordinate them. In science the laboratory supplies experience, a series of activities that provide data about a natural phenomenon to the investigator, who then interprets these data, and in so doing, develops an understanding of the phenomenon being investigated. In Einstein's description of science, laboratory activities provide the "experiences," the interpretation of which leads to the "logical system."

To appreciate fully what Einstein is saying, we will examine the teaching procedure used in teaching science in the *majority* of classrooms throughout the world—the inform-verify-practice (IVP) procedure. Usually this procedure begins with a lecture that orally delivers information to students about the concept to be learned and names the concept. The information and conceptual language can also be delivered through some media such as television, motion pictures or the printed page, but in all of these forms, the assumption is made that the language used has meaning for students. According to this teaching procedure, there need not be any prior experience to make the language meaningful other than a careful definition of terms, which is why textbooks carry carefully prepared vocabulary lists. Regardless of how the information is conveyed, in the first phase of this teaching procedure—*exposition*—the teacher tells the learner what is to be known. Reading has a prominent position in this teaching procedure. In other words, the first phase of the usual process—often called *exposition*—for teaching science requires that the teacher *inform* the students of what is to be learned.

In the second phase of the traditional exposition teaching procedure, learners usually are shown proof that what they have been told is true. Science includes perhaps the best procedure found in any discipline for students to test the authenticity of what they have been told. Apparatus and materials are available to do the needed testing. Thus, when students are told that a particular chemical reaction is exothermic, they can carry out the reaction and verify it for themselves. Such exercises are sometimes called experiments, but they are not true experiments because the outcome is known before the activity is carried out. These activities are simply verification and are extremely important to the exposition teaching procedure. The *verification phase* is the best opportunity students have to attach meaning to the language of the concept they have been given during the information-giving phase.

In the last phase of the exposition teaching procedure, students answer questions and problems in the textbook and may also take quizzes and do extra credit readings. The last phase rarely includes any further experience with the apparatus and materials of the discipline, and the activities are usually conducted on the verbal level. This phase of the exposition teaching procedure gives students an opportunity to *practice* using the information they have been given. The teaching in science in most schools is done with the inform-verify-practice (IVP) procedure.

Focusing attention on Einstein's description of science immediately reveals the first deficiency of the IVP teaching procedure. Students have no experiences to coordinate; they are informed about what they are to know. The experiences *someone else* has had are coordinated into a logical system and presented to them. The IVP teaching procedure tells students that science is a finished procedure—here are its products—that they are expected to know. Do not believe that the experiences students have during a verification laboratory are the kinds of experiences Einstein was talking about. In a verification laboratory, students simply reenact with materials—apparatus, chemicals, living things—what the textbook tells them. They are reliving someone else's experience, not having experiences of their own. The verification laboratory is further disqualified as a science experience because students know the outcome—Einstein's coordinated logical system—all the time the "laboratory" is in session. If Einstein is correct, we must claim that science cannot be taught with the IVP teaching procedure. A test of our interpretation follows.

Physicist Niels Bohr, who left his imprint on science by inventing the Bohr model of the atom, stated that "the task of science is both to extend the range of our experience and reduce it to order" (Booth, 1962), a description closely parallel to Einstein's. Both are concerned about experience with phenomena and reducing that experience to some form of order. The experiences students must have in doing science, according to Einstein and Bohr, must provide information, a precise description of the exploration phase of the learning cycle. The information gained from the exploration phase must be formed into a "logical system," according to Einstein, or reduced to order, according to Bohr. Both men are saying that in science, the information gained from exploration must be conceptually organized by the investigator. In other words, the practice of science requires that the investigator make conceptual inventions. The first two phases of the learning cycle, therefore, have their roots in the discipline itself. These phases and their sequences, according to Einstein and Bohr, are science.

Critics of the idea that science is a process of inventing explanations for phenomena found in the natural world will always say, "Yes, but where do the facts of science fit into that description of science?" The nineteenth-century French scientist Henri Poincairé addressed that question when he said: "Science is built up with facts, as a house is with stones, but a collection of facts is no more a science than a heap of stones is a house" (Kelly, 1941). Poincairé left little room for the argument that memorizing and being able to repeat the facts of science represents being educated in science; these activities—memorizing and repeating—do *not* represent science. Furthermore, teachers who concentrate on leading students to memorize the facts, laws, and principles of science—the IVP procedure—are not teaching science; the students have only the stones, not the house. In order to be educated in science students must have experiences in which they participate in

reducing to a logical system. They have then learned how to construct knowledge about the natural world—they have learned science. According to Poincairé they have built the house.

Science, then, is a process of finding facts, laws, principles, and concepts, but the content does not represent science. Perhaps science historian Duane Roller said it best: ". . . science is the quest for knowledge, not the knowledge itself" (Roller, 1970). Teaching what is called science without involving the students in a quest or search is not teaching science. Roller's statement and the foregoing explanation render the majority of elementary school textbooks labeled "science" useless to teach science.

Most assuredly, the exploration and conceptual invention phases of the learning cycle represent a quest. But what about expansion of the idea; are the activities in that phase representative of science? Probably not. To adhere to Einstein's, Bohr's and Roller's descriptions of science, which we do, the expansion phase of the learning cycle is not necessary. The exploration phase provides experience and the conceptual invention phases leads students to build a logical system.

Why, then, is the expansion-of-the-idea phase included in the learning cycle? There are two reasons. First, the mental functioning model of Piaget, which we discussed in chapter 2, demonstrates that after a new idea has been formulated (a "logical system"), thought has been put in accord with "things." This accommodation is followed by a period in which these new thoughts are organized and integrated with old thoughts. Or, as Piaget stated, thought is put in accord with thought. You will remember from chapter 2 that this process is called organization. Human beings will take new ideas and organize them with old ideas. Learning does not stop with Einstein's new logical system; it uses old logical systems to explain the new and in the process, revises the old systems. The expansion-of-the-idea phase of the learning cycle, therefore, represents how *content* ideas change as more and more concepts are learned. Those changes represent true knowledge construction.

There is a second reason for including the expansion phase in the learning cycle. Whenever we learn new ideas, we need to extend them to other related ideas and truly expand those ideas, which is probably another way of putting thought in accord with thought. Activities provide the opportunity each of us needs when we learn something new—we need practice with the new idea. Doing additional experiments, answering questions and reading about the new logical system or concept *after* it has been invented give us ample opportunity to practice.

The data presented here to lead *you* to conceptualize that when using the learning cycle as a teaching procedure science is being taught came from three scientists and a science historian. They clearly demonstrate that if science is to be taught, students must interact with the materials of the discipline to collect data and make order out of the data. The order students produce either is a conceptual invention or leads to it. **The learning cycle, therefore, is not a method of teaching science. The learning cycle comes from the discipline itself; it represents science. If science is to be taught in a manner that leads students to construct knowledge, they must make a quest. The learning cycle leads students on that quest for knowledge.**

A PERSISTENT COMPLAINT

Whenever science teaching is directed at implementing the "quest-for-knowledge," there are always complaints that less content will be "covered" than if the students read about the products science has produced in a textbook. The complaint is probably accurate, but it lacks validity.

The "lack-of-coverage" complaint is invalid because letting students read about the products

of science from a textbook is *not* science. What is said is being taught—science—is not taught.

There is also a second reason that the "lack-of-coverage" complaint—although probably accurate—should not overly concern teachers using the learning cycle. Earlier in this chapter, we demonstrated that the learning cycle leads to the development of the rational powers. Since the rational powers are the essence of the ability to think, students who have experiences which enhance that development are in a position to carry on their own education. Fostering that ability in students is the greatest service schools can perform for them. The Educational Policies Commission said it eloquently (E.P.C., 1961):

. . . education does not cease when the pupil leaves school. No school fully achieves any pupil's goals in the relatively short time he spends in the classroom. The school seeks rather to equip the pupil to achieve them for themselves.

Since the learning cycle leads to rational power development, which will, in turn, lead students to achieve their own goals, the "lack-of-coverage" complaint seems unimportant. Content is "covered" through the learning cycle, and if you need to reassure yourself, consult chapters 4 through 7 again.

W̶rite a paragraph that explains your concept of the "logical system" idea in Einstein's description of science. Use the data just presented.

ACTIVITIES IN THE PHASES OF THE LEARNING CYCLE

We have said the students explore, experience conceptual invention, and participate in expanding concepts. But specifically, what kinds of *activities* do they engage in? What do students actually do while exploring, inventing, and expanding the idea? What kinds of experiences

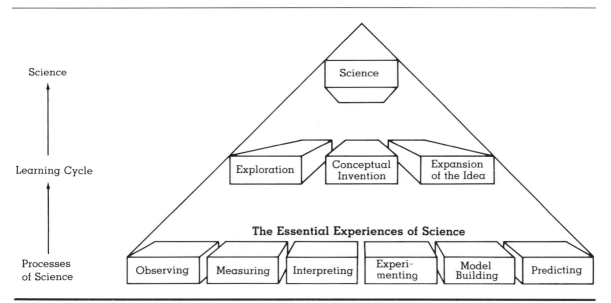

Figure 9-1   The basis of the pyramid of science is composed of the Processes of Science. These processes are essential in doing science.

does the teacher provide children in teaching with the learning cycle? We believe there are six specific essential experiences that would make classroom activities recognizable to a scientist as science. These essential experiences are: observing, measuring, interpreting, experimenting, model building, and predicting.

Figure 9-1 shows the relationship of these six essential experiences to the learning cycle and to science. As Figure 9-1 suggests, "Exploration," "Conceptual Invention," and "Expansion of the Idea" used together properly represent doing and learning science. These three major aspects can be further reduced to simpler processes, the six blocks at the base of the pyramid labeled "Essential Experiences."

The learning cycle can be depicted as two triangles and a rectangle as shown in Figure 9-2. All six "Essential Experiences" may be used in arriving at the idea—or concept—to be invented from the data collected during the "Exploration" phase. The processes, although not

used in equal amounts of time, are used in an order or combination that will culminate in the invented concept. For example, when exploring a new aspect of nature, an individual would logically begin by observing and measuring to procure information and then proceed to interpreting, predicting, experimenting, and model building. It is not reasonable, for example, to begin to use model building and predicting until some information is available and some interpreting has been done. After the *idea* has been grasped, all six of the "Essential Experiences" can again be used in "Expansion of the Idea."

Each of the six experiences is a process used in practicing science or learning science. As processes they are tools having certain basic components that identify them, whether they are being used to gather data or expand an idea. We will first explore each of the six processes by presenting a short description and then a learning cycle that focuses on a specific "Essential Experience." Each of the learning cycles we

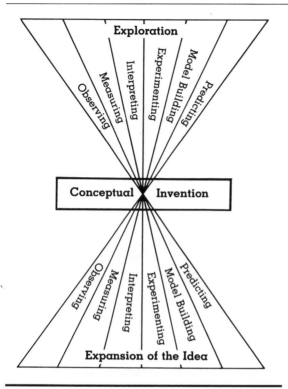

Figure 9-2 The Processes of Science are used in all phases of the learning cycle.

present provides students with more than one "Essential Experience," but one "Essential Experience" is the primary focus of each learning cycle.

Observing

If you are interested in acquiring information about an object you are not familiar with, the most obvious thing to do is look at it. Your observations can give you a great deal of specific information and can lead you to find other types of investigations that will give you much more. You can make observations in many ways. Feeling, squeezing, poking, rubbing, and listening are but a few of the methods (other than visual) that can be used to make observations. Observing is the first action the learner performs in

acquiring new information. The curriculum must provide opportunities for the learner to have extensive experience in making observations. How are such learning experiences provided?

If children are going to learn how to observe, they must be given the opportunity to watch, feel, squeeze, poke, and do other things that will enable them to describe the object they are observing. Furthermore, the object they observe must be one the children feel comfortable with and not so foreign that they are afraid of it or uncertain of what can or should be done with it. When young children go to school, they are probably more familiar with the objects in the environment than with anything else. The first observations children can be led to make, then, can be of the common things in their immediate environment. The environment contains many different shapes, but shape as a concept is usually not evident to children. The following learning cycle leads to the concept of shape. We have made the assumption that the children will not be reading, so we have written the following learning cycle for the teacher.[1]

Exploration
The children at their desks observe wooden blocks cut into triangles, circles, squares, rectangles, and diamonds. The children learn to describe the shapes of the various wooden objects. The teacher provides the shape label as needed. (Cardboard shapes may also be used.)

The teacher calls out a shape and each child holds up an object of that shape from the child's own tray.

Conceptual invention
The teacher collects many objects that are familiar to children, such as a plate, a cup, a picture, a book, a watch, a coin, a bell, et cetera. The teacher holds up one object at a time, then asks some child to describe the shape of the object.

---

[1] We will follow the procedure of using the titles for the learning cycle's phases of Exploration, Conceptual Invention, and Expansion of the Idea when the materials are written for the teacher. When the materials are written for the students, we will use Gathering Data, The Idea, and Expanding the Idea as titles.

After the teacher has gone over the collection of objects, she then verbally states the idea:

Objects have a shape.

Expansion of the idea

Have the children first find square objects in the classroom. Round, triangular, rectangular, and other shapes are found next.

Have the children observe and describe objects of a particular shape on the playgrounds, along the street, and at home. Be sure that both living and nonliving objects are included.

Measuring

After taking measurements of any object, investigators (adults or children) are able to make statements that are much more definitive than those they were able to make based only on qualitative observations. We cannot, for example, look at a plant today and specifically say it has grown a definite quantity since yesterday. Our senses might tell us that the plant has grown, but they certainly would not tell us how much. In order to be able to state how much a plant has grown in three days or in a week, we must be able to refine the measurements our senses allow us to take. Not only are our senses inadequate to make a measurement as small as that of daily plant growth, they are also woefully inadequate in accurately estimating large measurements, such as the distance to the sun, the velocity of sound, or the weight of an elephant. Measurements are necessary to extend our senses down to the infinitesimal and up to something approaching the infinite, because our senses are not reliable as measuring devices except in a very approximate way.

Measurements can be considered observations, but they are quantitative observations that can be repeatedly taken in the same manner at different times. Variations will occur in measurements because of growth in a living organism (if that is what is being measured) or inaccuracies or inconsistencies that occur in the application of the measuring standard. To enable pupils to learn how to use observations from quantative measurements, the elementary school science curriculum must provide appropriate learning experiences for pupils at all levels.

The following learning cycle has been used many times on the fourth grade level to lead children to understand the concept of average, which must be based upon measurements. These directions are written for the students.

Gathering data

Try this experiment. Mark a straight line for a starting line. Put your feet together with the toes of both feet on the starting line. Hop as far as you can with your feet together. Measure the distance you hopped in centimeters. Again, hop as far as you can and measure the distance. Make a record of the two distances.

Compare the two distances you hopped. If the distances are not the same, take a part of the longer distance and add it to the shorter distance. Make both distances the same. Compare this new distance with each of the distances you measured. How is the new distance different from each of the earlier distances?

Repeat what you did. Hop as far as you can. Then measure the distance. Hop again and measure the distance. Do this four times. After each time, make a record of the distance.

Now, take a part from each of the longer distances. Add these parts to the shorter distances until all four are the same. Make a record of this distance.

The idea

You made all four distances the same. To do this, you took parts from the longer distances. You then added these parts to the shorter distances. The new distance you obtained is called the

average.

The new distance is the *average distance* you can hop. In many experiments, you will report the average result. An average often provides accurate data and is usually better than the result of only one experiment.

When you listen to people talk, you will hear the word "average" used to describe almost everything. People talk about average driving speeds, average salaries, average food prices, and even average people. There is even an average number of letters on each full line of print on this page. Perhaps you can find out that average.

Averages are important in your school studies. You will be working with averages in many ways in your mathematics, science, and social science classes.

Expanding the idea

Try this. Add together the four distances you hopped. Divide the sum by four. The number you get is also called the average. Compare this average with the average you got by taking away and adding on.

Sometimes it is very hard to get an average by taking away and adding on. For example, suppose you wanted to know the average height of the pupils in your class. It would take a long time to find the average by taking away and adding on.

Think about how you could find the average height of the pupils. What numbers would you need to add together? What number would you divide by?

Understanding average

1. Find the average height of the pupils in your class. Find the average in centimeters. Find the average in inches.
2. Find out the number of pupils in five different classrooms in your school. What is the average number of pupils in each classroom in those five classrooms?
3. Determine the average age in months of the pupils in your class.
4. Find the average age of the members of your family. Which has more variation, the ages of your family or the ages of the students in your class?
5. One boy reported that the average time he spent coming to school each morning for one week was fifteen minutes. On one of the mornings it took twenty-two minutes. Explain how he could have an average time of fifteen minutes.

Interpreting

As data accumulate, a person who wishes to use them tries to make them understandable. In an elementary school classroom data interpretation has a variety of forms. In the learning cycle data interpretation usually follows observing and measuring. Interpreting can be as simple as grouping objects into heavy and light or deciding if an object is rough or smooth, or as complex as building a model to explain patterns in data. Interpreting is "making sense out of data."

In almost every case, interpretation leads to experimenting and predicting. If during the interpretation of data a pattern or trend is discerned or suspected, this pattern or trend can be stated as a possible generalization or an hypothesis. A carefully planned series of observations, measurements, and experiments can then be conducted to learn more about the relationships found.

Interpreting involves the discernment of the various factors that appear to affect an object or event. When plant growth is observed and considered, the factors of light and water are almost intuitively associated with it. But other factors such as temperature, soil type, and mineral content might also be involved. Isolating these important factors or variables is an essential aspect of interpretation. Discovering that a particular variable is not important represents a significant finding. For example, in working with a pendulum, students will find that the length of the string of the pendulum affects the period, but the weight of the object on the string does not.

The process of interpreting no doubt involves all ten of the rational powers of the mind and is one of the most educationally fruitful aspects of the learning cycle; but it is also one of the most abused parts. Teachers are usually willing to allow children to observe and measure, but when it comes to interpretation, teachers have a tendency to take over. Interpreting data is fun and exciting, but unless the students do it, the educational value is lost. Teachers can act as a guide, but they should let students interpret.

There are two procedures for teaching data interpretation—the individual method and the group method. In the individual method, each student keeps personal records and, with the assistance of the teacher or classmates, interprets, generalizes, and concludes from them. What the students receive from this procedure is directly dependent on them. In the group procedure, each student contributes personal findings to the entire group, and what the student gains is as much dependent on the data of others as it is on personal data. This latter method, in addition to being useful in demonstrating the value of working together, leads students to find the scientifically sound concept of the value of more than one viewpoint or set of measurements. While there are values to be gained from having students interpret their own data, these values, as well as several others, will also be achieved by group interpretation of data.

In the group approach to interpreting data, the teacher uses the chalkboard and serves as the class secretary. Each group of students states what it found, and the teacher records this. At the end of such a session many data are available for inspection and study. The entire class has the same data, and the attention of the entire group (including the teacher) can be focused on any piece of information. The class is then able to decide whether or not any of the variables being considered require the collection of additional information. This type of social interaction is important in learning and intellectual development.

Data interpretation frequently involves data organization. A collection of unorganized descriptions and measurements usually "makes no sense." Imagine a sports page randomly covered with bits of information about the scores of baseball games for the entire season. Before you could begin to discern a pattern, you would almost surely have to decide on some organizational scheme and then implement it. You might begin by deciding to count and record the total number of wins and losses for each team. After that, you might decide to serial-order the teams on the basis of most wins to least wins. The data would then begin to yield new information, which could not be obtained directly from the random pieces of data. The new information might be that Team A has won sixteen of its games while Team D has won only six of its games. The information showing the number of wins or losses by a team could be placed in a histogram, as shown in Figure 9-3. The histogram is just one technique to use in interpreting data. Teachers need to use those techniques that fit the kind of data that are to be organized.

The following learning cycle shows how interpretation was used to lead fifth-grade chil-

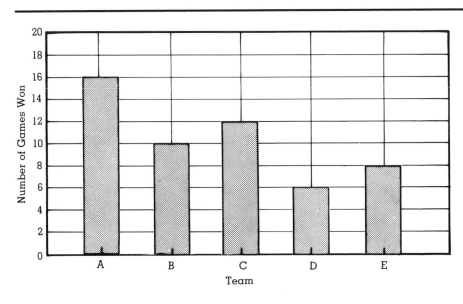

Figure 9-3 This is a type of histogram called a bar graph. The number of games won by each team can be readily compared.

dren to the invention of the extremely important concept of *community*. The children had collected data for some time about what happens to organisms in small terraria and aquaria. The information from the exploration phase had been placed on a chart. What follows are instructions for the children to use in interpreting data from the exploration in order to permit them to invent a concept and proceed through the invention and the expansion phases. All materials have been written for the students. (Renner, Stafford, and Coulter, pp. 326–331).

Gathering data
You have been organizing information on a chart in order to represent the relationships among the organisms in a certain area. Now it is possible to look at the chart and to think about each section. You can see how one section is related to other sections.

You should have a section for producers, sections for two kinds of consumers, one section for decomposers, one section for raw materials, and a place to indicate light. Check your work to see if you have included all the sections on the chart. Be sure that you have labeled all the sections.

Choose one section of the chart and imagine that it no longer exists. Imagine that the things represented there have all been destroyed. Write a paragraph about what might happen if that were true.

You have considered what would happen if organisms from an entire section in your chart were gone. Choose just one population. Imagine that all members of that population are gone. How would that affect any other population? Find a population that could be eliminated without an effect on any other population.

The idea
Plants and animals within a certain area are shown on your chart. The chart summarizes the interactions among the living things. The food cycle is an example of interaction and of a relationship among the plants and animals.

Organisms in an area interacting in this kind of relationship can be called a

community.

Write the word *community* at the top of your chart.

The word "community" is probably familiar to you. You probably live in an area which is called a community. In some ways, the meaning is exactly the same. The word "community" is a reference to the things which are close to you and with which you have some kind of relationship.

The term *biotic community* is applied to organisms that are dependent upon each other for survival. The word *biotic* means "of or having to do with life." A biotic community is a community of living things. . . .

Each part of a biotic community is dependent upon other parts. There are interactions among one living thing and other living things. There are also interactions among living things and the nonliving parts of the environment. One population is dependent upon another population. This dependency holds the community together.

Expanding the idea
Depending on where you live, you may have several different kinds of communities near you. But, regardless of the kind of community or of the populations which compose it, every community must have the sections which you have represented and labeled on your chart.

Write a paragraph predicting what would happen if you removed "light" from your chart. What would happen to the community? Give data to support what you think.

Think of some other kinds of communities. Choose a kind which is of interest to you and make a community chart which shows different organisms interacting in a food cycle.

Perhaps you will need to investigate organisms and food habits. Be sure that you have all the necessary parts of the community. Draw the arrows which show food transfer. When you are through, trade community charts with a classmate. Check to see that every organism listed in the community has a food source.

When listing organisms on your chart, be sure you list people as part of the community. Discuss how people interact in a community. Compare the effect of people on a community with the effect of other organisms.

Make a list of the ways people affect a community. Indicate whether each way is helpful or harmful. Discuss your list with others. Then change your list if you think you should.

Teaching with the IVP procedure instead of the learning cycle may bring up a problem associated with allowing pupils to interpret data.

The pupils might interpret the data incorrectly and arrive at a wrong conclusion. When an incorrect conclusion is reached using the learning cycle, what should you do?

Students must not be allowed to harbor an incorrect concept, but experience has shown that telling them they are wrong will not allow them to learn the concept correctly. The learners will probably seem to accept your decision as an adult authority, but they will probably not begin to disbelieve what their own collected information has indicated and accept what you say. If students are going to learn to classify, compare, evaluate, and use all their rational powers, they must be given experience in classifying, comparing, and evaluating without being made to feel that what they do is not really important because the teacher will decide whether or not their data are correct and interpret those data for them. If applying the rational powers to data produced by an experiment has the adverse affect of leading learners to an erroneous concept, there is only one way for the students to correct that concept for themselves. They must be provided with the opportunity to apply their rational powers to data from a second experiment that will contradict the first. The students must then decide which evidence is correct, although they have absolutely no basis for making such a decision. The only way they can approach a solution is to repeat both experiments or observations or measurements.

If the data from an experiment lead students to an incorrect concept, then they did something in the experiment improperly. Leading students to see the need to repeat the experiments will also give the class an opportunity to review their procedures. If class-determined procedures are carefully reviewed, the probability of repeating procedural errors (which will again result in learners' arriving at an unacceptable concept) will be reduced. If teachers are to lead learners away from a self-developed concept unacceptable to science, they must make a second experiment available that, although it uses a different route, will provide data to enable the learners to arrive at the acceptable concept.

One of the pervasive concerns of this book is that elementary school science experiences should contribute to the development of the childrens' rational powers. Data interpretation can make a contribution to that development. Educationally speaking, spending the time needed to make additional observations and measurements and allowing the children, through their own interpretation, to arrive at a correct result is more fruitful than shortcircuiting the process by rejecting their interpretation and supplying your own.

Experimenting

Often, when applied to observation and measurements, data interpretation leads to other science processes—experimentation, model building, and prediction. The results of using these processes require further interpretation.

When observations and measurements are initially interpreted, one or more possible trends, patterns, or relationships may be noticed or suspected. These possible relationships act as a guide to further explorations and are sometimes called "working hypotheses." These explorations, which will be designed to establish whether or not a relationship exists, must be carefully planned and controlled. When observations and measurements are made under planned and controlled conditions, an experiment has been done. Since experimenting requires controlled conditions, some data collection and data interpretation should precede it. The data used come from many sources, such as observations, measurements, and the interactions of objects under consideration "to see what happens." Without some data related to the experiment, the investigator would have no idea what to control or what to observe.

Experiments do, of course, provide data, and are an essential part of the *exploration* phase of the learning cycle. Students in a fourth-grade class had some familiarity with plant growth through simple observations. They had decided that certain factors were essential to plant growth and were ready to test them. The following is a series of experiments on plants designed for fourth graders. Notice how certain factors are controlled. Notice also how the directions or guidance given the children decrease as the experiments continue. The directions for students follow.

Gathering data

Fill three pots with soil. Plant three bean seeds in each pot. Give each pot the same amount of water.

Set one pot in full light. Turn a box over the second pot. That pot then will be in the dark. Turn a box over the third pot, but make a hole in the box. That pot will then be in a small amount of light.

Each plant will get a different amount of light. Be sure everything else is the same. You are testing only one variable. That variable is the amount of light.

Experiment

Repeat the experiment with light. But use grass seeds instead of bean seeds. Put twenty grass seeds in each of the three pots. Keep your records as carefully as you did before. Control all the variables as well as you can. What is the effect of light on grass? What do you conclude?

You have now done controlled experiments with plants and light. Except for light, all the conditions were the same. How does the amount of water a plant receives affect its growth?

Experiment

Again, plant beans in three pots. Keep all variables the same except the amount of water. Keep the soil in one pot fairly dry. Keep the soil damp at all times in the second pot. Keep water standing on top of the soil in the third pot.

Observe the growth of the plants. Keep a record of what happens in each pot. Combine your data with the data of others in your class. What do you conclude about water and bean plants?

Experiment

Get two small pots the same size. Decide on the kind of plant you would like to grow. You might like to plant sunflower seeds instead of bean seeds. Or you might like to try this experiment with a flower such as the zinnia.

Plant only two seeds in the first pot. Plant a great many seeds in the second pot. Care for the plants in both pots in exactly the same way. Your only variable is the number of seeds you planted in each pot.

Observe the growth of the plants. Keep a record of the growth. What information did you gather from the results of this experiment?

Experiment

Next, do an experiment to test the effect of temperature on plants. List the materials you will need. Plan how you will keep track of the results. Write a statement on what you conclude.

At the conclusion of this series of experiments, the idea (concept) "environmental factors" was used to focus on aspects of the environment that affect living things. The first two phases of the learning cycle have been completed.

Plan at least two or three "Expanding the Idea" activities which would follow the experiment just done to gather data and the introduction of the idea of environmental factors.

Model building

Whenever data are interpreted, some type of *explanation* results. Those making the explanation do not know if it describes *exactly* what the system that produced the data is like, but uncertainty is not particularly important at this point in the quest. What is *extremely* important is that the explanation explains the available data. The person producing the *explanation* has built a mental *model* on the basis of the available data. Observations and possibly measurements will have been made and data—which can come from experimenting—interpreted before model building begins. As soon as an experimenter thinks or says, "those data mean . . . ," he/she has begun the process of model building.

Quite evidently, preoperational children cannot build models, but early concrete operational children can begin to do so because they are beginning to stablize the thought reversal

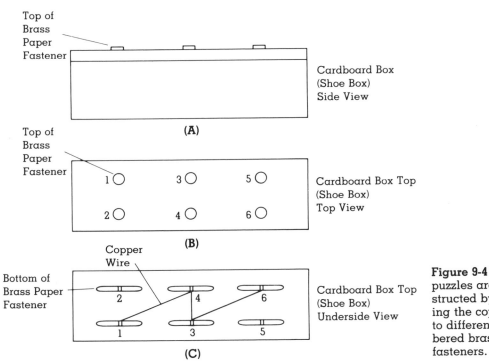

Top of
Brass
Paper
Fastener

Cardboard Box
(Shoe Box)
Side View

(A)

Top of
Brass
Paper
Fastener

1 ◯   3 ◯   5 ◯

2 ◯   4 ◯   6 ◯

Cardboard Box Top
(Shoe Box)
Top View

(B)

Copper
Wire

Bottom of
Brass Paper
Fastener

2   4   6
1   3   5

Cardboard Box Top
(Shoe Box)
Underside View

(C)

Figure 9-4 Different puzzles are constructed by attaching the copper wire to different numbered brass paper fasteners.

process. The following third-grade learning cycle on electricity demonstrates the process of model building. The directions are written for the students.

Gathering data
You are going to build an electrical puzzle. You will then exchange your puzzle with someone else. That person will solve your puzzle. You will solve the one you are given. The puzzle will come in a small box. *DO NOT* open the box.

To make your puzzle, you will need six metal paper fasteners, copper wires, and a small cardboard box. A shoe box will do.

Punch six holes in the box top. Number each hole. Put one paper fastener in each hole. Then connect some of the paper fasteners with wires. Make the connections on the underside of the box top (see Figure 9-4). You will need a circuit tester (Figure 9-5) to solve the puzzle. Study the directions given on Figure 9-5. Those directions will tell you how to make a circuit tester.

Be sure your circuit tester is working well. Touch the ends of the wires to two paper fasteners on your box which are connected. What do you observe? What do the data from your observations tell you?

Now exchange boxes with another group. DO NOT open the box they give you. Touch the tops of different pairs of paper fasteners. Draw a picture of what you found.

The idea
You found out something from the box you made. You found out something from the box you were given. Write one or two sentences telling what you found out.

Expanding the idea
Use your circuit tester. Go around the room. Touch the ends of the wires to different types of materials. What did you find out?

The children are building a model when they draw the picture of what they believe the

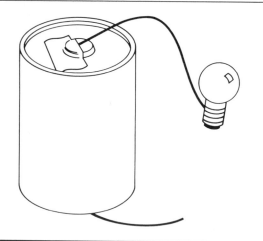

Figure 9-5 This system is called a "circuit tester." It is made of a flashlight cell, a bulb, two pieces of wire, and some tape. The bottom of the bulb is placed on one part of an object, while the wire from the bottom of the flashlight cell is touched to another part. If the light goes on, then the object completed the circuit.

inside of the unknown box looks like. Third-grade children *should not* be expected to find all of the connections in the box they are given. To do so they would have to test all possible pairs of the metal paper fasteners two at a time, a problem in combinatorial reasoning that requires formal operational thought. The children will find some connected pairs, and finding all the connected pairs of paper fasteners is not important. What is important is that the students use the data *they* have to draw the picture called for at the end of the "Gathering Data" (exploration) phase. When the children who built the box try to correct another group, the teacher should intervene and say something like: "You know because you built the box. But this group is explaining what their data tell them." All models are based upon the available data, and science contains many such models that have been changed frequently. The solar system and

the atom are perhaps the two most well-known models that have undergone frequent changes.

The conceptual invention is another model: "The metal paper fasteners must be connected before the bulb lights." The students will probably not say anything about the type of material that must be used to connect the paper fasteners. This information—which is not a model—will emerge from the "Expanding the Idea" phase of the learning cycle. Model building is a very creative process in science. The models of nature created by children or adults enhance understanding or explain some aspect of nature. Furthermore, the model-building process helps students build the quest-for-knowledge model of science and assists them in developing their rational powers *if* the model is based on the available data and *not* on what the answer should be.

Record (1) the air temperature (2) cloud condition of the sky (3) the humidity and the (4) rate and (5) direction of the wind for seven days. Also describe the weather each day. Build a model that explains the relationship between the weather and the five variables just listed.

Predicting

The interpretation of data, as you have seen, can lead to model building. Interpretations and models made from data also have another use. That use is exactly the same as the use that can be made of any past learning in increasing our ability to function more effectively in the future; that is, we use past learnings to *predict* what our future behavior should be. The interpretations we make of our past experiences form the basis of our everyday behavior. A common example illustrates this very well. When you are standing at a corner waiting to cross the street and the light regulating the opposing traffic turns red, you feel free (after a visual inspection) to cross. In the past you have had direct experience telling you that moving automobiles stop when confronted by a red light. From that data-interpretation experience, you predict that the moving automobiles you are watching will also stop when the traffic light turns red. You are so convinced your prediction is valid that you are willing to risk your own personal safety by stepping into the street in front of automobiles approaching the red light. This behavior on your part did not come without a great deal of experience, which you accumulated over a long period of time.

So it is with predictions that can be made from data derived from experiments. If children are going to learn to predict future events and base those on scientifically collected and interpreted data, they must be given the freedom to make predictions.

You have seen in this chapter how observing, measuring, interpreting, experimenting, and model building can each provide the focus for "Exploration," "The Idea," and "Expanding the Idea." But where and how does predicting fit into the learning cycle? Before we attempt to answer this question let us explore in greater depth just what a prediction is. A prediction is an estimate of the events to take place, or the results to be achieved, or both.

You will immediately recognize that the description of a prediction does not differ greatly from that of an hypothesis, and your observation is quite correct. There is, however, a fundamental difference between them. An hypothesis is generally based on very limited experience with a particular problem or situation; sometimes it is based on intuition. In other words, an hypothesis is an investigator's belief about what the answer to a question actually is. Although a great amount of evidence is not needed to support the investigator's personal belief, enough is needed to suggest further investigations and guidance for those investigations. Sometimes the information an experiment delivers in its early stages is not definitive enough to allow only one hypothesis to be stated; rather, the data suggest several hypotheses that can be tested. An hy-

pothesis, then, could be described as a tentative assumption stated to enable the investigator to test its validity. Stating hypotheses that are believed to be false is often useful in an investigation because proof of such falsity narrows the number of possible explanations for a problem.

Predictions, however, do not have the tentative, work-guiding nature of hypotheses; they are not stated for the primary purpose of being tested—hypotheses are. A prediction is made on the basis of ideas that have been tested over and over again. For example, weather predictions such as you have done are based on data from such variables as temperature, humidity, time of year, and wind velocity. The effect on weather of each of these factors has been thoroughly investigated, and while that investigation was progressing, many hypotheses about the effects of these factors were tested. Now, however, meteorologists understand the effect of the various factors upon the weather and need not hypothesize about them further. Rather, the effect of such thoroughly tested factors can now be used to predict the weather just as you did. An hypothesis, then, is an assumption that allows the validity of a generalization or model to be tested; a prediction is the use of tested generalizations or models in order to forecast the future behavior of an individual, the results of an experiment, or the outcome of an event. Obviously, predictions involve the use of thought reversals and, therefore, require concrete operational thought.

What is the value to students of learning how to predict? Why is experience in this area an essential part of their experience in science? Perhaps the most basic reason for including experience in predicting in science education is that prediction is a definite, integral part of the structure of the scientific discipline. In many ways, prediction is at the apex of the scientific processes; all that is done in a scientific investigation leads the experimenter toward the goal of stating the results of a similar situation in the future. Since we feel that the elementary school science curriculum must be recognizable as science by a scientist (the integrity of the discipline must be maintained), prediction must be a part of the curriculum.

What is necessary in order to make a prediction? Data must be gathered, classified, compared, analyzed, and evaluated. These data must then be synthesized into a general statement about the situation under consideration, which allows the investigator to reason from the general to the particular about what will happen in a future situation. This, of course, is deduction. In other words, making a prediction demands the use of the learner's rational powers. The experience of predicting, therefore, assists learners in the development of their rational powers and leads them to construct a more complete picture of the structure of the discipline of science than they would if predictions were not included. Prediction is, in a sense, a practical application of one's understanding of nature.

Now to the question of, "Where does predicting fit into the learning cycle?" As you can see, predictions are based on ideas that have been formulated primarily through interpretation, experimentation, and model building. The natural place of predicting, therefore, is in "Expanding the Idea." Then why, you might ask, is predicting listed in the "Exploration" triangle (Figure 9-2) as well as in "Expansion of the Idea"? No idea stands alone. Each idea is linked to others in the structure of science. Even when someone is expanding one idea, that person is gathering data with which to construct or invent a related idea. Thus, prediction fits meaningfully into both triangles.

In illustrating the process of prediction in the learning cycle, we will not develop an entire learning cycle. Rather, we include an activity that can be carried out with the Expanding-the-Idea phase of the learning cycle illustrating "model building." This activity is intended to be the last one the student experiences in the learning cycle.

Expanding the idea
Your teacher will give you a collection of various kinds of material. Write down the name of each type of material. Each material is to be placed between the wires of your circuit tester. *Before you do that* predict whether or not the bulb will light. Test the material with your circuit tester. Consider only the materials you were wrong about. Write down why you thought the bulb would light using the material.

FITTING THE ESSENTIAL SCIENCE EXPERIENCES INTO SCHOOL

Preoperational children can make observations and report them, but teachers must remember that these observations will be reported from a very egocentric frame of reference. These children should not be expected to be very objective. They will oftentimes ignore sound reasons obvious to an adult and use such transductive reasoning as "because I like it" or "don't like it" to group objects or make decisions about which plant is greener. Teachers must not come to believe that such children are slow learners or are doing unsatisfactory work in school. These children are just being preoperational. While they can engage in making relative measurements such as bigger than, smaller than, fatter than, longer than, and so on, they cannot use a ruler meaningfully because they do not have the ability to conserve length. But they can do elementary experiments. A child found an odd looking object among bean seeds and asked: "Is this a seed?" The teacher asked the child what happened to the other seeds they had planted. The child responded that those seeds had "made plants." The teacher led the child to plant the object and when it did not grow the teacher asked the child what she thought. The little girl said, "I guess is wasn't a seed." This is an experiment that late preoperational children can do.

Doing experiments that require *any* form of record keeping, interpreting data, building simple models, and making even elementary predictions require that students be capable of making thought reversals. This ability leads them to begin to conserve and give up transductive reasoning. In other words, for children to profit from essential science experiences other than observing, *very simple* experimenting, and interpreting—as we discussed earlier—they must have entered the concrete operational stage. Of extreme importance, however, is providing preoperational children with much experience observing and with other experiences from which they can profit. If preoperational children do not have these experiences with materials, their entry into the concrete operational stage will probably be delayed. Research showing this will be discussed in chapter 10.

The ability to reverse thinking processes, develop conservation reasoning, and give up transductive reasoning does not appear overnight. The degree of difficulty of the essential experiences from which children can profit becomes greater as the children move more deeply into the stage of concrete reasoning. Third graders still do not think like sixth graders!

References

Educational Policies Commission. *The Central Purpose of American Education.* Washington, D.C.: National Education Association, 1961.

Holton, Gerald, and H. Duane Roller. *Foundations of Modern Physical Science.* Reading, MA: Addison-Wesley Publishing Co., 1958.

Kelly, Harry C. *A Textbook of Electricity and Magnetism.* New York: John Wiley and Sons, 1941.

Renner, John W., Don G. Stafford, and Vivian Jensen Coulter. *ACTION.* Encino, CA: Glencoe Publishing Co., 1977.

Roller, Duane. "Has Science a Climate?" *Sunday Oklahoman* (Oklahoma City, Oklahoma), February 22, 1970.

CHAPTER TEN

RESEARCH
WITH THE
LEARNING CYCLE

W e have already seen that Jean Piaget established the first two phases of the learning cycle when he discussed the activities students must undertake during assimilation and accommodation, although Piaget did not, to our knowledge, use the name learning cycle for this teaching and curriculum construction procedure. Robert Karplus deserves credit for adding the learning cycle's third phase, which he originally called *discovery*, and later referred to as *concept implementation*. After using the learning cycle with students from kindergarten through graduate school, we have concluded that in the third phase, the concept is expanded from the immediate investigation to other areas of knowledge. Hence, we named this phase expansion of the idea; when preparing materials for elementary school students we have called the phase expanding the idea. The credit for the original formulation of the learning cycle concept, however, belongs to Piaget and Karplus.

Karplus implemented the learning cycle by organizing and directing the Science Curriculum Improvement Study (SCIS), which produced a kindergarten through sixth grade elementary school science curriculum. The SCIS used the learning cycle as both an organizational principle and a teaching procedure, and much research has been done with the SCIS materials. In this portion of the chapter we will report on the research done at the University of Oklahoma with which we have been associated. Because the SCIS materials depend on the learning-cycle

TABLE 10-1

COMPARISON OF EXPERIMENTAL AND CONTROL GROUPS ON THE DATA PROVIDED BY THE TEACHER

Data	Experimental Group	Control Group	Data	Experimental Group	Control Group
Average IQ, Otis-Lenon	103.2	106.2	Number of children in sample with readiness scores between 64 and 63 (average)	12	14
(Above average group) Number of children in sample with IQ above 111	17	21	Number of children in sample with readiness scores between 45 and 63 (average)	23	19
(Average group) Number of children in sample with IQ between 88 and 111	33	34	Number of children in sample with readiness scores between 24 and 44 (low normal)	12	5
(Below average group) Number of children in sample with IQ below 88	10	5	Number of children in sample with readiness scores below 24 (low)	1	1
Number of children who attended kindergarten	42	48	Average score on readiness test	59.23	65.60
Number of children in sample with metropolitan readiness scores above 76 (superior)	12	21	Average chronological age in months at time of first test	76.83	77.00

model, the research reported here is an evaluation of that model.

There is one difference between the learning cycles you experienced in chapters 4 through 7 and the learning cycles prepared by the SCIS. In the learning cycles you experienced, all the phases are put together in one whole and the teacher determines what a lesson should include. But the SCIS materials are organized into chapters, and each chapter could be an exploration, an invention, or a discovery lesson. This organizing concept is important only because it could make each learning cycle cover a longer period of time than that necessary for the learning cycles you have experienced. The research results that follow, however, should be thought of as the result of elementary school student experience with the learning cycle.

THE LEARNING CYCLE AND INTELLECTUAL DEVELOPMENT IN ELEMENTARY SCHOOL SCIENCE

You were introduced to the Piaget-designed conservation tasks in chapter 1. The results of administering these tasks to children assess the movement of thought from the preoperational stage to the concrete operational stage. The first of the research projects (Renner et al., 1973, pp. 300–309) conducted during the first semester of the 1968–69 school year used the conservation tasks as evaluative criteria with a sample of 120 first graders, 60 in the experimental group and 60 in a control group. The experimental and control groups were exposed to the same educational program in everything *except* science. The experimental group was given the SCIS first-grade program consisting of the units *Material Objects* and *Organisms*; the control sample used a science textbook.

Each of the 120 first graders was given a pretest using the six conservation tasks—num-

ber, liquid amount, solid amount, length, weight, and area—during the first week of school. A posttest of the same tasks was given five months later. The same experienced evaluator conducted all the testing.

The experimental and control groups were compared on the basis of IQ, kindergarten attendance, age, and readiness scores. The comparison of the two groups is summarized in Table 10-1. The data show that the control group occupies a favorable position on every basis of comparison. Based on these data, one would predict that the control group would outperform the experimental group, but the data collected from the pre- and posttests show that this is not the case. In fact, the experimental group outperformed the control group in total gains in conservation by 140 to 92. The difference is statistically significant at the .01 level of confidence.

Table 10-2 shows the numerical increase in conservations in each of the six test areas. The experimental group outgained the control group on every conservation task. On two tasks (number and length) the difference in the gain was statistically significant at the .01 level of confi-

TABLE 10-2

PRETEST AND POSTTEST TOTALS FOR EXPERIMENTAL AND CONTROL GROUPS

Conservation Area	Experimental Group		Control Group	
	Pretest	Posttest	Pretest	Posttest
Number	13	50	15	37
Weight	3	13	1	8
Liquid amount	5	25	5	19
Solid amount	5	26	5	22
Length	3	30	0	11
Area	6	31	13	34
Total conservations	35	175	39	131
Total gain in conservations		140		92

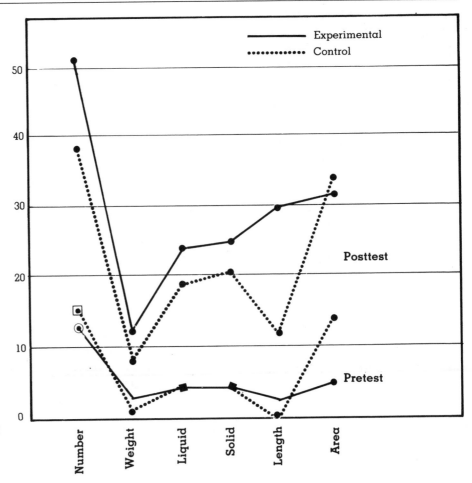

Figure 10-1 Total Conservations for Each Sample by Task.

dence. Figure 10-1 compares the Control and Experimental groups on their ability to conserve before (pretest) and after (posttest).

The data support the conclusion that the rate of attainment of conservation reasoning is significantly enhanced by the experiences made possible by the first-grade program of the SCIS. Since the SCIS curriculum and teaching plans are based on the learning cycle, we can extend the foregoing conclusion to say that the use of the learning cycle with the SCIS materials enhances intellectual development.

THE LEARNING CYCLE AND THE DEVELOPMENT OF THE ABILITY TO USE THE PROCESSES OF SCIENCE

In this research, a comparative study was made of the performance of SCIS students and non-SCIS-oriented students on a series of process-centered tasks. Two groups of elementary students were identified for testing in making the comparison. One group—the non-SCIS group—

had only a textbook exposure to science; in this research, the conventional textbook-centered curriculum was considered to be nonprocess oriented. Students in both groups had been in their respective science programs for nearly five years at the time the comparison was made.

The validity of the study was dependent on how adequately the investigators controlled the several variables other than the science programs that might contribute to the development of science processes. Obviously, one method for controlling these factors was to match the subjects on as many factors as possible; a matched pair would be comparable on all factors, except science instruction, that could promote the development of science processes. Individuals from the two groups were matched on the four factors of intellectual level, chronological age, sex, and socioeconomic level. Through this process, thirty matched pairs were ultimately selected for the comparison. Table 10-3 illustrates comparative data for the two groups.

In addition to the foregoing factors used in establishing individual comparability, the following factors were also used to strengthen the comparability of the two groups.

1. *Readiness for Learning.* The subjects in the study had scores, recorded from readi-

ness tests they had taken upon entering their first year of school, which indicated that there was no statistical difference between the two groups of subjects in their readiness to learn.
2. *School Organization.* The subjects in both groups had been exposed to the same school-organizational structure during their school years prior to the study. All the students in the study had been in self-contained classrooms until grade five, when they encountered departmentalized approaches.
3. *Curricular Organization.* The curriculum programs in mathematics, social studies, and language arts were essentially the same for all students in the study. Only the science approaches seemed to be different for the two groups.

Critical consideration of the preceding factors indicated that none presented any overt advantage to the students in developing the ability to use the processes of science. We reasoned, then, that if any difference was found to exist between the groups in process abilities, it could be attributed to the type of science curriculum used. The investigators concluded, therefore, that the students, as selected from the two groups,

TABLE 10-3

COMPARATIVE DATA FOR THE TWO GROUPS

Comparative Factor	SCIS Group	Textbook Group
Mean IQ	119	119
IQ range	86–134	80–140
Mean chronological age	128 mos.	129 mos.
Sex	18 female and 12 male pairs	
Socioeconomic level	28 middle-class and 2 upper-class pairs	

were comparable on all but one of the controllable factors that might influence the development of process abilities. That one factor, the difference in how they learned science, is what this research study tested.

The comparison of the two groups, which in actuality was a comparison of the SCIS and the textbook approaches, was made by comparing student performance on process-oriented tasks. The children from the two groups were compared according to their ability to use the science processes of observation, classification, measurement, experimentation, interpretation, and prediction. These processes represent five of the six essential experiences in science. At the time the research was done, no commercial test instrument was available to evaluate these processes. Consequently, an instrument had to be constructed. The process instrument prepared consisted of seventeen tasks that required the student to function in each of the previously identified process areas. Each task was completely designed around a performance problem, and the child was provided with the necessary materials to successfully attack the problem. While attempting to solve the problem, the child was involved in physical and mental manipulation of the materials while also using specific science processes.

The instrument had a reliability coefficient of 0.64 for internal consistency and was judged to be highly valid (Weber and Renner, 1972). Its validity was judged by a panel of nationally recognized science educators. The statistical significance of their judgments ranged from 0.0082 through 0.000013. The discriminatory power of the test was 0.43.

The instrument was individually administered to each of the sixty students in the study. In each of the seventeen tasks, a student had two opportunities to score one point: an acceptable performance earned one point, and an unacceptable performance earned no points. Consequently, a student could score thirty-four points by successfully performing all thirty-four tasks

on the seventeen items. The following sample items are representative of the total instrument and illustrate the scoring procedure.

Process task—Observation
Materials: One piece of clear, transparent plastic sheeting that measures 8×5 inches.
Administrative Procedure: Hand the plastic sheet to the child.
Instructions to the child: Describe this object.

Scoring
1. Give one point if four properties are given.
2. Give one point if eight or more properties are given.

Process task—Prediction
Materials: A rubber band, a small piece of stiff wire, a support stand, a ruler, graph paper, string, and four hardware washers.
Administrative Procedure: Give the materials to the child.
Instructions to the child: You have four hardware washers here.
How far would eight of these washers stretch this rubber band?

Scoring:
1. Give one point if the child determines how far the four washers will stretch the rubber band.
2. Give one point if, based on his measured data, the child gives an answer for the stretch that would be caused by eight washers.

The raw scores for all students in each group were totaled and used in the statistical treatment of the comparisons. The scores from the SCIS group were statistically compared to those from the textbook group in each of the selected process areas. Thus, the two groups were compared on the ability to use those science processes previously mentioned. The comparisons and the resulting significance for each process are found in Table 10-4.

As the data in Table 10-4 demonstrate, the probability that the differences found between the SCIS and non-SCIS groups are chance is nonexistent. All the differences in performance using the science processes favor the SCIS group. Our interpretation of these data led us to the conclusion that the SCIS program is superior to

TABLE 10-4

RAW SCORES AND STATISTICAL SIGNIFICANCE

Process	SCIS Score	Textbook Score	Statistical Probability	Significant
Observing	114	63	0.000072	Yes
Classifying	103	71	0.0007	Yes
Measuring	104	52	0.0007	Yes
Experimenting	124	53	0.000013	Yes
Interpreting	113	97	<0.05	Yes
Predicting	131	79	0.0002	Yes
Total	689	415	0.000002	Yes

a textbook program in aiding children to develop the ability to use processes of science. Children who have studied the SCIS curriculum will be better observers, classifiers, measurers, experimenters, interpreters, and predictors than will children who have studied science through a textbook approach. Again, the conclusion from this research can be extended: the learning cycle curriculum and teaching procedures are superior to those used with a conventional textbook.

THE INFLUENCE OF THE SCIS PROGRAM ON STUDENT ACHIEVEMENT IN MATHEMATICS, READING, AND SOCIAL STUDIES

The student populations used in this research were the same ones used in the science process research reported earlier. Matched pairs of students were not used in this study; all students were in their fifth year at the two participating schools. Forty-six students from the school using the SCIS materials and 69 students who had studied science only from a textbook comprised the two populations. As was said earlier, the curricula for mathematics, social studies, and language arts were essentially identical for all

115 fifth-grade students. Only the science programs were different, and the fact that they were markedly different enabled us to study the impact of the learning-cycle centered program on student achievement in the three other curricular areas. The decision was made to focus the research on reading rather than on the entire language arts area. The research investigated the degree to which a learning-cycle-centered science curriculum—SCIS—contributes to learning in the subject areas of reading, mathematics, and social studies.

The *Stanford Achievement Series*, 1964 edition, was administered to each group of pupils during the month of September, the first month of entry into the fifth grade. Scores in mathematics concepts, skills, and applications, and word meaning and paragraph meaning were obtained by utilizing Form W of the Intermediate I battery. Data concerning achievement in social studies skills and content were obtained by administering Form W of the Intermediate II battery. According to information available from previous test scores, teachers, and principals, all the students included in the study were progressing normally in their school work. None had exhibited any evidence of unusual or abnormal discipline, social, or emotional problems.

Using the *Stanford Achievement Series*, raw

scores of the two sample groups were analyzed. The statistical analysis consisted of testing for significant differences in academic achievement among the subjects under investigation.

This study revealed the following major findings:

1. No difference was found in the understanding of mathematics concepts between two student groups.
2. There was no difference in mathematics skills between the two groups.
3. There was a difference in mathematics applications between the two groups, which favored the SCIS group and is evidence that children learn to manipulate data in problem-solving situations through the data handling experiences required in the learning cycle.
4. No significant difference between the two groups in social studies content was evident.
5. There was a significant difference in the curricular area of social studies skills, which favored the SCIS group. This finding is analogous to that of mathematics applications. Social studies skills involve interpretation of graphs and tables, reading maps, and interpreting posters; in other words, these skills essentially require the ability to assimilate data for problem-solving.
6. There was no significant difference between the two groups in the area of word meaning.
7. The available evidence supports the inference that the SCIS group excelled the other groups in determining paragraph meaning.

As a result of the statistical treatment in all seven academic areas investigated, the general hypothesis—no difference between the groups—was rejected. The evidence very strongly suggested a difference between the two groups in the areas of mathematics applications, social studies skills, and paragraph meaning. On the other hand, no significant difference was determined in mathematics skills and concepts, social studies content, and word meaning.

Of particular interest is the observation that, in academic areas where differences were determined—mathematics applications, social studies skills, and paragraph meaning—there is a common thread. In the case of mathematics applications, performance on the instrument was determined by the ability to apply mathematical knowledge and to think mathematically in practical situations. The author-stated goal of the social studies skills test is to test "knowledge in action." The paragraph meaning test purported to provide a measure of the pupil's ability to comprehend connected discourse involving varying levels of comprehension. The common thread, then, is that each area requires a level of thought transcending mere recognition and recall. Apparently, children who have had an SCIS—and thereby learning cycle—experience tend to utilize the higher powers of thinking more effectively than those who have not had such an experience.

The finding of no significant difference in social studies content, mathematics skills, and word meaning was not particularly astonishing. Again, there is a common thread in the fact that each area emphasized proficiency in skill development. Mathematics stresses computational skills; word meaning considers factual knowledge of synonyms and simple definitions; basically, social studies content is factually oriented. In this regard, it is interesting to note that children in an inquiry program perform *at least as well as* children in a completely traditional setting. In fact, a defensible conjecture would be that the traditional group would perform better, since the tests tend to reflect the outcomes expected in noninnovative programs. Obviously, quite the opposite is evident; the children in an experimental science program performed adequately in all areas and exceeded the traditional groups in three. In the data that have just been presented there is a very important thread: the experimental group scored significantly better on paragraph *meaning*, mathematics *application* and social studies skills, i.e., in using such skills as map and globe skills to *solve problems*. If you carefully consider what is being said, the children in the experimental group excelled the control group in one ability only—the ability to inquire and to use the thinking needed to accomplish it. That is what the SCIS program and the learning cycle have done for the children in the experimental group.

We believe that these conclusions should be made known to every teacher, school administrator, and anyone else who has contact with and responsibility for the elementary schools in this country. These data provide an unequivocal answer to the school people who say, "We just don't have time or cannot afford to invest in the resources to teach science." The truth of the matter is that any school that teaches science using the learning cycle model is teaching much more than good science; it is also teaching reading, mathematics, and social science. In fact, schools cannot afford *not* to teach science using this model.

A LEARNING-CYCLE BASED PROGRAM IN SCIENCE AND READING READINESS

As we worked with the SCIS first-grade physical science program called *Material Objects*, we were struck by its similarity to a reading readiness program. We were also reminded of a statement made by Professor Millie Almy of Teachers College, Columbia University, as she studied children's conservation reasoning (Almy, 1966, pp. 139–140): ". . . the finding in our studies of a rather substantial correlation between performance in conservation tasks and progress in beginning reading suggests that, to some extent, similar abilities are involved. A program designed to nuture logical thinking should contrib-

ute positively to readiness for reading." The word that interested us most was "readiness." Earlier in this chapter we demonstrated that the SCIS first-grade program leads children to an increased ability in conservation reasoning. According to Almy's inference then, children who have had experience with the SCIS learning-cycle-based program should be more ready to read than those who have not. We then asked this question: Is the SCIS first-grade program an effective reading-readiness program?

In order to answer this question, we used control and experimental groups from selected first-grade rooms in one school system. Because of the way the schools in that system are constituted, there was no reason for us to believe that one room of children was any different from any other room. The students in the control group used a commercial reading readiness program and no science program; at the same time, the experimental group used the *Material Objects* unit during several periods a day and no reading readiness program. Both groups were given the Metropolitan Reading Readiness Test at the beginning of the school year as a pretest, and six weeks later as a posttest. This posttest coincided with the completion of the *Material Objects* unit by the experimental group. All teachers involved in the research had previously attended a summer workshop in elementary school science emphasizing the SCIS approach and had taught the *Material Objects* unit for one year.

Table 10-5 shows the pre- and post- scores for both groups and the gains in each score. The experimental group out-gained the control group in total score and in all subtest areas except copying. These gains are also shown graphically in Figures 10-2 and 10-3.

In light of the greater gains by the experimental group in five of the six subtest areas, one is almost compelled to ask how a science program can outperform a reading readiness program when compared on reading readiness standards. The answer lies in the examination of

TABLE 10-5

METROPOLITAN READING READINESS SCORES (PRE-, POST-, GAIN)

	Control			Experimental		
	Pre	Post	Gain	Pre	Post	Gain
Word meaning	11.09	11.53	0.44	9.54	11.16	1.62
Listening	11.56	12.90	1.34	11.45	12.89	1.44
Matching	10.56	12.28	1.72	9.67	12.48	2.81
Alphabet	11.56	15.50	3.94	10.86	15.16	4.30
Numbers	15.96	19.68	3.72	15.27	20.21	4.94
Copying	10.68	12.12	1.44	10.56	11.86	1.30
Total	71.41	84.01	12.60	67.35	83.76	16.41

Figure 10-2
Average Gain in
Metropolitan Subtest
Scores.

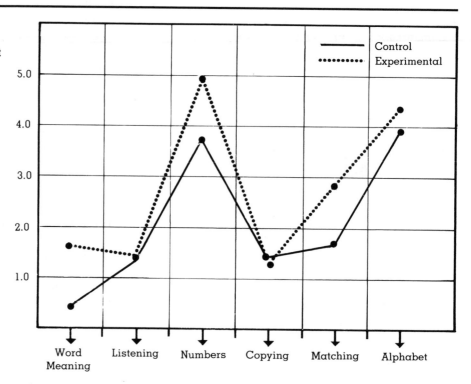

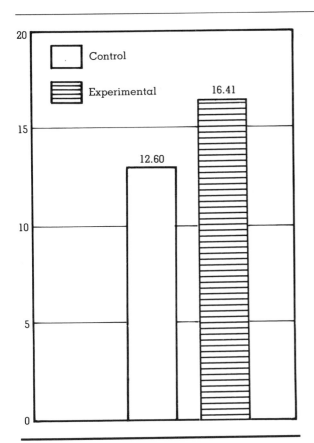

Figure 10-3 Average Gain in Total Metropolitan Score

two factors: the nature of the *Material Objects* unit and the purpose of education.

The experimental group outperformed the control group in the areas of word meaning, listening, matching, and numbers for the simplest of reasons: the members of the experimental group, through the use of the *Material Objects* unit, were able to have concrete experiences in each of these areas to the limit of their interest and ability. The children learned to match because they were allowed to match the properties of objects with the objects themselves, which they could grasp, manipulate, and even alter. They developed skills in listening because they

listened not so much to the teacher as to their peers describing, classifying, and discussing experiences. They learned word meaning when they or the teacher invented words to describe experiences with objects. They gained number skills as they ordered objects or groups of objects serially. In other words, they engaged in learning through the learning cycle. They were outgained on the copying subtest because they didn't do much copying; instead, they were encouraged and allowed to think. At present, we have no explanation for the superior gains of the experimental group on the alphabet subtest, although the data show superior gains.

The second factor, the purpose of education, was covered in chapter 9. The purpose that runs through and strengthens all other educational purposes—the common thread of education—is the development of the ability to think.

If you accept this statement as we do, its implication is undeniable: in order to learn to read, a child must first develop some ability in the reasoning process. A person need not be able to read in order to reason, but is the converse true, that a person must be able to reason in order to read? We feel that this is indeed true, and our research supports our conviction. Almy (1966) found that progress in beginning reading is related to performance on the conservation tasks. We demonstrated earlier that the use of the *Materials Objects* unit would accelerate the attainment of conservation abilities. The research described here shows that the classroom use of *Material Objects* can develop reading readiness. The conclusion to this investigation seems apparent: to best teach reading, first teach thinking as represented by conservation reasoning. The combination of the work reported here with Almy's findings strongly implies that conservation abilities are good indicators of reading readiness.

The research data and interpretations presented above demonstrate that the learning-cycle-based SCIS program leads children to develop an understanding of the nature of science and to begin achieving the central purpose of education. The data also suggest that other school subjects profit from students' experience with the learning cycle and with the materials used in this curriculum development and teaching procedure. The argument has been advanced that it is the experience with the materials used with the learning cycle, and not the learning cycle itself, which produces the research results just reviewed. This argument is unimportant to us because the learning cycle cannot be used *without* materials. Furthermore, we hypothesize that if students were given the materials and told to learn from them they would explore the materials, invent explanations, and then see where else those explanations are useful and interesting. We believe that the learning cycle is the *natural* way to learn.

RESEARCH ON THE LEARNING CYCLE WITH THE ANTHROPOLOGICAL MODEL

Are classrooms accomplishing what in the previous nine chapters we've said could be accomplished? We had the opportunity to "test" the learning cycle in the classroom in the following study using the anthropological-research model.[1]

Anthropological research—also known as ethnographic or qualitative research—is an investigative process produced to gain a picture of the "way of life" of a group of people (Rist, 1979). The groups of people in this research are elementary school science teachers and their students. "Way of life" refers to the science classroom environment. In anthropological research field work, two data-gathering strategies are participant observation and interviews with individuals in the environment. These strategies allow the researcher to obtain firsthand knowledge about the groups of people in question. Anthropological research allows the researcher to "get close to the data," thereby developing the analytical, conceptual, and categorical components of explanation directly from the data (Filstead, 1970, p. 6). The following research is well suited to an anthropological model because it involves both observation of teachers' classrooms and analysis of individual interviews conducted with students.

During the summer preceding the fall in which the research reported here was done, twenty-six elementary school science teachers attended a National Science Foundation sponsored workshop. During the workshop they experienced the structure and use of the learning-cycle-teaching and curriculum-construction procedures that, as we have shown, were developed from Piaget's functioning model. In the research, sixteen teachers from the group of twenty-six constituted the experimental group. The experimental group was asked to list names of teachers from their school that 1) had had approximately the same amount of teaching experience, 2) taught the same grade level, and 3) taught science using the traditional exposition procedure. From these lists, teachers were randomly selected by grade to constitute the control group. Random samples of students from both the experimental and control teachers' classrooms—kindergarten, first, second, third, and fifth grades—were interviewed from the fifth through the eleventh week of the school year.

The students were interviewed using the Piagetian conservation reasoning tasks of weight, length, and liquid amount that were referred to earlier. In interviews, students were also asked to describe nine objects, which enabled researchers to collect data about the students' 1) usage of property words, 2) organization of information or knowledge, and 3) willingness to talk. The nine objects included a magnet, a marble, a seashell, a wooden square, a wooden triangle, a plastic bar, a lead bar, a steel bar, and a cotton ball. All interviews were tape-recorded.

---

[1] We are grateful to Dr. Suzanne Bryan Methven for her assistance in doing and reporting this research.

Classroom observations of the teachers in the experimental and control groups were made to determine the teaching procedures they used with their students. The criteria used to judge the teaching procedures included 1) classroom activities, 2) the teacher's function in the classroom during these activities, 3) the student's function during these activities, and 4) the sequence of activities throughout a science unit (Grzybowski, 1985).

The students in the experimental classroom were given the opportunity to explore materials, to observe and record related data, to interact with their peers and the teacher while gathering information from the materials, and to use the concept developed from the materials in additional settings and with additional materials. The students in the control classrooms were presented with an oral explanation of the concept prior to any actual experience with the materials. At the beginning of a class, the control students were informed about what they were supposed to see. During the laboratory activity itself, the control students had little or no opportunity to interact with their peers, to interact with their teacher, or to use the concept in additional settings and with additional materials.

Interview data collected from experimental and control students demonstrate noticeable differences. When a control kindergarten student was shown a magnet and fifteen nuts and asked to describe these objects to the researcher, he responded as follows: "They are screwdrivers, and they're all little." When given identical instructions with the same objects, an experimental kindergarten student responded: "One of these small ones are different from all of these other small ones and is more rounder. The big, black magnet is bigger than the others, and it's also a different color." When shown the same magnet and nuts, an experimental first-grade student responded: "They're metal, they're round, they got sharp ends," while a control first-grade student simply said: "I forgot." When shown a marble and asked to describe it, a control first-grade student responded: "It's round and has colors in it." An experimental first-grade student responded as follows when given identical instructions with the marble: "It's smooth, and it's kind of little. It's yellow. It has a little bit of dirt on it. It has a tiny hole in it." A lead bar, a steel bar, and a green plastic bar were all shown to another first-grade control student and another first-grade experimental student. Each student was asked to describe them to the researcher. The control student responded: "You can play with them, you can spin around on them." The experimental student responded: "They're silver, one is green, they're straight, they got hard ends, they can't bend." When shown a wooden square and asked to describe it, a second-grade control student responded: "It's a square. You can make walls and floors out of squares. Paper is square. Doors are square." While a second grade experimental student responded: "It's flat, square, and has sharp edges. When you hold it like this, it's a diamond shape. It's smooth, and it's made out of wood."

The responses of the experimental students demonstrate that they are much better able to use property words than the control group students. When shown a marble and asked to pick it up, feel it with their fingers, look at it closely, and describe it to the researcher, the control group usually responded: "It could be used to play with or in games," while the experimental group noted: "It is round, yellow, and would roll." The experimental group was also better able to focus on the object in question and talked only about that object, while the control group often brought in additional irrelevant information. When describing the seashell, for example, a control child noted that "it was pretty, could be used in decorations, and could be hung from a net thing," information we consider irrelevant in describing the seashell. The experimental group was also much more willing to talk to the researcher, perhaps because of the increased amount of social interaction they had in the experimental classroom both with peers and with their teacher. Several control students gave no answer to the majority of the questions, but such an incidence of nonresponse was not found in the experimental group.

These differences are further exemplified in the following responses dealing with the description of a cotton ball from children in kindergarten through fifth grade. A kindergarten experimental child responded: "It's white, and it looks like a snake. It is soft," while a kindergarten control child said: "It's soft. You can put it in your ears when your ears hurt. It can tear apart." One first-grade experimental child responded: "It's soft. It's white. It has a little bit of fuzz on the end. You can roll it into a ball," while a first-grade control child said: "It's squishy. It's bendy. It's soft." A second-grade experimental child said: "It's soft, it's white, you can bend it, you can stretch it, you can break it," while a

second-grade control child responded: You can put medicine on it and put it on your leg." A second-grade experimental child responded: "It's real soft. It kind of pulls apart. Looks like people have been pulling it a lot." Another second-grade control child said: "You can take it apart easy. You can wad it up, and you can also—it's soft. You can make a neat design with it. It keeps blood from coming out of you." A third-grade experimental child responded: "It's furry, white, bendable, breakable, and has different colored spots on it." A third-grade control child said: "It's white. It's soft. You can bend it. You can squeeze it." A fifth-grade experimental child responded: "It has dirt spots on it. It's soft. It has things sticking out. It twists and bends in different directions. It comes apart. It has a hole in the middle." A fifth-grade control child responded: "It is long. It's soft and cushiony."

Although the children from the two groups

TABLE 10-6

CONSERVATION ABILITIES OF EXPERIMENTAL AND CONTROL GROUPS

Experimental

Grade	Sample Size	Conservation of		
		Length	Weight	Liquid Amount
Kindergarten	10	1	4	3
First	39	20	22	18
Second	40	32	32	21
Third	39	36	31	27
Fifth	10	9	9	8

Control

Grade	Sample Size	Conservation of		
		Length	Weight	Liquid Amount
Kindergarten	10	4	5	5
First	19	10	10	8
Second	30	25	21	16
Third	30	27	24	20
Fifth	10	10	9	9

seem quite different in their responses, the data in Table 10-6 indicate that the intellectual development levels of both the experimental and control students were approximately the same.

These data demonstrate that the experimental students are better able to organize their knowledge, express themselves, and use the property concept. These research results lend strong support to the inquiry classroom as opposed to the exposition classroom. Since the central purpose of American education is to develop in our youth the ability to think, some of these data you just read indicate that drastic changes must take place in numerous elementary school classrooms if this goal is to be achieved. Those data also show, however, that changes can take place.

References

Almy, Millie. *Young Children's Thinking.* Teachers College, Columbia University; Teachers College Press, 1966.

Filstead, W. J. *Qualitative Methodology.* Chicago: Markam, 1970.

Grzybowski, E. B. Research in progress.

Renner, John W., Don G. Stafford, William J. Coffia, Donald H. Kellogg and M. C. Weber. "An Evaluation of the Science Curriculum Improvement Study." *School Science and Mathematics,* April, 1973, 291–318.

Rist, R. C. On the Means of Knowing: Qualitative research in Education. *New York University Education Quarterly.* 10 (4): 17–21,179.

Weber, M. C., and John W. Renner. "How Effective is the SCIS Program?" *School Science and Mathematics.* 72(8): 729–734, November, 1972.

APPENDIX

APPENDIX

PROTOCOLS FOR FORMAL OPERATIONAL TASKS

PREFACE

The interviewing protocols included here measure the degree of concrete or formal thought a student has attained. These protocols have been taken from the work of Jean Piaget and Barbel Inhelder. The adaptations of the tasks to apparatus and indigenous conditions have been made by the authors and other persons associated with the Science Education Center, University of Oklahoma. Any items in the protocols which are at variance with formal thought should not be accredited to Piaget and Inhelder but to those interpreting how their tasks should be used in interviewing situations.

CONTENTS

Conservation of Volume   204

Combinatorial Reasoning   205

Correlational Reasoning   207

Exclusion of Irrelevant Variables   208

Probabilistic Reasoning   209

Proportional Reasoning   210

Separation of Variables   211

We are grateful to Ms. Jean McGregor Cate for her assistance in preparing these protocols.

Conservation of Volume[1]

Materials:

Two test tubes and materials that will hold them vertically, two metal cylinders, *exactly* the same size but different in weight, that will fit into the test tubes, strings to lower the metal cylinders into the test tubes, water, medicine dropper.

The materials are placed in front of the student. The interviewer should explain the task as follows:

"Here are two test tubes that are exactly the same, and the level of water in them should be the same. Make sure you are satisfied that the water levels are the same in both tubes. If you need to change one of the levels you may use the medicine dropper to make them equal.

"Here are two metal cylinders that are the same size. You will notice one is just as big around and just as tall as the other." (Demonstrate this.) "Hold one of them in each hand and tell me how they are obviously different." (The answer should be weight.)

"We are going to put one cylinder in each tube. Each cylinder will sink all the way to the bottom of its tube. What will happen to the level of the liquid when the cylinders are submerged in the tubes?" (The answer should be that the water levels will rise.)

1. The interviewer then asks: "Will the heavier cylinder raise the water level more? Will the lighter cylinder raise the water level more? Or will both cylinders raise the water levels the same?"
2. The interviewer asks why the subject believes as he/she does, and has the subject explain the answer he/she chose.
3. The interviewer lowers the lighter cylinder into a tube.
4. The interviewer then has the subject lower the heavier cylinder into a tube and observe the water level.
5. If the subject predicts incorrectly (or correctly giving the wrong reason) the interviewer asks what he/she thinks caused the levels to come out equally.

Scoring:

IIA The subject makes an incorrect prediction or predicts correctly and gives the incorrect reason; can't explain the results when he/she sees the experiment performed.

IIB The subject makes an incorrect prediction or predicts correctly and gives the incorrect reason (as in IIA); however, when the subject sees the experiment performed he/she realizes the correct explanation.

IIIA The subject predicts correctly and gives a correct reason.

IIIB This task does not require IIIB level of thought.

---

[1] *Piaget's Theories: Conservation*, John Davidson Films, San Francisco; and Jean Piaget, Barbel Inhelder and Alina Szeminska, *The Child's Concept of Geometry* (New York: Harper and Row, 1960), chapter 14.

Combinatorial Reasoning

1. THE ELECTRONIC TASK (ET)

Materials: see Deluca.

The interviewer puts the materials in front of the student and says, "Here is a metal box with four switches, a push button, and a light bulb. By placing one or more switches in the 'on' position you can turn the light on if you push the button. I would like you to work with the switches and find as many different ways as you can to turn the light on. Do you have any questions?" After the student has responded the interviewer says, "You may begin." During the experiment, the interviewer uses questions such as the following:

1. "Have you tried all possible ways to turn the light on?"
2. If the answer is no, the interviewer says, "Please continue to find all possible ways to turn the light on."
3. If the subject stops again, the interviewer goes back to the first question.
4. If the answer to the first question is yes, the interviewer says, "all right" or "good."
5. The interviewer then says, "Find out the function of switches 1 and 3 in turning on the light."
6. The interviewer then asks the student to identify the function of switches 2 and 4 by saying, "Find out the function of switches 2 and 4 in turning on the light." The subject's reasoning pattern and his proof in identifying the function of the switches are important. The subject may be questioned to insure that he/she demonstrates some form of proof for the role of these switches.

Scoring:

IIA The subject simply tries combinations of a single switch with the push button (i.e., combinations of twos) or by taking them all together. If the light is turned on it will be by chance and the light will be attributed to a single switch. At this level combinations remain incomplete and "the idea of constructing combinations two by two or three by three, etc. does not occur to them" (Inhelder and Piaget, 1958, p. 112).

IIB The IIB subject has the attributes of IIA, with the addition of some $n \times n$ combinations with the push-button switch or $n \times n \times n$ combinations with the push-button switch. These combinations are obtained by random selection strategy or empirically, and the subject still attributes the light to one particular switch.

IIIA At this level the subject does not deal with the problem by "random selection strategy," rather he uses a systematic method in the use of $n \times n$ combinations. The subject realizes that the light results from a combination of switches rather than one switch. Moreover, the subject does not stop when he/she has succeeded in lighting the bulb but continues to complete other possible combinations.

IIIB The construction of combinations and proofs is organized in a more systematic way with greater speed. The subject in this category is able to determine the role of the various switches and demonstrate some form of proof for the role of each switch.

2. COLORED BEADS TASK (PIAGET AND INHELDER, 1951, P. 163)

Materials:

Five sets of colored plastic beads: blue (B), green (G), orange (O), yellow (Y), and White (W).

The Colored Beads Task was designed by Piaget to test for the presence of combinatorial reasoning. The Colored Beads Task was considered to be content free, since working with materials such as several colored beads does not depend on the students' background and major area of specialization. Evaluations of combinatorial reasoning by the Colored Beads Task have also been made by Hensley (1974, p.32) and Kishta (1978). The subject is presented with the five sets of colored beads and has the opportunity to generate all possible combinations of beads, taking them two at a time, three at a time, four at a time or all five at a time, as listed in Table 1. The interviewer must check to be sure that each set contains beads of the same color, and must be sure that the sets of beads are placed in front of all the subjects in the same order (B, G, O, Y, W). To generate all possible combinations requires the successful use of combinatorial reasoning. Regarding the function of the involving factors in the combinations, there is no neutral or inhibitor element in the Colored Beads Task. In the Colored Beads Task all combinations are considered to be the right answer.

The protocol for this task is a modified form of the protocol developed by Hensley (1974, p. 33). The rack of five sets of beads is placed in front of the subject and the interviewer says, "Here are five plastic containers, each containing beads of different colors. Your task is to make groups of beads. A group has two or more beads of different colors. Also, a group will not have more than one bead of the same color. The order in which you place the beads makes no difference. Blue and orange, orange and blue are the same. Using as many beads as you wish, I would like you to make as many different groups of beads as you can. Do you have any questions?" After the student responds the interviewer says, "You may begin." During the experiment the interviewer uses questions such as the following:

1. "Have you made all possible groups of beads?"
2. If the answer is no, the interviewer says, "Please keep trying to make as many different groups as you can."
3. If the subject stops again, the interviewer goes back to the first question.
4. If the answer is yes, the interviewer says, "all right," and the experiment terminates at this point.

TABLE 1

COMBINATIONS OF THE FIVE COLORED BEADS:

BLUE (B), GREEN (G), ORANGE (O), YELLOW (Y), AND WHITE (W)

BG	GY	BGO	BYW	BGOY	BGOYW
BO	GW	BGY	GOY	BGOW	
BY	OY	BGW	GYW	BGYW	
BW	OW	BOY	GOW	BOYW	
GO	YW	BOW	OYW	GOYW	

Scoring:

The scoring procedure for this task is a modified form of the scoring method used by Hensley (1974, p. 34). In particular, the limits of the total number of combinations necessary to pass the task at each of the four developmental sublevels IIA, IIB, IIIA, and IIIB were adopted from the Hensley scoring method.

IIA The subject is able to make most of the bead pairs (combinations of twos). He/she might combine the beads three at a time, four at a time, or all five at a time. Nevertheless, the IIA subject does not complete more than three combinations of higher orders.

IIB The subject is able to generate the ten bead pairs or all of the beads together. He/she completes some higher combinations without any systematic approach, but no more than eighteen total combinations.

IIIA The new innovation which appears at substage IIIA is the introduction of systematic method in the use of $n \times n$ combinations. The IIIA subject completes between nineteen and twenty-two combinations in a systematic way. The minimum number of combinations to pass the task at IIIA level was also reported to be nineteen in Hensley (1974, p. 36) and Kishta (1978).

IIIB The subject has the attributes of substage IIIA, but combinations are organized in a more systematic fashion from the start and with greater speed. At substage IIIB, the subject generates more than twenty-two combinations.

Correlational Reasoning[2]

Materials:

Sets of cards with fat or thin rats with green or red tails. The numbers shown represent the number of cards required for each trial.

Trial 1: 7 fat rats with red tails
2 fat rats with green tails
3 thin rats with red tails
8 thin rats with green tails

Trial 2: 2 fat rats with red tails
8 fat rats with green tails
8 thin rats with red tails
3 thin rats with green tails

Trial 3: 6 fat rats with red tails
9 fat rats with green tails
4 thin rats with red tails
6 thin rats with green tails

The interviewer begins with the following introduction: "A scientist recently conducted an investigation of the rats that inhabit a series of small islands in the South Pacific. On the first island he visited, he found that all the rats were either quite fat or quite thin. (Show examples to the student.) Also, all the rats had either green tails or red tails. This made the scientist wonder if there might be a connection or a relation between the size of the rats and the color of their tails. So he decided to capture some of the rats and observe them to see if there was some connection." The interviewer hands the first of three sets of data cards to the student.

The interviewer asks the student to examine the cards and check to see if there is, in fact, a relationship. Students initially unable to proceed may be given assistance in classifying the cards into four categories. The interviewer allows a few moments for the student to explore and categorize the cards. The interviewer may ask, "Are there more fat rats than thin rats?" "Are there more rats with green tails than with red tails?" "Do you find any connection between the thin rats and the tail color?" The student

[2] We extend our thanks to Dr. Anton E. Lawson, Arizona State University, for his assistance in preparing this protocol.

then is asked to explain any relation found. If the student shows some success on the first set of data, two additional trials may be presented.

Scoring:

IIA Multiple classification of incidents is implied in the subject's response. The student describes various events qualitatively: "I don't know, because there are some rats of each kind"; "I think there is no connection. There are seven rats with green tails and three with red tails and there are two thin rats with green tails and eight with red tails."

IIB Multiple classification of incidents is implied, and the incidents are compared in the subject's response. The number of cases is compared: "The island made them have different colors and shapes, because there are more rats with green tails than red, and more fat rats than thin."

IIIA Beginning of correlational reasoning using probabilities or proportionalities appears in the subject's response. The subject compares the incidences in two pairs, "There are more red fat than green fat, and more green thin than red thin rats."

IIIB A satisfactory solution of the problem with a clear identification of the mathematical relationships being used for the comparisons is apparent in the subject's response. The student identifies and/or compares two ratios: "More small rats have green tails by eight/three, and more large rats have red tails by seven/two"; "With red tails the rats are more likely to be small—about 80 percent—and with green tails the rats are most likely to be big—70 percent"; the subject compares the number of confirming cases or disconfirming cases.

Exclusion of Irrelevant Variables

PENDULUM EXPERIMENT (INHELDER AND PIAGET, 1958, PP. 67–79)

Materials:

Ring stand with ring, three strings of different lengths and three weights (50 gms, 100 gms, and 150 gms).

The interviewer places the materials in front of the student and says, "Here are the materials to make a pendulum. You may hang a string on the stand, place a weight on the string, and swing the pendulum. (Show the student.) I would like you to work with the materials to determine what controls how fast the pendulum swings." Ask the student to identify the variables. If students cannot name all of the possible variables,

i.e., push, drop, weight, length of string, point them out for them.

During the experiment the interviewer uses questions such as the following:

1. Have you tried all of the possible ways to change the speed of the pendulum swing?
2. What things have you changed to see if the pendulum swing speed changes?
3. What factor(s) control(s) the rate with which the pendulum completes its swing?
4. Why did you choose the (one of the four factors) to test?

Scoring:

IIA Variations in the motion of the pendulum attributed to the push it is given when starting. The length of the string may be mentioned as somewhat affecting the rate, but is not singled out. Several variables are varied simultaneously.

IIB Variations in the motion of the pendulum are explained as an inverse relationship between the length of the string and the motion of the pendulum. Variables are not isolated. "The longer the string, the slower its motion." "The shorter the string, the faster its motion."

IIIA The student separates the variables, such as length of string, the size of the weight, the height from which the weight is released, and the force of the push, but the student has difficulty in controlling each while experimenting. An hypothesis may be formed that variation is caused by the length of the string, yet the student will qualify its role.

IIIB The student separates the variables and formulates an hypothesis that leads to the exclusion of all factors except the length of the string.

Probabilistic Reasoning

Materials:

Squares—four yellow; five blue; three red.
Diamonds—two yellow; three blue; seven red.
Box.

The interviewer provides a box to which blue, red, or yellow squares and blue, red, or yellow diamonds are added. The interviewer begins by explaining to the subject that different numbers of squares and/or diamonds will be added to the box. The subject will be asked several problems. The interviewer continues:

1. Put *two yellow squares* and *two blue squares* in a box. Shake the items and ask, "What are the chances of my drawing a *blue square* on the first draw?"
2. Put *one each of red, blue, and yellow squares* and *two each of red, blue, and yellow diamonds* into a box. Shake the items and ask, "What are the chances of my drawing a *square of any color* on the first draw?"
3. Put *five blue squares, four yellow squares, and three red squares* into a box with *three*

blue diamonds, two yellow diamonds, and four red diamonds. Shake the items and ask, "What are the chances of my drawing a *red piece (either a square or a diamond)* on the first draw?"
4. Using the same items as in number 3, ask, "What are the chances of my drawing a *blue diamond* on the first draw?"
5. Using the same items as in number 3, add *three more red diamonds* and ask, "What are the chances of my drawing out a *yellow square* on the first draw?"

Scoring:

IIA: The subject is unable to answer the first question.

IIB: The subject is able only to give the 2:1 proportion response to the first question.

IIIA: The subject identifies a 1:3 proportion.

IIIA: The subject states that a 1:7 proportion is present.

IIIB: The subject identifies the 1:6 proportion when *all other* proportions are identified correctly.

Proportional Reasoning

EQUILIBRIUM IN THE BALANCE (INHELDER AND PIAGET, 1958, CHAPTER 11)

Materials: see source note above.

The apparatus is placed in front of the student. The interviewer says, "Here is a bar that is balanced at the center. Notice that there are seventeen evenly spaced hooks on each side of the balance point on which to hang weights. We are going to do some balance tasks. I'll hang a weight on one side and ask you to balance the bar by hanging a weight or weights on the other side. You can hang weights on different hooks or on the same hook if you wish. The weights can be hooked together to suspend them from the same hook."

The interviewer proceeds with the following steps:

1. "First, I'm going to hang a 100 gram weight on the sixth hook." (Count from center.) "I want you to place a 100 gram weight on the other side to make the bar balance." The interviewer holds the bar level while the subject is hanging the weight, and before releasing it asks this question: "Why did you hang the weight on the ——— hook?"

2. "I'm going to leave my 100 gram weight on the sixth hook and give you two 50 gram weights. Where will you hang your 50 gram weights to balance my 100 gram weight?" The interviewer holds the bar level while the subject decides where to place the two 50 gram weights and places them. Before releasing the bar, the interviewer asks: "Why did you hang the 50 gram weights on the ——— hook (or hooks)?"

3. "Now, I'm going to hang a 100 gram weight on the sixth hook." (Count from center.) "I want you to take a 50 gram weight and hang it on the other side to balance the bar." The interviewer holds the bar level while the subject is placing the weight. While holding the bar level, the interviewer asks: "Why did you hang the weight on the ——— hook?"

4. "Next, I'm going to hang a 120 gram weight on the third hook." (Count from center.) "Hang a 40 gram weight on the other side to make the bar balance." The interviewer holds the bar level while the subject is placing the weight. Still holding the bar level, the interviewer asks: "Why did you hang the weight on the ——— hook?"

5. "Now I'm going to hang a 70 gram weight on the tenth hook." (Count from center.) "Hang a 100 gram weight on the other side to make the bar balance." The interviewer holds the bar level while the subject is placing the weight. Still holding the bar level, the interviewer asks: "Why did you hang the weight on the ——— hook?"

If the interviewer is unsure of his/her judgment regarding the interviewee's success after using the 70/100 weight combination, a good way to test it is to place a 60 gram weight on the sixth hook and give the subject 40 grams. The procedure followed is the same as that given above.

Suggested amendments: balance

The magnitude of the weights and distances can be changed, provided the proportions of 1:1, 1:2, 1:3, and a more complex one (e.g., 3:2, 7:10) are retained.

Scoring:

IIA: The subject is not successful with anything beyond step 2.

IIB: The subject is successful with the two-to-one[3] proportions of step 3. The explanation must include the use of the proportion concept.

IIIA: The subject is successful in balancing the bar using the weights and distances outlined in step 4. The explanation must include the proportion concept.

IIIB: The subject is successful in balancing the bar using the weights and distances outlined in step 5. The explanation must include the proportion concept. A student who solves the problem using a rule such as weight times distance on one side equals weight times distance on the other side is using an algorithm, without necessarily using a proportion. If this is evident, the subject is told, "Give me another solution using weight and distance in some other way." If the student cannot satisfactorily explain this using proportions, a lower score is given, depending on the last level for which a satisfactory explanation was given.

---

[3] Piaget and Inhelder infer (*Growth of Logical Thinking*, chapter 11) that the successful completion of the 2:1 proportion task is a characteristic of the IIIA category. Warren Wollman and Robert Karplus ("Intellectual Development Beyond Elementary School V: Using Ratio in Differing Tasks," *School Science and Mathematics*, no. 7 (November 1974):593–611) have shown the 2:1 proportion concept to be attainable at the IIB level.

Separation of Variables

BENDING RODS (INHELDER AND PIAGET, 1958, CHAPTER 3)

Materials: see source note above.

The apparatus is placed in front of the subject and the interviewer uses an explanation such as the following:

"I have an apparatus and I want to show you how it works. I can pull the rods back and forth and make them as long or as short as I want. The effective length is from here out." (Demonstrate.) "The screws must be loosened in order to move the rods." The interviewer allows the subject a few moments to explore the apparatus, and makes sure the subject understands that adjusting the lengths of the rods is permitted.

The interviewer says: "Look at the rods and tell me in as many ways as you can how the rods are different." The interviewer leads the subject to state the three ways the rods are different and explains that these differences are called variables. If the subject does not find all the variables, the interviewer explains what they are. At this point the weights are introduced, and the subject is shown how the weights will bend the rods. The interviewer now restates the four variables.

The interviewer next says: "Do some experiments to show me the effect of each one of the four variables on how much the rods bend." The interviewer is inviting the subject to demonstrate at least one experiment to show the influence of one of the variables on the bending of the rods. That is a category IIIA characteristic.

If the subject does not reach the IIIA level, the interviewer should provide the opportunity to reach the IIB level. A good question to lead back to IIB is: "Take one thick rod and one thin rod and make them bend the same amount, using two equal or identical weights." The subject in category IIB solves this problem by logical multiplication and explains why. The intuitive feeling is present that long-thick balances short-thin. The IIA student does not demonstrate logical multiplication.

After one experiment controlling variables has been done and after the subject is established at the level IIIA, a good question to use in leading the subject is: "What else can you do to test the other variables?" The interviewer may precede this question with: "There are three more variables. Do you remember what they are?"

A good question to lead the subject during the task, but not before the subject has had the opportunity to set up an experiment, is: "What can you do to prove that the material (or length, or diameter) of the rod is important in determining how much it will bend?"

A good question to conclude the interview for this task is: "Is there anything else you want to do with this apparatus?"

Questions to be asked during the entire interview after each experiment the subject attempts are:

"What are you showing with that experiment?"

"What variable is your experiment dealing with?"

"How does your experiment show what variable you are testing?"

Scoring:
IIA: The subject cannot explain logical multiplication.
IIB: The subject can explain logical multiplication (intuitive feeling that long and thick balances short and thin).
IIIA: The subject does at least one experiment that proves the effect of at least one variable.
IIIB: The subject solves the entire problem.

References

DeLuca, F. P. "Application and Analysis of an Electronic Equivalent of Piaget's First Chemical Experiment." *The Journal of Research in Science Teaching* 16:1–11, 1979.

Hensley, J. H. *"An Investigation of Proportional Thinking in Children from Grades Six Through Twelve."* Unpublished Doctoral Dissertations, University of Iowa, 1974.

Inhelder, Barbel, and Jean Piaget. *The Growth of Logical Thinking.* New York: Basic Books, 1958.

Kishta, A. E. "Proportional and Combinatorial Reasoning in Two Cultures." *Journal of Research in Science Teaching* 15:11–24, 1978.

Piaget, Jean, and Barbel Inhelder. *The Origin of the Idea of Chance in Children.* New York: Norton, 1951.

ACKNOWLEDGMENTS

ACKNOWLEDGMENTS

We are grateful to the people listed below for the use of their artwork. Every effort has been made to locate the sources of illustrations and photographs.

ILLUSTRATIONS

David Cunningham: 125

James Curran: 68 bottom, 69, 71 top, 127

Kate M. Flanagan: 68 top left, 72 top, 75, 95 top, 96 top and middle, 103, 104 bottom left, 105, 113 bottom, 123, 137

Barbara Hack: 134

Heather Preston Kortebein: 71 middle and bottom, 72 middle and bottom, 74, 118 top, 120, 121

L. Marek: 52

Lianne Ruppel: 68 top right, 79, 89, 90, 94 top left, 104 top and bottom right, 106 top, 113 top, 114 bottom, 118 middle

Bonnie Russell: 80 top, 131

Clifford Spohn: 119 top

Maria Szmauz: 38, 54, 76, 80 bottom, 81, 109 (original by Bob Haydock), 110, 111, 114 top, 115, 118 bottom, 188, 194, 195

Teaching Science in the Elementary School, Third Edition, John W. Renner and Don G. Stafford (Harper & Row 1979): 4, 12, 14, 15, 16, 17, 18, 31, 33, 35, 37, 40, 42, 138, 140 top, 171, 172, 175, 179, 180

Jan Wills: 119 bottom

PHOTOGRAPHS

Marshall Berman: 83, 136

Albert J. Copley/ Visuals Unlimited: 94 top right and bottom, 95 bottom, 98, 122 top and bottom, 130

John D. Cunningham/Visuals Unlimited: 96 bottom, 106 bottom

George Fry III: 126

Peter Oglivie: 129, 132

H. Oscar/Visuals Unlimited: 101

Rachel Thompson: 78

Jane Wattenberg: 86, 87, 88, 140 bottom, 141

INDEX

INDEX

Abstract thinking, 22–24
  vs. concrete concepts, 20
Acceleration, 26
Accommodation
  defined, 32
  direct experience and, 50
  teacher's role in, 158
"Accord of thought," 32
Actions, 6–7
  vs. operation, 6–7, 9, 20
Adey, Philip, 56
Age
  intelligence quality and, 7
  preoperational stage and, 18
Almy, Millie, 193, 195
Animal homes, 149–51
Anthropological model, 196–99
Aquarium, building, 68–70
Assimilation
  of concepts, 49–50
  defined, 31
  demonstration and, 161–62
  development process and, 46–47
  exploration and, 161
  of facts, 48
  guided, 157
  importance of, 43
  teaching and, 34, 46–47
  thinking ability and, 167
  understanding and, 31–32
Assumptions, reasoning from, 24

"Back-to-the basics" theory, 22
Bending rods experiment, 211–12
Binet Laboratory, 7
Biological sciences
    concepts in, 59–62, 67
    first grade learning cycle, 68–70
    second grade learning cycle, 71–73
    third grade learning cycle, 74–77
    fourth grade learning cycle, 78–82
    fifth grade learning cycle, 83–85
    sixth grade learning cycle, 86–91
Bohr, Niels, 169
Breathing, 78–82
    model of, 52–53

Calendar, 98
Cantu, Luis L., 55
Centering, 11, 12, 13
Circuit testers, 141
Circulation system, 89–90
Classification, 20–21
Cognitive processes
    Piaget's theory of, 5–6
    preoperational stage and, 9–10
Colored bead task, 206–7
Combinatorial reasoning, 23
    measuring, 205–7
Concept implementation, 185
Concept misplacement, 55
Concepts
    in biological sciences, 59–62, 67
    concrete, 50–51, 52, 53–55, 156
    defined, 48–49
    in earth sciences, 59, 62–64, 93
    flexible, 51–53
    formal, 51, 52, 53–56, 156
    incorrect, 177
    for kindergarten children, 143–44
    measuring understanding of, 53–55
    in physical sciences, 59, 62–64
    types of, 49–51
Conceptual invention, 36, 37, 48
    model building and, 180
    observing and, 172–73

teaching and, 38, 158
    thinking ability and, 167
Conceptualization, 49
Concrete concepts, 21, 50–51, 52, 156
    measuring understanding of, 53–55
Concrete operational thinkers, 21–22
    assimilation by, 31–32
    in elementary school, 155–56
    formal operational thought and, 23, 24–25,
        54–55
    hypotheses and, 47
    mental structures used by, 34
    model building by, 178–79
    science experiments and, 24
    teaching, 34
Conservation reasoning, 14, 20–22
    effect of learning cycle on, 187–88
    evaluation of, 196
    in preoperational children, 11
    reading readiness and, 193
Conservation tasks
    area, 15–17
    length, 17, 19
    liquid, 15, 26
    number, 14–15, 19, 46
    solid amount, 15
    volume, 24, 39–40, 204
    weight, 17–18
Content
    culturally imperative, 159
    defined, 39
    intellectual level and, 42
    learning cycle and, 169–70
    rational powers and, 166
Correlational reasoning, measuring, 207–8
Correspondence, 20–21
Cubits, 157, 159
Culturally imperative content, 159
Culture, intellectual development and, 42
Current, electrical, 139–40

Data gathering, measuring and, 173
Data interpretation, 174–77
    predicting and, 180–81

Data organization, 175
Decentering, 20
Decomposition, 83–85
Deduction, 13, 182
Deferred imitation, 10
Development, learning and, 45–47
Development learning, 30. *See also* Knowledge
    construction; Intellectual development
Direct experience
    concepts and, 50, 52
    importance of, 156
Directions
    vs. free exploration, 39
    how to give, 156–58
    oral vs. written, 160
Discovery, 185
Disequilibrium, 50
    defined, 32
    role in learning, 32–33
    transductive reasoning and, 46
Drawing, preoperational stage and, 10

Earth sciences
    concepts in, 59, 62–64, 93
    first grade learning cycle, 94–97
    second grade learning cycle, 98–100
    third grade learning cycle, 101–2
    fourth grade learning cycle, 103–7
    fifth grade learning cycle, 108–12
    sixth grade learning cycle, 113–16
Educational Policies Commission (E.P.C.),
    165–66, 170
Educational transmission, 42
Egocentrism, in preoperational children, 11
Einstein, Albert, 167–68, 169
Electric currents, 35–36, 139–40
Electricity, 138–42
Electronic task (ET), 205
Energy, 134–37
    understanding concept of, 50–51
Environmental input
    processing, 30–31
    structures and schemes and, 31–32

Equilibration, 32
    importance of, 43
Equilibrium, 32
    dynamic nature of, 33
Equilibrium in balance experiment, 210–11
Ethnographic research, 196–99
Evaluation, of student's learning, 162–64. *See
    also* Research
Examinations, 163–64
Exclusion of irrelevant variables, measuring,
    208–9
Expansion-of-the-idea phase, 37
    demonstration and, 161–62
    experimenting and, 178
    importance of, 169–70
    interpreting and, 176
    learning cycle activities and, 171
    measuring and, 174
    observing and, 173
    origin of concept, 185
    teaching and, 38, 158–62
    thinking ability and, 167
Experience, importance of, 156
Experimenting, 171, 177–78
Experiments, in inform–verify–practice (IVP)
    teaching, 168
Explanation, model building and, 178–80
Exploration, 37
    assimilation and, 161
    benefits of, 39
    defined, 34
    demonstration and, 161–62
    experimenting and, 177–78
    importance of, 169
    learning cycle activities and, 171
    observing and, 172
    teaching and, 38, 156–58, 161–62
    thinking ability and, 167
Exposition, 168

Facts, defined, 48
Fantasy, in preoperational children, 22
Fifth grade
    biological sciences concepts, 61

Fifth grade (*continued*)
    biological sciences learning cycle, 83–85
    earth sciences concepts, 63–64
    earth sciences learning cycle, 108–12
    physical sciences concepts, 65–66
    physical sciences learning cycle, 134–37
First grade
    biological sciences concepts, 60
    biological sciences learning cycle, 68–70
    earth sciences concepts, 62
    earth sciences learning cycle, 94–97
    physical sciences concepts, 64
    physical sciences learning cycle, 118–21
Flavell, John H., 6, 39
Flexible concepts, 51–53
Food, and food chain, 74–77
Formal concepts, 23, 51, 52, 156
    measuring understanding of, 53–55
    teaching as concrete, 156
    concrete operational thinkers' learning of,
        54–55
Formal operational thinking, 22–24, 50–51, 52
    concrete operational thought and, 23, 24–25
    evaluating, 203–12
    lack of, in elementary school, 155–56
    mental structures used in, 34
    models and, 52–53
Fossils, 103–7
Fourth grade
    biological sciences concepts, 61
    biological sciences learning cycle, 78–82
    earth sciences concepts, 63
    earth sciences learning cycle, 103–7
    measurement learning cycle, 156–58
    physical sciences concepts, 65
    physical sciences learning cycle, 129–33
    preparing learning cycle for, 156–58
Freedom of the mind, 166
Fronts, weather, 113–16
Frustration, vs. disequilibrium, 32
Functioning, 33, 169

Galen, 86
Gases, 125–28

Generalizations, 49
Geology, 103–7
Grammar, teaching, 23
Guided assimilation, 157
Guilford, J. P., 54

Harvey, William, 86
Heart, 86–91
Herron, J. Dudley, 55
Hypotheses
    learning to state, 23, 47
    predicting and, 181
    working, 177
Hypothetico-deductive thought, 23

Induction, 13
Inform–verify–practice (IVP) procedure, 168,
    169
    data interpretation and, 176–77
Inhelder, Barbel, 203
Instructions. *See* Directions
Intellectual development. *See also* Reasoning;
        Thinking; *specific levels*
    accelerating, 26
    factors affecting, 25–26, 42–43
    first (sensimotor) level of, 8–9, 10
    fourth (formal operational) level of, 22–24
    learning cycle and, 187–88
    learning limitations, 55–56
    model, 40–42
    moving from one state to another, 25
    science content and, 24–26
    second (preoperational) level of, 8–20
    teaching method and, 10
    third (concrete operational) level, 20–22
Intelligence
    age-specific, 7
    as dynamic, 40
    invariants of, 33
Interiorized actions, 7
Interpreting, 171, 174–77
    predicting and, 180–81
Invariants, defined, 33

Invention, conceptual, 36
Irreversibility, 11, 13. *See also* Reversibility

Karplus, Robert, 185
Kindergarten
    concepts in, 143–44
    learning cycles for, 143–51
Knowledge, defined, 5, 6
Knowledge construction, 6, 49, 170
    defined, 5
    learning model, 30–34
    teaching and, 34–38

Language
    development of, 8
    preoperational stage and, 10
Lawson, Anton E., 55
Learning
    cognitive theory base for, 5
    development and, 45–47
    disequilibrium and, 32–33
    model of, 5
    vs. reciting, 29
    vs. training, 30
    understanding and, 29–30
Learning cycle
    activities in, 170–82
    alternate form of, 38–39
    for biological sciences, 59–62, 67–91
    conservation task performance and, 187–88
    defined, 37
    demonstrations and, 161–62
    for earth sciences, 59, 62–64, 93–116
    evaluation of, 185–99
    intellectual development and, 187–88
    for kindergarten children, 143–51
    for physical sciences, 59, 64–66, 117–42
    planning, 160
    predicting in, 182
    preparing, 155–64
    rational powers and, 166–67
    reading readiness program in, 193–96
    research with, 185–99

school achievement and, 191–93
science and, 167–70, 188–91
significance of, 165–83
student evaluation and, 162–64
teaching and, 37–38, 161–62
thinking ability and, 167
Learning model, 30–34
Linguistic transmission, 42
Liquids, 125–28
Logic. *See* Reasoning
Logical-mathematical experience, intellectual
    development and, 25–26, 42
Lung capacity, 80–81
Lungs, 78–82

Magnetism, 122–24
Map reading, 108–12
Material Objects (physical science program),
    193–96
Mathematics
    logical-mathematical experience, 25–26, 42
    reversibility and, 11
Matter, states of, 125–28
Maturation, intellectual development and, 25,
    42
Measurement, 156–58
Measuring, 171, 173–74
Memorization
    vs. learning, 169
    reversibility and, 11
    vs. understanding, 5, 10
Mental images, preoperational stage and, 10
Mental operations, 5, 6–7
Mental representation, in preoperational chil-
    dren, 20
Mental structures, 30–31
    change in, 33–34
    building, 31
    development process and, 46
    environmental input and, 31–32
    intellectual level and, 42
    organization of, 32
Metric system, 159–60
Metropolitan Reading Readiness Test, 193

Mixtures, 129–33
Model building, 171, 178–80
Models
  formal thought and, 52
  used with direct experience, 52–53
Mold, 83–85

Object permanency, 8
Observing, 171, 172–73
  evaluation of, 190
Oklahoma, University of, 185
  Science Education Center, 203
Operations, 6–7
  vs. action, 6–7, 9, 20
  concrete, 14
Oral instructions, 160
Organization, 169
  of mental structures, 32
Origin of Intellect, The: Piaget's Theory (Phillips), 9

Pendulum experiment, 208–9
Perception-boundedness, 9, 12, 14
Phillips, John L., Jr., 7, 9, 33, 39
Physical experience, intellectual development
  and, 25, 42
Physical sciences
  concepts in, 59, 64–66, 117
  first grade learning cycle, 118–21
  second grade learning cycle, 121–24
  third grade learning cycle, 125–28
  fourth grade learning cycle, 129–33
  fifth grade learning cycle, 134–37
  sixth grade learning cycle, 138–42
Physiological maturation, intellectual development
  and, 42
Piaget, Jean, 5–6, 30–34, 37, 40, 42, 43, 45,
  155–56, 169, 185, 203
  intellectual level model of, 7–26
  Psychology of Intelligence, The, 9
Plants, growing, 71–73
Poincairé, Henri, 169

Predicting, 171, 180–82
  evaluation of, 190
  vs. hypothesizing, 181
  value of, 181
Preoperational thinkers, 9–20
  assimilation and, 46–47
  characteristics of, 11–20
  identifying, 14–20
  learning cycles for, 143–44
  mental schemes used by, 33–34, 47
  nonassimilation of concrete operational ideas
    by, 31
  science and, 182–83
  science experiments with, 24
  teaching, 34
  transductive reasoning in, 46
Probabilistic reasoning, measuring, 209
Programmed-learning materials, 43
Properties, 118–21
  ability to explain, 197–99
  of mixtures, 129–33
Proportional reasoning, measuring, 210–11
Propositional reasoning, 23
Protocols, for formal operational tasks, 203–12
Psychology of Intelligence, The (Piaget), 9
Pulse, 86
Purser, Roger K., 55

Qualitative research, 196–99
Questions, used in evaluations, 162–63

Rational powers, 166
  developing, 166–67, 177
  interpreting and, 174
  predicting and, 182
Reading readiness, learning cycle program in,
  193–96
Reality
  formal operational thought and, 24
  sequences, 6
Reasoning. See also Intellectual development;
  Thinking
  age-specific, 3–6

Reasoning (*continued*)
  from assumptions, 24
  combinatorial, 205–7
  concrete, 21–22
  conservation, 14, 20–22
  correlational, 207–8
  deductive, 13
  inductive, 13
  model of, 5
  probabilistic, 209
  proportional, 210–11
  propositional, 23
  with the structured whole, 23, 52
  transductive, 13
Reciting, vs. learning, 29
Record keeping, importance of, 162
Renner, John W., 55
Research, 185–99
  anthropological model for, 196–99
  Science Curriculum Improvement Study
    (SCIS), 185–96
Reversal, 20
Reversibility, 7, 11–13, 20
Rocks and soil, 94–97
  earth history and, 103–7
Roller, Duane, 169

Schemes
  defined, 31
  development process and, 46–47
  environmental input and, 31–32
  in preoperational children, 47
Science
  ability to use processes of, 188–91
  definitions of, 167–69
  intellectual levels and, 24–26
  learning cycle and, 167–70
  nature of, 167
  preoperational stage and, 13
Science concept rating, 56
Science Curriculum Improvement Study
    (SCIS), 185–86
  ability to use science processes and, 188–91
  intellectual development and, 187–88
  school achievement and, 191–93

Science Education Center, University of Okla-
    homa, 203
Seasons, 98–100, 145–46
Second grade
  biological sciences concepts, 60
  biological sciences learning cycle, 71–73
  earth sciences concepts, 62
  earth sciences learning cycle, 98–100
  physical sciences concepts, 64–65
  physical sciences learning, 122–24
Sedimentary rock, 105
Self-regulation, 32
Semiotic functions, 10
Sensimotor level, 8–9
  vs. preoperational level, 10
Separation anxiety, 8
Separation of variables, measuring, 211–12
Seriation, 20–21
Shapes, 147–48
Shayer, Michael, 56
Signifiers, 9–10
Sixth grade
  biological sciences concepts, 61–62
  biological sciences learning cycle, 86–91
  earth sciences concepts, 64
  earth sciences learning cycle for, 113–16
  physical sciences concepts, 66
  physical sciences learning cycle for, 138–42
Skinner, B. F., 43
Social interaction, 197–98
Social transmission, intellectual development
    and, 25–26, 42–43
Soil and rocks, 94–97
  earth history and, 103–7
Solids, 125–28
Standard unit of measure, 156–58
Stanford Achievement Series, 191–92
States in a transformation, 11, 12–13, 20
States of matter, 125–28
Stimulus-response (S–R) model, 43
Structured whole, reasoning with, 23
Structures. See Mental structures
Student achievement, effect of SCIS program
    on, 191–93
Student evaluation, 162–64

Summer and fall, 145–46
Symbolic functions, 10
Symbolic play, 10

Teaching
    concrete concepts and, 21
    conservation concept and, 19–20
    demonstrations, 161–62
    inform–verify–practice (IVP) procedure for,
        168, 169
    intellectual development and, 10
    model, 34–38
Temperature, concept of, 51–52
Thinking. See also Intellectual development;
        Reasoning
    improving ability, 199
    learning cycle and, 167, 192–93
    reading readiness and, 195
    school's role in developing, 165–66
Third grade
    biological sciences concepts, 60–61
    biological sciences learning cycle, 74–77
    earth sciences concepts, 62–63
    earth sciences learning cycle, 101–2
    physical sciences concepts, 65
    physical sciences learning cycle, 125–28
Thought reversal. See Reversibility

Training, vs. learning, 30
Traits, intellectual development levels and, 9
Transductive reasoning, 13, 19, 182
    disequilibrium and, 46
    in preoperational children, 11
Transformation, states in, 11, 12–13, 20

Understanding
    assimilation and, 31–32
    concrete reasoning and, 22
    vs. memorization, 5, 10
    as necessary part of learning, 29–30

Variants, 31, 42
Verbal evocation. See Language
Videotapes, vs. exploration, 161–62
Volcanoes, 101–2

Way of life, 196
Weather fronts, 113–16
Working hypotheses, 177
Written conceptual inventions, 158
Written instructions, 160

Year, 98–100